# Slavery &
# Abolition
## in Early
## Republican
## Peru

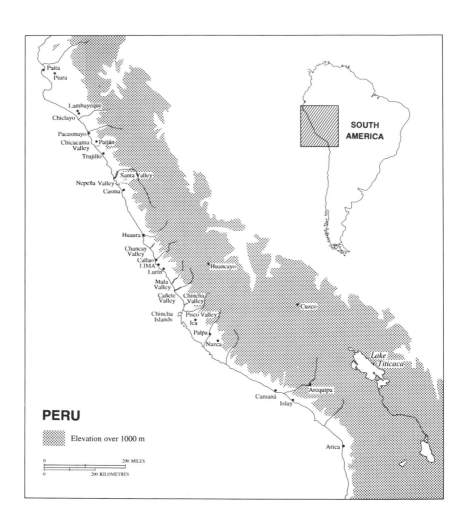

Paita
Piura

Lambayeque
Chiclayo

Pacasmayo
Chicacama
Valley          Paiján
Trujillo

Santa Valley
Nepeña Valley
Casma

Huaura
Chancay
Valley
Callao
LIMA            Huancayo
Lurín
Mala
Valley
Cañete          Chincha
Valley          Valley
Chincha         Pisco Valley
Islands         Ica                 Cuzco
                Palpa
                Nazca

                                    Lake
                                    Titicaca

                        Arequipa
                Camaná
                        Islay

SOUTH
AMERICA

                                    Arica

## PERU

Elevation over 1000 m

0                    200 MILES
0              200 KILOMETRES

# Slavery & Abolition

## in Early Republican Peru

Peter Blanchard

A Scholarly Resources Inc. Imprint
Wilmington, Delaware

The paper used in this publication meets the minimum requirements of the American National Standard for permanence of paper for printed library materials, Z39.48, 1984.

©1992 by Scholarly Resources Inc.
All rights reserved
First published 1992
Printed and bound in the United States of America

Scholarly Resources Inc.
104 Greenhill Avenue
Wilmington, DE  19805-1897

**Library of Congress Cataloging-in-Publication Data**

Blanchard, Peter, 1946–
    Slavery and abolition in early republican Peru / Peter
Blanchard.
        p.    cm. — (Latin American silhouettes)
    Includes bibliographical references and index.
    ISBN 0-8420-2400-X. — ISBN 0-8420-2429-8 (pbk.)
    1. Slavery—Peru—History—19th century.  I. Title.
    II. Series.
HT1147.B58  1992
306.3'62'0985—dc20                                        92-4999
                                                            CIP

Peter Blanchard is an associate professor in the Department of History, University of Toronto. His other publications include *The Origins of the Peruvian Labor Movement, 1883–1919* (University of Pittsburgh Press, 1982) and *Markham in Peru: The Travels of Clements R. Markham, 1852–1853* (University of Texas Press, 1991).

# Contents

Acknowledgments, ix

Introduction, xiii

1  Independence, 1

2  The Importance of Slaves, 19

3  The Slaveholders' Counterattack, 37

4  Slave Life, 63

5  Slave Resistance, 95

6  Capitalism, Industry, and Immigrants, 127

7  Abolitionist Pressure, 151

8  Foreign Involvement, 171

9  Abolition, 189

10  The Aftermath of Abolition, 211

Bibliography, 227

Index, 239

# Acknowledgments

The roots of this book and, consequently, the debts I have incurred in writing it can be traced back at least to 1980 when I began the research for it, perhaps even further. They might go back to 1970 and my first months as a graduate student at the University of London. A prominent Latin Americanist from the United States, then on sabbatical leave in England, was invited to give a paper at the seminar chaired by Professor R. A. Humphreys. Rather than enlightening us about some aspect of his present research, the speaker chose to advise us on how to publish an article, since he recently had ended a stint as editor of a well-known Latin American journal. Two things about that talk remain with me: first, that it went on interminably; and, second, that he made some dismissive remarks about works on slavery, a subject that he claimed had been covered completely in recent years and was no longer of academic interest. His views were at best undiplomatic, for among those present was Leslie Bethell, who recently had completed his book on the Brazilian slave trade. They were also of questionable accuracy, as shown by the numerous path-breaking works on slavery that have appeared subsequently. Even at the time, his views raised eyebrows. My supervisor, John Lynch, pointed out to me afterward that much remained to be done on the subject, including a work on the abolition of slavery in Peru.

Perhaps that comment remained in my subconscious, for ten years later, as I began contemplating where to turn now that my work on the early years of the Peruvian labor movement was nearing completion, the idea came back to me. I remained interested in Peruvian workers, but I wanted to examine an earlier period and restrict myself to a particular section of the labor force. The slave population seemed an obvious choice. After some deliberation, I decided to concentrate on Peru's slaves after independence and to study the various pressures and developments that led to abolition in 1855.

It was not a decision that attracted universal approval. Evaluators of the various bodies to whom I turned for financial assistance seemed to think, like the American academic, that slavery was not a subject worth supporting, suggesting instead that I concentrate on Peru's Indian population. As a result, I am saved the usual paragraph acknowledging grant-awarding institutions. Two exceptions were the Social Sciences and Humanities Research Council of Canada, which awarded me travel grants assisting research trips to Peru and England, and the Humanities and Social Sciences Committee of the University of Toronto, which provided a grant for the accompanying map.

I am deeply indebted to the staffs of the following archives, libraries, and institutions: in Lima, the Biblioteca Nacional, the Archivo General de la Nación, the Archivo Arzobispal, the Archivo de la Cámara de Diputados, and the Instituto Riva-Agüero; in Arequipa, the Archivo Departamental de Arequipa; in Trujillo, the Archivo Departamental de La Libertad; in London, the British Library, the Public Record Office, the Royal Geographical Society, the Wellcome Institute for the History of Medicine, the Senate House Library, the Institute of Historical Research, the University College London Library, and the Institute of Latin American Studies; and in Toronto, the University of Toronto libraries and the Cartography Department of the University of Toronto, which drew the accompanying map. In addition, special thanks are due Félix Denegri Luna, of Lima, who once again permitted me to use his private library. He dug out relevant works, even amid the disorder produced by the construction of a much-needed addition for his remarkable and expanding collection, and suggested where to find other material.

Several colleagues, particularly Martin Klein, Michael Wayne, Jock Galloway, and Ann McDougall, have assisted me over the years. They served as sounding boards for some of the ideas contained herein and provided information on different slave societies and experiences. Finally, my biggest debts, and the ones most difficult to repay, are to my wife and son. Joanna helped finance my research by continuing to work while I was away conducting my research. She also offered numerous suggestions for improvements in the manuscript. Together with Adam, she has kept the various and sundry demands of completing this book in proper perspective.

# Introduction

In January 1855 the government of Peru began implementing a decree that formally abolished slavery throughout the country. Its actions brought an end to an institution that had arrived with the first Spanish conquistadores over three hundred years earlier and had survived the succeeding centuries with remarkable resilience. In the waning years of the colony, hints of the demise of slavery were increasingly apparent, and antislavery legislation passed by the independence leaders in the early 1820s seemed to sound its death knell. Slavery, however, had assumed a role of vital importance during the colonial period, and separation from Spain did not alter that reality, so that while slavery faced serious challenges at the time of independence, it managed to survive and even flourish for another three decades.

The following study examines Peru during the years from independence to abolition, focusing upon the changing fortunes of slavery and of the slave population. At that time the only legally enslaved people in Peru were African-born blacks and their American descendants. Their continuing enslavement indicated the importance of slavery to the new republic as well as the strength of the slaveholders and their supporters. Slaves were still viewed as an essential component of the labor force and a significant economic resource. Possession of slaves remained an indicator of social status. Consequently, slaveholders made a determined effort to ensure that slavery did not follow the path of colonial rule, using their influence in the new republic to make certain that the institution survived.

For Peru's slaves the survival of slavery after independence meant that little had changed in their lives. They were still property and treated as such. Most slaves tried to cope by accommodating themselves to the system. They took advantage of the few opportunities they had to lighten their burden, saving their small earnings to buy their freedom or that of their loved ones, or serving their masters loyally in the hope that this would be rewarded with manumission. Other slaves found the system intolerable and responded, like many of their colonial forebears, by actively resisting. Many ran away, others turned to crime, still others attacked their oppressors, and a few even resorted to rebellion.

The situation was hardly a propitious one for the slaves, but it was not entirely lacking in hope. Mounting pressures were undermining slavery and working toward its eventual demise. Throughout the colonial period the Spanish Crown had tried to restrict and control slavery, although with limited success. In the later years of the colony, it renewed its efforts, largely in response to Great Britain's crusade against the slave trade. The definitive attack on slavery began with Peru's independence and the antislavery legislation introduced by the independence leaders. Over the next three decades the pressures mounted, both internally and externally, until abolition finally occurred in 1855.

With the advantage of hindsight one might argue that abolition was inevitable, but at the time the government decision came as something of a surprise: Neither the slaveholders nor the slaves had anticipated it or prepared for it. The surprise reflected, in part, the ineffectiveness of Peru's campaign for abolition. The Peruvian struggle lacked the drama and intensity that marked movements in other slaveholding countries. No prominent figures emerged to lead it; no formal abolitionist party was formed; no extensive debate, either moral, philosophical, or practical, took place about the effects of slavery and abolition; no significant socioeconomic developments occurred to weaken slavery and convert large numbers of slaveholders into proponents of free wage labor; no threat of racial warfare transformed apprehensive Peruvians into abolitionists; no apocalyptic civil war destroyed slavery and the supporting way of life.

Peruvian slavery might be said to have died a natural death. However, that death did not occur completely of its own volition and at a selected time. It was the result of a gradual loss of support by the defenders of slavery and of small victories by the antislavery forces. Those forces may have been hesitant, uncertain, unfocused, and disunited, but during the three decades covered by this study they began to confront the opposition and to alter the environment in which slavery had flourished. The resistance of the slaves, the expanding influence of liberals and modernizing sectors of society, the increasing pressures of abolitionist elements, the availability of alternative workers and new sources of capital, and the continuing influence of the British antislavery crusade all helped to weaken slavery in Peru. Of these, the most important was the resistance of the slaves. Their actions did not reach the level of threatening the nation with racial warfare, but by running away, buying their own freedom, taking complaints to the courts, and challenging their owners in a variety of other active and passive ways they made more and more of Peru's slaveholders acutely aware of the costs of slavery and the fact that it could not survive much longer. They stimulated white abolitionists into renewed activity, made government officials increasingly aware of the immorality and irrationality of the system, and, together with the other antislavery forces, prepared the groundwork for the abolition decree and its grudging acceptance by the slaveholders.

The weakness of Peru's antislavery forces may have delayed emancipation, but at the same time it prevented the development of more bitter animosities among Peruvians and avoided the bloodshed that marked abolitionist struggles in other countries. Already split by numerous ideological, economic, and regional differences that produced almost continuous political instability through the early years of the republic, Peru's elite had no desire to create even more divisions among themselves. They wanted to preserve slavery because the slaves were important as workers and investments, and also because they saw value in maintaining the ways and institutions of the past. A bitter fight over abolition would have hurt their political and economic power and might have led to even more significant and fundamental changes. This they were determined to avoid.

The resilient strength of the landholding elite constitutes part of a broader issue that is one of the themes of this study: the continuing influence of the past. It was responsible for many of the problems faced by Peru during these early critical years and in subsequent decades. Colonial institutions and traditions managed to withstand the trauma and dislocations of independence and maintain their influence over Peru and Peruvians. They lay at the root of the conservatism that dominated the country through the early nineteenth century and was still very much in evidence thereafter. Thus, although abolition brought an end to one colonial institution, its effect was limited. It did not destroy the accompanying social attitudes, assumptions, and structures, which continued to affect the lives of all Peruvians including the former slaves.[1]

The lack of change following abolition might give the impression that the Peruvian example was a "nonevent," a term that has been used to describe the concurrent movement in Venezuela.[2] To describe Peruvian abolition as such, however, would unjustifiably belittle the efforts of those who struggled to achieve abolition. It also would ignore the fact that an exploited and oppressed group in Peru had successfully battled the odds against them. Their victory indicated that, despite the obstacles, rigidities, and restrictions of the Peruvian system, change was possible and improvements could be won. It provided a measure of hope to all those who wanted to advance their own status, better the lives of their families, and influence the direction of their country.

In its gradualism and preservation of the status quo, the abolition of slavery in Peru resembled what was occurring in other Latin American countries at approximately the same time and in much the same way. Many comparisons and contrasts could be made with the slavery systems and abolitionist struggles in these neighboring countries and in the Western Hemisphere as a whole, for the literature on slavery is voluminous. Works by David Brion Davis, Eugene D. Genovese, and Orlando Patterson provide an excellent introduction to the subject, as well as stimulating insights and useful bibliographies.[3] For Latin America the literature is less extensive but still extremely rich, as the following selection of monographs indicates. Much of the recent literature has as a central aim the refutation of two older but still influential works, *The Masters and the Slaves* by Gilberto Freyre and *Slave and Citizen* by Frank Tannenbaum.[4] Comparing the slavery systems in Latin America and the United States, Freyre and Tannenbaum concluded that slavery in Spanish America and Brazil had been much more humane than the American version, that the slaveholders had been more compassionate, and that, as a result, abolition had been easier to accomplish. Their conclusions, however, have been widely criticized. General surveys of Latin American slavery by Herbert S. Klein, Rolando Mellafe, and Leslie B. Rout, Jr., provide an overview and synthesis of many of the important issues and themes, and present data that directly challenge the Freyre-Tannenbaum thesis.[5]

More specific works that reveal the exploitative nature of black slavery during the colonial period are those by Frederick Bowser on Peru, Colin A. Palmer on Mexico, Stuart B. Schwartz on Brazil, and William Frederick Sharp on Colombia.[6] Writers focusing on the nineteenth century and developments leading to abolition who have explicitly challenged Freyre and Tannenbaum include Robert Edgar Conrad, Peter L. Eisenberg, Mary C. Karasch, Robert Brent Toplin, and Franklin W. Knight.[7] Similar impressions that Latin American slavery was as harsh if not harsher than its American counterpart emerge from works by those who have concentrated on the social aspects of slavery and slave society, such as Katia M. de Queirós Mattoso and Verena Martínez-Alier. The same is true of one of the few firsthand accounts— although a rather controversial one—by a Latin American slave, the Cuban Esteban Montejo.[8]

By presenting a more accurate picture of Latin American slavery, these and other writers have uncovered many of the differences that existed among and within the slaveholding societies. At the same time, they have found certain common patterns and themes that tie Latin America together. One issue that has attracted particular attention has been the relationship between slavery and the dominant economic activity of a region. Philip D. Curtin's general examination of the "plantation complex" is a useful overview, while more specific works on the same theme include those by Eisenberg and Schwartz on the Brazilian sugar industry, Manuel Moreno Fraginals and Laird W. Bergad on the Cuban sugar industry, Francisco A. Scarano on the Puerto Rican sugar industry, and Stanley J. Stein and Warren Dean on the Brazilian coffee industry.[9] The study of this relationship also has drawn historians into an examination of slavery's decline, to see whether and how the two were connected. Conclusions have varied. Peru provides something of a contrast, for its slave population was relatively small and few slaves were involved in the primary economic activities of the country. Nonetheless, parallels can be drawn between its coastal planter class, which depended on slaves, and those of Brazil and Cuba.

A second economic relationship that has attracted scholarly attention has been the link between capitalism and slavery. Following in the footsteps of Eric Williams and his

provocative work, *Capitalism and Slavery*, writers have tried
to tie the demise of Latin American slavery to the spread of
Western capitalism.[10] Foremost among these is Moreno
Fraginals who has concluded that, in Cuba, industry and
slavery were incompatible, and that the rise of the one led to
the decline of the other. However, others have taken issue
with this explanation of Cuban abolition, most notably
Rebecca J. Scott.[11] She has argued for a broader approach,
stressing the complexities and the gradualism of the abolitionist process, elements that are at the center of other works
on abolition, including those by Eisenberg on Brazil and
John V. Lombardi on Venezuela.[12] A combination of internal
and external factors led to the destruction of Latin American
slavery. Foremost among the latter was the role of foreign
nations, particularly Great Britain, in the abolition of the
slave trade. Leslie Bethell has studied this issue for Brazil,
while David R. Murray has done the same for Cuba.[13] More
numerous and, to Scott's mind, more important were the
internal factors. She has cited, for example, the availability
of alternative sources of labor as a factor in Cuban abolition,
while Toplin has underlined the importance of the organized
abolitionist movement in weakening Brazilian slavery. Both
have stressed the contribution of the slaves to the process,
another important theme in the literature. Slave resistance
ranged from the informal and covert, which Scott argues was
vital to Cuban abolition, to the more open and violent, such
as La Escalera rebellion in Cuba, which has been examined
by Robert L. Paquette.[14] Open and violent resistance may or
may not have been critical to Brazilian abolition; opinions
differ according to whether one accepts the views of Toplin or
Eisenberg.

The route to abolition may have varied, and different
writers may have concentrated on different milestones along
the way, but all agree that Latin America's slaves obtained
nothing other than their freedom when abolition was achieved
at last. The dominant sectors of society made no effort to
remunerate the slaves for their years of exploitation or to
ease their passage to freedom. As George Reid Andrews has
shown in the case of Buenos Aires, the discrimination and
racism that developed during the centuries of slavery continued long after its collapse.[15] These same barriers confronted blacks throughout Latin America, and in some areas
they continue to do so to the present day.

The controversies that appear in the literature, while serving as a stimulus for further research, indicate how difficult it is to generalize about Latin American slavery. Significant differences existed in both time and space, even within a single country, and numerous other variables differentiated parts of the region. Nevertheless, comparisons can and should be made, for they provide a framework into which slavery and Afro-American studies can be placed. In the case of Peru, its slavery system and abolition process replicated some of the patterns evident in other countries, but they also had their own particular characteristics. These reflected the peculiarities of the country and the way slavery had developed for over three hundred years before it finally collapsed in 1855. Its demise had seemed imminent in 1821, when Peruvian independence was declared, but because of the nature of the country and its slavery system, abolition would take another thirty-four years to accomplish. Those years and the developments that occurred in them are the focus of this book.

## Notes

1. Others have noted how the past has continued to influence developments in Latin America. See, for example, Susan M. Socolow, "Recent Historiography of the Rio de la Plata: Colonial and Early National Periods," *Hispanic American Historical Review* [hereafter cited as *HAHR*] 64 (1984): 114. The issue has prompted some historians to reconsider the traditional periodization of Latin America, arguing that independence does not mark as significant a break as other events. For the domination of conservative groups and conservative values in early republican Peru see Paul Gootenberg, *Between Silver and Guano: Commercial Policy and the State in Postindependence Peru* (Princeton, 1989).

2. See John V. Lombardi, "The Abolition of Slavery in Venezuela: A Nonevent," in *Slavery and Race Relations in Latin America*, ed. Robert Brent Toplin (Westport, 1974), 228–52.

3. David Brion Davis, *The Problem of Slavery in the Age of Revolution, 1770–1823* (Ithaca, 1975); David Brion Davis, *Slavery and Human Progress* (New York, 1984); Eugene D. Genovese, *Roll, Jordan, Roll: The World the Slaves Made* (New York, 1976); Orlando Patterson, *Slavery and Social Death: A Comparative Study* (Cambridge, 1982). I owe more to these writers than my few references to their works indicate.

4. Gilberto Freyre, *The Masters and the Slaves: A Study in the Development of Brazilian Civilization*, trans. Samuel Putnam (New York, 1946); Frank Tannenbaum, *Slave and Citizen: The Negro in the Americas* (New York, 1946).

5. Herbert S. Klein, *African Slavery in Latin America and the Caribbean* (New York, 1986); Rolando Mellafe, *Negro Slavery in Latin America*, trans. J. W. S. Judge (Berkeley, 1975); Leslie B. Rout, Jr., *The African Experience in Spanish America: 1502 to the Present Day* (Cambridge, 1976).

6. Frederick P. Bowser, *The African Slave in Colonial Peru, 1524–1650* (Stanford, 1974); Colin A. Palmer, *Slaves of the White God: Blacks in Mexico* (Cambridge, 1976); Stuart B. Schwartz, *Sugar Plantations in the Formation of Brazilian Society: Bahia, 1550–1835* (Cambridge, 1985); William Frederick Sharp, *Slavery on the Spanish Frontier: The Colombian Chocó, 1680–1810* (Norman, 1976).

7. Robert Edgar Conrad, *The Destruction of Brazilian Slavery, 1850–1888* (Berkeley, 1972); Peter L. Eisenberg, *The Sugar Industry in Pernambuco: Modernization without Change, 1840–1910* (Berkeley, 1974); Mary C. Karasch, *Slave Life in Rio de Janeiro, 1808–1850* (Princeton, 1987); Robert Brent Toplin, *The Abolition of Slavery in Brazil* (New York, 1975); Franklin W. Knight, *Slave Society in Cuba during the Nineteenth Century* (Madison, 1970).

8. Katia M. de Queirós Mattoso, *To Be a Slave in Brazil, 1550–1888*, trans. Arthur Goldhammer (New Brunswick, 1986); Verena Martínez-Alier, *Marriage, Class and Colour in Nineteenth-Century Cuba: A Study of Racial Attitudes and Sexual Values in a Slave Society* (Ann Arbor, 1989); Esteban Montejo, *The Autobiography of a Runaway Slave*, ed. Miguel Barnet, trans. Jocasta Innes (New York, 1973). See also Robert Edgar Conrad, *Children of God's Fire: A Documentary History of Black Slavery in Brazil* (Princeton, 1983).

9. Philip D. Curtin, *The Rise and Fall of the Plantation Complex: Essays in Atlantic History* (Cambridge, 1990); Manuel Moreno Fraginals, *The Sugarmill: The Socioeconomic Complex of Sugar in Cuba, 1760–1860*, trans. Cedric Belfrage (New York, 1976); Laird W. Bergad, *Cuban Rural Society in the Nineteenth Century: The Social and Economic History of Monoculture in Matanzas* (Princeton, 1990); Francisco A. Scarano, *Sugar and Slavery in Puerto Rico: The Plantation Economy of Ponce, 1800–1850* (Madison, 1984); Stanley J. Stein, *Vassouras: A Brazilian Coffee County, 1850–1890* (New York, 1970); Warren Dean, *Rio Claro: A Brazilian Plantation System, 1820–1920* (Stanford, 1976).

10. Eric Williams, *Capitalism and Slavery* (Chapel Hill, 1944).

11. Rebecca J. Scott, *Slave Emancipation in Cuba: The Transition to Free Labor, 1860–1899* (Princeton, 1985).

12. John V. Lombardi, *The Decline and Abolition of Negro Slavery in Venezuela, 1820–1854* (Westport, 1971).

13. Leslie Bethell, *The Abolition of the Brazilian Slave Trade: Britain, Brazil and the Slave Trade Question, 1807–1869* (Cambridge, 1970); David R. Murray, *Odious Commerce: Britain, Spain and the Abolition of the Cuban Slave Trade* (Cambridge, 1980).

14. Robert L. Paquette, *Sugar Is Made with Blood: The Conspiracy of La Escalera and the Conflict between Empires over Slavery in Cuba* (Middletown, 1988).

15. George Reid Andrews, *The Afro-Argentines of Buenos Aires, 1800–1900* (Madison, 1980).

# 1

# Independence

On July 28, 1821, before a massed audience in Lima's Plaza de Armas, the Argentine liberator General José de San Martín declared: "Peru from this moment is free and independent by the general wish of its people and the justice of their God-defended cause."[1] In fact, almost five more years would pass before the last royalist troops finally surrendered, yet San Martín's declaration marked a turning point in Peru's struggle to end three hundred years of Spanish rule. For the Peruvian people, independence meant that they were now free to decide for themselves their country's future, free to choose their own political system, free to decide what economic route to follow, and free to organize social relations as they saw fit. With San Martín's arrival in Lima and his dramatic pronouncement, the most common word on the lips of the Peruvian people seemed to be *libertad*, freedom.

For Peru's fifty thousand black slaves, however, the celebration of independence was a mixed blessing. *Libertad* may have meant freedom for the nation; it did not mean freedom for all the people who made up that nation. Although Peru had been liberated from Spanish rule, its slaves remained fettered to their owners. Hopes of emancipation were raised at the time of independence, as gestures were made toward abolishing slavery, but after all the fighting had ended and independence had been irrevocably secured, another three decades would pass before the slaves, too, would share in the freedom that was being celebrated in 1821.

Three decades of further struggle, exploitation, and frustration may seem a long time, especially since abolition appeared virtually assured in the early 1820s. Yet, compared with what occurred in other slaveholding nations, the time span was not exceptional. Peru abolished its system almost contemporaneously with Colombia, Ecuador, Venezuela, and the Argentine Confederation, a decade before the United States (where antislavery pressures were much stronger), and over a quarter of a century before Cuba and Brazil. Moreover, in light of slavery's deep roots in Peru, some delay and resistance were to be expected, for slavery had been an important institution for over three hundred years, and proslavery forces were determined that it should continue.

The history of black slavery in Peru can be traced back to the arrival of the first Europeans, in the sixteenth century. African slaves accompanied Francisco Pizarro in his conquest of the Inca empire in 1532, and their numbers grew over the following years and decades as conquistadores and settlers spent some of their gold and silver on this expensive form of property. The possession of black slaves was something of a status symbol to the Spaniards, but from an early date slavery also had an important economic basis. Slaves came to constitute a significant sector of the labor force, especially along the coast, where the Indian population rapidly declined following the conquest. They grew much of the food on the farms and estates that supplied the expanding Spanish coastal cities; they labored on the plantations that by the later colonial period were producing commercial crops such as sugar and grapes; and they made up a large percentage of the work force in the urban centers, where they were domestic servants, artisans, and manual laborers. They filled virtually every occupation from sailor to wet nurse. If a particular job lacked workers, slaves were found to learn the skill, thereby filling the gap and, simultaneously, increasing the slaves' value. As a result of their skills, adaptability, and value, black slaves within one hundred years of their arrival in Peru had been transformed from a luxury into a vital necessity.[2]

Slaves not only helped to establish Spanish rule in Peru but also left their distinctive mark on the colony. Attempts by the conquerors to eradicate the slaves' African heritage proved unsuccessful, and some cultural elements were transferred and adopted, most notably in religious celebrations, music, and dance. The slaves may have accepted Christianity, but they managed to retain some aspects of their African religions; certain of their superstitions and deities survived, and they continued to rely on the intercession of black sorcerers. More surprising but probably more effective in the transfer of African culture were the *cofradías* or religious brotherhoods that sprang up among the black population. Initially the brotherhoods were established by the religious orders to stimulate Christian beliefs and to organize celebrations for a particular saint, but independent confraternities also appeared, such as the Cofradía de los Congos Mondongos, that clearly sought to maintain or foster African ties. Some brotherhoods accepted members only from a particular tribal group, providing an obvious means for cultural transfer, while their celebrations, regardless of the membership or ties, reached out to an even wider audience. The festivities had a definite African flavor, created in large part by the accompanying music in which the wooden *cajón* or drum, of African origin and played almost exclusively by blacks, beat out the rhythms for their dances. These, too, were of African origin. One such dance was the *zamacueca*, the forebear of today's better-known *marinera*, apparently a favorite of Simón Bolívar and still popular on the Peruvian coast in the midnineteenth century. Cultural remnants such as these survived in the slave quarters of the plantations and in the black barrios of urban centers. The ties may have been weakening by the late colonial period as the influx of African slaves came to an end, the brotherhoods lost their exclusively African characteristics by admitting other racial groups into their celebrations, and most free Afro-Peruvians chose Spanish culture as their model. Nevertheless, elements remained, providing a focus for a separate black identity and a stimulus to slave resistance during and after the independence period.[3]

Late in the colonial period, as cracks began to appear in the imperial structure, slavery was still a thriving institution in the viceroyalty, and the desire to acquire slaves was as strong as ever. Efforts were made to maintain the slave trade, and the Crown responded with such legislation as a 1796 decree that eliminated duties on slaves imported into Peru. Eleven years later, slavery supporters made the case to Madrid that 1,500 slaves of both sexes needed to be supplied annually to meet existing demands.[4] Ricardo Palma has written that 65,747 slaves, costing at least 300 pesos each, were imported between 1790 and 1802 so that the slave population continued to grow, perhaps by as much as 25 percent between 1795 and 1826.[5] Most of these imports were probably of American, not African, origin because of the risks of the transatlantic trade owing to the Napoleonic Wars and the intensifying British crusade against the slave trade. According to one report, the fifteen hundred slaves who arrived

in Peru annually between 1799 and 1810 were imported from
Buenos Aires and Chile.[6] Despite the difficulties in obtaining
them, slaves remained as important as they had been two
centuries earlier. They still constituted a significant portion
of the labor force on coastal plantations and truck farms;
they were a major component of the laboring population in
many urban centers, virtually monopolizing certain occupations such as wet nurse, food vendor, and water carrier; and
they were the domestic servants in numerous urban and
rural homes.[7]

Nonetheless, although slavery remained very much alive
in Peru, with significant support for its retention and even
for its expansion, there were signs that the institution's days
were numbered. The Crown had long tried to limit slavery
and force owners to try to find alternative workers. Royal
legislation had tightly circumscribed slavery since the beginning of the colonial era, and new efforts were being made
as colonial rule waned. In 1789 the Crown introduced a code
dedicated exclusively to colonial black slavery that "did as
much as could possibly be done . . . to guarantee the rights
and privileges of slaves 'as human beings.' " It obligated
owners to provide their slaves with food, housing, clothing,
medical assistance, and religious instruction and to allow
them days of rest. It limited the amount of work that could be
demanded and the length of the workday, and it restricted
the use of corporal punishment. These kinds of restrictions
were not original, and their reissuance suggests that past
legislation had been either ineffective or ignored. This also
proved to be the case with the new code, for the Crown
resisted challenging slave owners who were determined to
operate the system as they wished, not as the Crown ordered.[8] Nevertheless, pressure from Spain continued, and in
1812 the last slaves of the colonial era arrived in Peru.[9] Five
years later, in response to British pressure, Ferdinand VII
abolished the slave trade altogether, driving up slave prices
to an average of 600 pesos and raising serious doubts about
slavery's future in Peru.[10]

Antislavery pressures were also developing within the
colony. Perhaps the most notable attack of the late colonial
period occurred during the Indian rebellion of 1780–81. Its
mestizo leader, José Gabriel Condorcanqui, more commonly
known as Túpac Amaru II, may not have been a committed
abolitionist, but he realized the potential value of mobilizing
the black population and offered to free any slave who joined

him. His brother, Diego, was more generous, issuing an
abolition decree in September 1781, although his motives
may have been equally opportunistic and few slaves seem to
have been attracted.[11] Slaves, meanwhile, were taking matters into their own hands to weaken the institution. They
sought to secure their freedom by buying it, by claiming it
through the courts on the grounds that their owners had
mistreated them, by cultivating close personal ties with their
owners, and, when all else failed, by running away. These
forms of resistance and accommodation were not new. They
had been a part of Peruvian slavery since the beginning of
the colonial era, but the fact that slaves continued to resort to
them as the Spanish Empire crumbled indicates that they
were not passively awaiting a change in their status; rather,
they were willing to force the issue.[12]

With the outbreak of the wars of independence, the slaves
found themselves in a confusing and contradictory situation
regarding their future. On the one hand, events during the
wars suggested that the end of Spanish rule would also mark
the end of slavery, as initiatives taken during the struggle
were designed to weaken and ultimately to destroy the institution. On the other hand, wartime developments produced
pressures in the opposite direction, in support of slavery, to
ensure that it would continue after the fighting had stopped.

The struggle for Peruvian independence was a long and
complex affair that clearly revealed the basic conservatism of
those who would emerge to rule the new nation.[13] As fighting
spread through Spanish America, Peru remained a bastion of
royalism with only a small minority of the elite supporting
independence. The rest remained loyal to the Crown, in large
part because of their fear of social unrest. Confronting Peru's
small white population was an agglomeration of Indians,
mestizos, blacks, and other castes who outnumbered the
whites by eight to one, who had been exploited for generations,
and whose growing alienation had led to numerous rebellions
in the late colonial period.[14] As a result, Peru was one of the
last colonies to declare itself independent, and then it did so
unwillingly and largely in response to outside pressures.
First, the Argentine, José de San Martín, invaded with an
army of Argentinians and Chileans and declared Peru independent; then a northern army under the direction of the
Venezuelan, Simón Bolívar, secured the military victories
that guaranteed Peru's independence. The fact that a second
invasion was necessary underscored the continuing resis-

tance to separation from Spain, and even after the defeat of the last Spanish forces the response of many Creoles remained at best lukewarm. Peru was a reluctant convert to independence. According to Timothy Anna, it staggered into republicanism "impelled by forces it could not control, afraid of the future but burdened by the past."[15]

Nevertheless, despite the resistance and the desire of many Peruvians to retain much of their colonial heritage, the independence period was not without its pressures for change. This was certainly the case where slavery was concerned. The underlying essence of the period was a call for freedom and equality, both of which held a special appeal for slaves. One of the first suggestions that fundamental changes were about to occur came with the Spanish liberal constitution of 1812. It accepted equality between Spaniards and Creoles and contained a provision permitting persons of African descent to become citizens.[16] It was never implemented, and the restoration of Ferdinand VII in 1814 brought an end to the liberal experiment. However, it helped to galvanize colonial desires for greater self-rule, which were only intensified by the return to absolutism.

The confrontation between liberals and absolutists in Spain had important implications for the colonies. It split the royalist forces and alienated many Creoles who now realized that the only sure way to protect their interests was to secure control themselves. Thus, throughout Spanish America the liberal-absolutist confrontation helped to increase the number of those supporting independence and to ensure the ultimate success of the patriot forces. In the case of Peru, it provided local support for San Martín's invasion in 1820 and his proclamation of independence in the following year.

With San Martín in charge, the slavery system in Peru faced its most serious challenge to date. That challenge came as something of a surprise, for previously San Martín had demonstrated little in the way of abolitionist sympathies. In fact, he is reported to have opposed universal manumission and questioned the mental capabilities of blacks. Moreover, in Peru his actions were circumscribed by his desire not to alienate the creole slaveholders, whose support was essential for the success of his movement and who were already suspicious of independence.[17] Nevertheless, by 1821 he seems to have come to the conclusion that slavery and the slave trade should be destroyed. His conversion may have been a product of liberal connections in Argentina and Chile, or it may have been an opportunistic gesture to win slave support for the independence cause.[18] Because of the constraints upon him, he could not abolish slavery at a stroke, but he introduced a series of decrees that he believed would sow the seeds for its eventual and complete destruction.

The first of these, issued on August 12, 1821, was a law of the free womb. Under it, all children born of slaves in Peru after July 28, 1821, would be free. In its preamble, San Martín attacked the slave trade as an "ancient abuse" and presented the decree as the first step toward the slaves' ultimate freedom. He noted that

> when men have been excessively abused and had their rights violated for a long time, a grand act of justice, although not completely compensatory, will provide at least the first steps toward the acquisition of the most sacred of all rights. A substantial proportion of our population is today looked on as a salable commodity and subject to the calculations of a criminal traffic: Men have purchased men, without any sense of shame. . . . It is obvious that time itself, which has sanctioned this [trade] will destroy it, but I would be irresponsible to my public conscience and to my private feelings if I did not prepare for this future, merciful reform.

At the same time, he recognized the need to be conciliatory to the owners, refusing to set a date for complete abolition.[19]

San Martín's second decree, issued on November 20, restated the Crown's decree of 1817 that ended the slave trade. Responding to "the philanthropic principles that every government of the civilized world has now adopted, desirous of avenging the human race for the outrages it has suffered during the centuries of error and obscurantism that have passed now and forever," the government ordered that any slave who arrived on the soil of independent Peru be freed.[20]

As a result of the decrees, Peru's slavery system seemed doomed, for slaves could not be reproduced. No new supplies could be introduced from without, nor could they be created within the country. Slavery would not disappear overnight, but within a generation it should be on the verge of extinction. The decrees warned owners that they were going to have to consider alternative forms of labor and alter the nature of their labor relations, but it gave them time to adapt to the new state of affairs.

San Martín introduced a number of other laws that were designed to help the slaves. One that followed from his first decree set out regulations concerning the upbringing of the children he had freed. The *libertos*, as they were called, were to be cared for, educated, and trained by their masters, the owners of their mothers, until they reached the ages of twenty for females and twenty-four for males. In return the *libertos* were obligated to serve their masters until they reached the assigned age, at which time they could remain or seek work elsewhere. Both sexes gained full citizenship rights when they became twenty-one.[21]

The aim here may have been to ensure protection for the newly freed children of slaves until they could fend for themselves, but it also had negative implications. Most notably it placed a specific group of blacks under the control of slave owners who faced the prospect of an irreversible decline in their slave labor force. The *libertos* constituted a potential alternative source of labor and by law were obligated to their masters. Thus, they were open to the latter's exploitation. The legislation, therefore, assisted in the perpetuation of a coercive labor system, not in its elimination as San Martín seemed to envision.

Other decrees, although more in reaction to immediate developments, also indicated San Martín's determination to undermine slavery. In September 1821, in response to the threat of a royalist advance on Lima, he issued a call for volunteers and offered freedom to any slave who joined and distinguished himself in the patriot army. With the passing of the threat, he decreed that on September 7 in future years the names of twenty-five slaves who had joined in Lima's defense were to be drawn by lot and freed in recognition of their patriotism, with the state remunerating the owners. Slaves who joined his army after this decree could also obtain their freedom. When owners took to hiding or imprisoning their slaves to retain possession of their valuable property, San Martín legislated that any owner found guilty of preventing a slave from enlisting would lose his or her property in the first instance and be exiled in perpetuity in the second, while the slave making the denunciation would be freed. San Martín seemed to be risking the enmity of Peru's slaveholders in issuing this law, and he challenged them again in early January when he decreed that any hacendado who hid a deserting slave—with the obvious aim of using the deserter as a worker—would face the loss of his property. He also freed the slaves of those Spaniards and Americans who had left Peru, and in October he prohibited the use of the lash.[22]

The groundwork for the destruction of Peruvian slavery was now in place, and San Martín's successors built on these foundations with further legislation that helped the slaves and provided new opportunities for manumission. The marquis of Torre Tagle, who took over the administration of the government in early 1822, recruited slaves on a number of occasions when royalist forces once more threatened Lima. He also prohibited slaves from being compelled to work on holidays, with a 100-peso fine for noncompliance; offered freedom in exchange for three years of military service to the slaves of Spanish bachelors who had been expelled from Peru; and freed slaves who denounced their owners for gambling.[23] Some of the more important changes affecting slavery were incorporated in Peru's first constitution, promulgated in November 1823. It declared that anyone born or arriving in Peru was free, abolished the slave trade, and denied citizenship to any foreigner involved in the slave trade.[24]

When Simón Bolívar, Spanish America's other great liberator, assumed direction of Peru's independence movement in September 1823, the slaves had reason to expect a continuation and even intensification of the liberalizing trends. Bolívar had become a proponent of abolition during the course of his struggles to achieve Venezuelan independence. Initially, he had shown little sympathy, displaying the attitudes and prejudices of Venezuela's aristocracy, of which he was a member. But by 1816, in response to political pressures and the realization that Venezuelan independence could not be achieved without slave support, his views had changed. The turning point seems to have occurred in February of that year, when he promised the president of America's first black republic, Haiti, to free all the slaves in the lands that he liberated. His motivation may have been more opportunism than a newly found humanitarianism, for in return he obtained the arms and supplies he required to carry out his revolution.

The nature of his conversion has produced differing views about his feelings toward slavery and his commitment to abolition. Some charge that Bolívar, like San Martín, considered emancipation solely as a means to bolster his army and secure independence; that he saw independence as a benefit primarily for the white population; that he feared a bloody slave revolt such as had occurred in Haiti and offered freedom only to forestall similar events in Spanish America;

that he opposed the creation of a black-dominated government in Venezuela and made military service a condition of emancipation to reduce the size of the black population; and that he viewed freedom not as a right but as a reward for previous sacrifice, so that slaves had to fight before being emancipated. As late as 1826 the British consul in Peru reported that Bolívar was a firm believer in albocracy, government by whites, since "experience has taught him that though South America is at length freed from her oppressors, if the principles of liberty are too rapidly introduced, anarchy and the destruction of the white inhabitants will be the inevitable consequence."[25] On the other hand are those who have seen Bolívar as a proponent of racial equality and as someone who was aware of the absurdity of an independence movement that maintained a section of the population in chains.[26] Whatever his true feelings, he arrived in Peru with an abolitionist reputation, arousing hopes of further reforms.

These hopes were soon dashed, for Bolívar did little to help the slaves, raising further doubts as to the extent of his conversion. He produced only two legislative initiatives of note, and they provided few benefits. On March 24, 1824, he issued an order that permitted slaves to change their owners.[27] Then, following the military victories at Junín and Ayacucho that definitively secured Peru's independence, he appointed a junta of hacendados from the Lima area to produce a set of regulations concerning rural slaves. The aim was to repair the damage done to agriculture by the war while ensuring that the slaves, whose labor would be crucial to that recovery, were treated with "humanity and justice." Issued on October 14, 1825, the regulations established a ten-hour workday for field hands, from 6:00 A.M. to 6:00 P.M. with a two-hour lunch break, and similar limitations for other workers in the rural sector. Slaves working "overtime" had to be paid as if they were free. The lash could be used as punishment, but no more than twelve times and blood could not be drawn. Married women and those over fourteen could not be whipped, nor could married men over fifty or those who had children over fourteen. Stocks and shackles could be used as alternative forms of punishment. For serious crimes, such as murder and rebellion, the slave had to be tried in a court of law. Owners were required to provide a daily ration of one pound of flour, one pound of beans, and meat if any was available; a set of clothes annually; medical care; and religious instruction. Slaves were forbidden to carry arms or enter towns without permission. Permission also was required for them to carry machetes, axes, or knives. Finally, the local police were responsible for seeing that these regulations were enforced through regular visits to the estates and interviews with the slaves.[28]

Perhaps nothing more should have been expected of Bolívar. He may have felt that sufficient legislation had been passed already for the slaves. The existing decrees, laws, orders, and regulations had touched all aspects of slave life and threatened the continued existence of slavery. The liberators had hesitated only in taking the final step of ordering the immediate and complete abolition of slavery. Complete abolition, however, would have unleashed fierce creole opposition, and the liberators were determined to avoid this at all costs. Their primary goal was independence, not abolition, and to achieve this they required the support of the creole population. The Creoles' opposition to independence had not weakened during San Martín's protectorate. In fact, by the time Bolívar arrived in 1823 the country was on the point of returning completely to the royalist fold.[29] One reason for this was the attack on the slavery system, which had convinced many slaves to join the rebel forces in expectation of manumission. As early as 1818 the viceroy of Peru commented that slaves were "openly decided for the rebels, from whose hands they expect liberty."[30] Although San Martín was reported to have been disappointed by the number he attracted, by January 1822 the majority of his army of between four thousand and five thousand conscripts was said to be slaves. Some claimed that slaves made up his entire army. Children as well as adults seem to have joined; in Pisco, slave mothers were reported to have given their children to officers to secure their children's freedom. And the flow continued after San Martín's departure, as ninety blacks from the Huaral and Sayán area assisted the patriot army in defeating a royalist force in April 1824.[31]

Slaves also fought on the royalist side, and for much the same reason they fought for the rebels. The royalists offered freedom in return for six years of service. In 1821, Viceroy José de La Serna conscripted fifteen hundred slaves from the valleys south of Lima with the promise of complete freedom at the end of the war. They were appraised and their owners compensated by the Crown.[32] The recruits may have been lured by the offer of freedom, but they were not always successful in achieving the goal for which they risked their lives. In one perhaps apocryphal case, a slave serving with the royalist forces asked for his freedom as a reward for wounding the patriot general, Antonio José de Sucre. Instead he was ordered shot, the royalist commander explaining that it was not right to have "canaille" like this attacking generals.[33]

While many slaves obtained their freedom through military service, others took advantage of the chaos of the independence period to achieve the same end by different means. Many simply ran away and then, frequently, turned to crime in order to survive. Weapons were easily obtained, as both royalist and republican owners were arming their slaves to defend their estates. Other slaves acquired weapons by enlisting and then deserting, while still others were armed during the recruiting drives when royalist forces threatened Lima. The result was further insecurity and chaos, particularly in the countryside where estate owners were fleeing, leaving their remaining slaves to fend for themselves. Many of these slaves joined the growing bands of guerrillas and highwaymen who were infesting the countryside and even threatening urban centers. No one seemed willing or able to suppress them. In September 1824, before Bolívar arrived in Lima to take charge and restore some degree of order, the British business community urged the landing of English marines to prevent what they feared was an imminent uprising by urban blacks.[34]

The loss of slaves through enlistment, confiscation by one side or the other, and flight left the country's slaveholders, especially those who were estate owners, in a precarious financial position. They also had lost their animals and seed, and their crops had been destroyed. Coastal agriculture was virtually in ruins. One can understand why they had little affection for San Martín and why his successors chose not to introduce additional antislavery laws.[35]

Deepening the hostility of the Creoles and further limiting the options available to the liberators was the country's desperate economic situation. By the late colonial period the prosperity that had marked the sixteenth century had long passed, and Peru was now a poor sister among its Spanish-American relatives. The situation worsened with the outbreak of the independence struggles, as mines were flooded and destroyed, fields were left untilled, communication and supply lines were disrupted, property was abandoned, and money disappeared in the baggage of departing capitalists. The new republican government thus had few financial resources to draw upon, compelling it to resort to frequent forced loans and requisitions in order to run the government and supply the army. The sums collected were insufficient to meet the various needs. Moreover, the requisitions antagonized those who were compelled to pay. Their animosity was an important factor in the political instability, machinations, and loss of support that blocked San Martín from securing the complete independence of Peru and eventually convinced him to withdraw in favor of Bolívar.[36]

The financial crisis also ensured that abolition did not proceed at a faster pace. Whatever money was available to San Martín and his successors was directed into the war effort; nothing was left for humanitarian gestures such as freeing slaves, nor for compensating slave owners. There is no indication that the liberators considered uncompensated emancipation. It was probably contrary to their beliefs, and strategically it made no sense at all, for it would have alienated further those who already were upset by the antislavery legislation and the economic crisis. The only property some Creoles had left was their slaves. To be threatened with the complete, uncompensated loss of this final source of wealth would have driven them immediately and irrevocably into the royalist camp.

Aware of the hostilities they had aroused, Peru's liberators began taking steps to reassure the Creoles, particularly the slaveholders. Some of their decrees had a short life span, especially those that had mobilized the slaves. In part this was because the threat had passed, although it was also a response to the objections of owners who wanted their workers returned.[37] Other complaints gave rise to new legislation. In October 1822 the constituent congress declared that slaves owned by private citizens could not be used on public works. Peru's first president, José de la Riva Agüero, was particularly active in assisting slaveholders: He rescinded decrees that allowed the recruitment of slaves, arguing that it was hurting the poor. He also prohibited the further conscription of slaves and ordered that those in service be returned to their owners or that restitution be paid.[38]

Under Bolívar the policy of assisting the owners intensified. Now that the political situation had been resolved, there was a general desire to reestablish order and restore the country's economic base. Past legislation, such as the annual freeing of twenty-five slaves and the regulation of rural slaves, was ignored or forgotten; the 1823 liberal constitution was never applied; and taxes on estate owners were reduced or eliminated.[39] New legislation restored controls over the slaves and nullified earlier liberal laws. A September 1825 decree compelled slaves to carry identity cards. The decree's stated aims were to clarify ownership and to catch those slaves who were claiming freedom on the basis of a false military record. It urged humane treatment for slaves, especially the elderly, but ordered that those who failed to carry their identity cards were to be recruited into the army or forced to work until claimed by their owners. In November the government restricted the rights of slaves who had served in the army by limiting freedom to those who had enlisted before November 5, 1824, and were still in service, along with those who had been invalided out of the army or who had been freed for some other reason; the rest were to be returned to their owners. In April 1826 the government tried to protect slaveholders further by threatening hacendados who lured slaves away from neighboring estates with a fine of twice the wage they paid the fugitive slave.[40]

Slavery continued, although the number of slaves was not large. At the end of the Independence Wars, Peru's slave population numbered around 50,400, or only 3.8 percent of the country's 1,325,000 inhabitants. There were also 40,000 free blacks. The number of slaves subsequently declined. In 1855, at the time of abolition, the government agreed to pay compensation for 25,505 blacks. Several thousand of them—one source reckons 6,000—were *libertos*, so the total number of slaves had fallen to around 19,000, or less than 1 percent of Peru's 2,000,000 inhabitants.[41]

While the size of the slave population was not large, most of the slaves, unlike the Peruvian population as a whole, were concentrated on the coast. They resided in the narrow river valleys running between the Andes and the Pacific Ocean, particularly in those valleys located between Piura in the north and Ica in the center-south, with the largest group in the Lima area. A survey in 1845 calculated that the slave population for the country then numbered 20,000, with 4,500 slaves in the Lima region; 2,500 in Chancay and Santa; 2,000 in each of Ica, Pisco, and La Libertad; 1,950 in Cañete; 1,500 in Chincha; and another 3,500 spread through the interior working as domestic servants.[42] Their concentration on the coast meant that, despite their overall small numbers, they comprised a significant portion of the population in specific areas and were consequently important in those areas. The most obvious example of this was the department of Lima. A 1796 census counted 17,881 slaves in the area, which translates into an impressive 28.4 percent of the local population. The figure may have been inflated, or the decline of the slave population following the termination of the slave trade and the dislocations of the Independence Wars may have been as extensive as some commentators claimed, for by 1820 there were only 8,539 slaves in the area, a much reduced 13.4 percent of the population. This decline was dramatic, but slaves still made up a significant proportion of the local population, and they continued to do so for the next decade. In 1836 there were 7,798 slaves in the area, amounting to 12.4 percent of the population.[43]

Thus, slavery was still a thriving institution in Peru decades after independence. It survived despite the apparent desires of the liberators, the extensive legislation they had passed that attacked the very roots of the slavery system, and the inclusion of their principal antislavery decrees in the constitutions of 1828 and 1834.[44] It survived despite the contribution of the slaves to the independence struggles and the pressure of those who argued after the end of the struggles that any slave who had "exposed his life for the liberty of the republic," regardless of the length of time, deserved his freedom. "Slavery," they charged, "is opprobrious to humanity, and it would be the most stupid contradiction to fight so gloriously for freedom on the one hand while maintaining slavery on the other."[45]

Others, no doubt, shared these sentiments, but in the first years after independence slavery's opponents lacked the necessary resources to challenge the system successfully. San Martín and the other liberators may have laid the groundwork for slavery's demise, but they had failed to supply the coup de grace. As a result, slavery continued. It remained a vitally important institution, and Peru's slaveholders were still a powerful and influential group who were determined that slavery should survive as long as possible.

## Notes

1. Quoted in Jorge Basadre, *Historia de la república del Perú, 1822–1933,* 6th ed. (Lima, 1969–70), 1:1. This and all other translations from Spanish that appear in this volume were prepared by the author.

2. For the most thorough examination of slavery in early colonial Peru see Bowser, *African Slave.* See also James Lockhart, *Spanish Peru, 1532–1560: A Colonial Society* (Madison, 1968), chap. 10; and Alberto Flores Galindo S., *Aristocracia y plebe: Lima, 1760–1830 (estructura de clases y sociedad colonial)* (Lima, 1984), 108–9.

3. Bowser, *African Slave,* 333, chap. 9; Henry E. Dobyns and Paul L. Doughty, *Peru: A Cultural History* (New York, 1976), 129; Christine Hünefeldt, "Los negros de Lima: 1800–1830," *Histórica* 3 (1979): 21–26; Fernando Romero, "Papel de los descendientes de africanos en el desarrollo económico-social del Perú," *Histórica* 4 (1980): 84; Juan Manuel Ugarte Eléspuru, *Lima y lo limeño,* 2d ed. (Lima, n.d.), 105, 112–13, 132–36, 140, 153–55.

4. J. R. Fisher, *Government and Society in Colonial Peru: The Intendant System, 1784–1814* (London, 1970), 148; Gaspar Rico y Angulo, *Proyecto relativo al comercio, suerte y servidumbre de los esclavos, inclinado a su transición oportuna a libres, durante el tiempo que debe continuar la introducción en territorios españoles* (Cádiz, 1813), 33.

5. These and the other statistics quoted are of questionable accuracy, but they give a general idea of numbers and trends. Ricardo Palma, *Tradiciones peruanas: colección completa* (Lima, 1957), 18:187; Dobyns and Doughty, *Peru,* 153. John Fisher gives a different picture. He has written that despite continuing demand and supportive legislation, few slaves were imported from the 1790s onward. See Fisher, *Government and Society,* 148–49.

6. *El Peruano,* December 16, 1826.

7. For slavery in the late colonial period see Flores Galindo, *Aristocracia,* chap. 4; and Hünefeldt, "Los negros de Lima," 27–49.

8. Manuel Labarthe, "Castilla y la abolición de la esclavitud," *Publicaciones del Instituto "Libertador Ramón Castilla"* (1955): 9; Luis Felipe Paredes, "Castilla y la abolición de la esclavitud," *Revista Universitaria* 109 (1955): 11. For the 1789 slave code see Herbert S. Klein, *Slavery in the Americas: A Comparative Study of Virginia and Cuba* (Chicago, 1967), 78–84.

9. Flores Galindo, *Aristocracia,* 103. Other sources say the last slaves of the colonial era arrived in 1814.

10. Palma, *Tradiciones* 18:187.

11. For more on the Túpac Amaru rebellion see Lillian Estelle Fisher, *The Last Inca Revolt, 1780–1783* (Norman, 1966); and Scarlett O'Phelan Godoy, *Rebellions and Revolts in Eighteenth Century Peru and Upper Peru* (Cologne, 1985), chap. 5. For the tactical nature of Túpac Amaru's abolitionism see Leon G. Campbell, "Social Structure of the Túpac Amaru Army in Cuzco, 1780–81," *HAHR* 61 (1981): 685 n. 22; and John Lynch, *The Spanish American Revolutions, 1808–1826* (London, 1973), 165.

12. Bowser, *African Slave,* chaps. 8, 10; Hünefeldt, "Los negros de Lima," 36–49.

13. The various details and problems of Peru's independence struggle are outside the scope of this study. For more information see Timothy E. Anna, *The Fall of the Royal Government in Peru* (Lincoln, 1979); and Lynch, *Spanish American Revolutions*, chaps. 5, 8.

14. Leon G. Campbell, "Recent Research on Andean Peasant Revolts, 1750–1820," *Latin American Research Review* 14 (1979): 3–49; Lynch, *Spanish American Revolutions*, 164; O'Phelan Godoy, *Rebellions and Revolts.*

15. Anna, *Fall of the Royal Government*, 179–83, 238.

16. Concerning the constitution see ibid., 82–85.

17. Lynch, *Spanish American Revolutions*, 275; Rout, *African Experience*, 169; Núria Sales de Bohigas, *Sobre esclavos, reclutas y mercaderes de quintos* (Barcelona, 1974), 108.

18. Pablo Macera, "Las plantaciones azucareras andinas (1821–1875)," in Pablo Macera, *Trabajos de historia* (Lima, 1977), 4:74–75.

19. *Gaceta del Gobierno de Lima Independiente*, August 18, 1821. The law was similar to that issued in Argentina in January 1813. See Andrews, *Afro-Argentines*, 48.

20. *Gaceta del Gobierno* (Lima), November 28, 1821.

21. Ibid., December 5, 1821.

22. *Gaceta del Gobierno de Lima Independiente*, September 5, 26, October 27, November 21, 1821, January 12, 1822.

23. *Gaceta del Gobierno* (Lima), January 26, February 2, March 9, 30, April 17, May 15, 1822, August 9, 1823.

24. Basadre, *Historia* 1:19, 68, 231, 235–36; Fredrick B. Pike, *The Modern History of Peru* (London, 1967), 54–55.

25. Ricketts to Canning, 2, April 25, 1826, Foreign Office files, 61/7, Public Record Office, London, England (hereafter cited as F.O., followed by file number).

26. Harold A. Bierck, Jr., "The Struggle for Abolition in Gran Colombia," *HAHR* 33 (1953): 365–73; Lombardi, *Decline and Abolition*, 40–42, 46; Lynch, *Spanish American Revolutions*, 262.

27. Perú, *Colección o catálogo de leyes, decretos, ordenes, reglamentos e instrucciones, dictadas desde el año de 1820 hasta el de 1831* ([Lima], n. d.).

28. Perú, *Colección de leyes, decretos y ordenes publicadas en el Perú, desde su independencia en el año de 1821* (Lima and Huaraz, 1831–1853), 2:96–97; *Gaceta del Gobierno de Lima*, October 16, 1825. See also Basadre, *Historia* 1:236–37; and César Gutiérrez Muñoz, "El reglamento de 1825 y la situación del esclavo en el Perú republicano," *Enseñanza de la Historia* 3 (1972): 10–19.

29. Anna, *Fall of the Royal Government*, 220–21.

30. Quoted in ibid., 151. See also Rowcroft to Planta, 3, July 2, 1824, F.O. 61/2.

31. Anna, *Fall of the Royal Government*, 196, 202; Francisco Javier Mariátegui, "Anotaciones a la historia del Perú independiente de don Mariano Felipe Paz Soldán (1819–1822)," in *Colección documental de la independencia del Perú. Tomo XXVI. Memorias diarias y crónicas*, ed. Félix Denegri Luna (Lima, 1971), 2:46; Rowcroft, private, June 22, 1824, F.O. 61/2; *Gaceta del Gobierno* (Trujillo), May 1, 1824. Some of the blacks in San Martín's army had accompanied him from Argentina. See Andrews, *Afro-Argentines*, 117–18.

32. Anna, *Fall of the Royal Government*, 172; "Virreynato, 1821: alistamiento de negros," Lima, February 18, 1821, Oficina de Investigaciones Bibliográficas, D5985, Biblioteca Nacional, Lima, Peru (hereafter cited as BN, followed by file number).

33. Nicolás Rebaza, *Anales del departamento de La Libertad* (Trujillo, 1898), 96.

34. Rowcroft to Maling, 14, September 2, 1824, F.O. 61/3; *El Comercio*, April 27, 1841; Anna, *Fall of the Royal Government*, 197; Flores Galindo, *Aristocracia*, 224–26.

35. *Gaceta del Gobierno* (Lima), April 3, 1825; Palma, *Tradiciones* 18:188.

36. Timothy E. Anna, "Economic Causes of San Martín's Failure in Lima," *HAHR* 54 (1974): 657–81. For Peru's late-colonial poverty see Anna, *Fall of the Royal Government*, chaps. 1, 8, 9.

37. For examples of decrees that were revoked see Perú, *Colección de leyes* 1:200.

38. *Gaceta del Gobierno* (Lima), October 12, 1822, March 8, May 21, 1823.

39. Labarthe, "Castilla y la abolición," 17; Sales de Bohigas, *Sobre esclavos*, 120. Since they named the local officials, rural slaveholders maintained virtually complete control over the implementation of regulations concerning rural slaves. See Alberto Ulloa y Sotomayor, *La organización social y legal del trabajo en el Perú* (Lima, 1916), 62.

40. *Gaceta del Gobierno de Lima*, April 28, September 22, November 24, 1825, April 12, 1826.

41. Basadre, *Historia* 1:208, 4:113; Dobyns and Doughty, *Peru*, 171; Santiago Tavara, *Abolición de la esclavitud en el Perú* (Lima, 1855), 29. For an analysis of population figures and censuses in the early republic see Paul Gootenberg, "Population and Ethnicity in Early Republican Peru: Some Revisions," *Latin American Research Review* 26 (1991): 109–57.

42. Enclosure with Adams to Aberdeen, Slave Trade (hereafter cited as ST), 5, August 4, 1845, F.O. 84/595.

43. P. Emilio Dancuart, *Anales de la hacienda pública del Perú: leyes, decretos, reglamentos y resoluciones; aranceles, presupuestos, cuentas y contratas que constituyen la legislación y la historia fiscal de la república* (Lima, 1902–1908), 2:15; *Memorias de los virreyes que han governado el Perú, durante el tiempo del coloniaje español* (Lima, 1859), 6:6–9, table 3; Fernando Romero, "El mestizaje negroide en la demografía del Perú," *Revista Histórica* 28 (1965): 244.

44. Basadre, *Historia* 2:86, 300.

45. "Expediente promovido por D. Vicente del Castillo solicitando le se devuelto un esclavo negro de su propiedad llamado Manuel del Castillo, enrolado en la artilleria," Archivo General de la Nación, Lima, Peru (hereafter cited as AGN), 1826, O.L. 145-56.

# 2

# The Importance of Slaves

Slavery survived in Peru for more than thirty years after independence because the government and the dominant elite continued to view it as an institution that was of vital importance to themselves and to the nation as a whole. The early republican governments were convinced that it was essential to the country's economic recovery and prosperity; members of the elite believed that it was crucial to their personal wealth and social position. A conservative group with strong ties to the institutions of the past, the elite considered slavery a viable labor system and slaves a valuable investment that had to be protected. After independence slaves were still a major component of the labor force on the estates and farms and in the urban centers along the coast, just as they had been during the colonial period. Many of them worked as domestic servants, ensuring the smooth operation of urban and rural households. As property, they represented a significant financial investment that could be converted into a substantial return if they were sold or rented. They could be used as collateral for loans or mortgages. Furthermore, many Peruvians believed that slaves were the most efficient and, more important, the cheapest laborers available, a critical factor during the financially troubled times that marked Peru's first decades as an independent nation. Government leaders, slave owners, and other influential members of the population remained committed to the proposition that slavery was beneficial, even essential, to the well-being of both themselves and the country.

In their considerations of slavery, contemporary observers tended to concentrate on Peru's rural slaves, largely because agriculture was in the midst of a profound crisis and slaves were seen as vital to its recovery. Estates had suffered greatly during the wars of independence, giving rise to report after report on the poor state of the rural economy. The British consul to Peru, Charles Milner Ricketts, wrote in 1826 that "at present on whatever point it may be viewed the scene is dismal, and the appearance such as if the country had just suffered from one of those dreadful earthquakes which lay all in ruin and devastation. The lands are waste, edifices to be rebuilt, the population diminished, the government unstable, just laws to be established, new capital to be raised, and tranquillity to be secured." Areas that had been profitable in the past were now in a state of decline. Ricketts noted that in the Pisco region,

> the cultivation of sugar was once carried on to a considerable extent; on one estate alone when General San Martin landed with the expedition from Chile, 1,200 slaves were employed in its manufacture; the number is now reduced to 300 and these principally aged persons and children. So much indeed has the population been diminished by the late war that the cultivation of the vine and sugar-cane is not more than one fourth of what it formerly was.[1]

Elsewhere in the center-south the situation was the same. The San José de la Nazca estate and its annex, La Ventilla, were described in 1828 as "a lamentable picture." The land was abandoned, the slave population was demoralized, and the vineyards were destroyed. At San Jacinto de la Nazca the estate house was in ruins and the slaves were naked and starving; San Regis was "totally abandoned." In the Cañete Valley, slaves were in short supply. Only the Montalván estate, owned by the exiled Chilean independence leader Bernardo O'Higgins, was "in a thriving state," and this was because his slaves were "protected from impressment." However, even O'Higgins had difficulty retaining them. By 1846 his estate possessed only 138 slaves, a far cry from the 600 it had boasted twenty-four years earlier. Similar diminutions were evident on estates around Lima. Between 1836 and 1846, Santa Beatriz's slave population fell by 45 percent, Monterrico Grande's by 86 percent, and those of other estates by amounts that ranged between these two extremes.[2]

The agrarian desolation reflected the owners' inability to make their lands pay. In the 1820s many estates were operating at a loss or showing only a minimal profit. Records from San José de la Nazca and San Javier de la Nazca, two former Jesuit estates that now were run by the state, reveal that during the four-year period from 1825 to 1828, San José lost 6,504 pesos, as expenses totaled 10,918 pesos, with income amounting to only 4,414 pesos. Between 1824 and 1829, San Javier suffered a loss of 9,602 pesos, with expenses of 22,851 pesos and income of 13,249 pesos. The single bright spot during these years was 1827, when San Javier recorded a profit, but it amounted to only 363 pesos, the equivalent of the price of one slave or the annual return on two rented slaves.[3]

The passage of time saw few improvements in the overall picture. A British observer during the 1830s noted abandoned villas, farms, and gardens on the road from Callao to Lima and blamed the country's chronic political unrest for their state. In the same decade, the only thing of value on San José and San Javier seemed to be their slaves. A Chilean visitor in 1846 still found abandoned and uncultivated fields around Lima and in the Cañete Valley, and he, too, blamed the continuing political chaos, as well as a lack of capital and a shortage of slaves.[4] The following year the minister of government, José Gregorio Paz Soldán, told congress that "agriculture on the coast is in a lamentable state of decadence. On some haciendas there are sufficient slaves for farming, but the double action of manumission and death is resulting in their disappearance."[5] Six years later, President José Rufino Echenique announced to the nation's legislators:

> Agriculture continues improving from the state of prostration to which the wars of independence and the subsequent internal convulsions reduced it, but I cannot say to you that it has made great progress.
> The lack of capital, workers, and markets has disheartened those dedicated to the cultivation of the land . . .
> Almost all the haciendas, especially on the coast, comprise extensive plots, of which a large part is left uncultivated. The principal products like sugarcane and *aguardiente* have lost their markets, and the other produce is sold at prices so low that they are rarely adequate to cover costs.[6]

Despite the dismal picture of a rural economy reduced to self-sufficiency or limited largely to local markets, not everyone was pessimistic about the country's agricultural prospects.[7] Some were willing to take a risk and rent estates. The social status associated with landholding may have served as sufficient inducement for many. Others may have had alternative sources of income to offset the costs of running an estate even at a loss, but most were probably reckoning that they could make the land pay, and pay handsomely, for rents (despite a decrease since the colonial period) were still substantial. In 1825 the Augustinian order leased its Monterrico Grande estate for four years with an option for five additional years at a rent of 1,500 pesos the first year, 2,000 the second, and 3,000 thereafter. The contract included fourteen slaves who were to remain on the estate but stipulated that if a slave died or was removed for public service the rent would be reduced by 6 pesos monthly. In the 1830s the Augustinians set 5,000 pesos as the rent for one of their estates, while other landlords were probably asking similar or even larger amounts. In many cases the financial demands were too great for the leaseholders to meet.

Most rental contracts during the first fifteen years after independence were terminated before the contract had expired. For example, Henry Swayne, a Scottish trader and longtime resident of Peru, in 1837 arranged a mortgage with Narciso de la Colina, the lessee of the Buenamuerte order's estates in the Cañete Valley, to try to assist the estates' recovery. Despite the injection of capital and the importation of machinery from Europe, returns failed to cover expenses, so that when Colina died shortly thereafter, he owed 350,000 pesos. Swayne, however, remained confident that landholding could be profitable. He had the lease transferred from the Colina family and negotiated with the order to rent the estates and their slaves for 28,000 pesos annually for twenty-seven years. He had the advantage of being able to call on his merchant house and his ties with other traders, both locally and in London. Nevertheless, his willingness to commit himself to such a substantial rent suggests that by the 1840s the agrarian picture was finally beginning to improve.[8]

Although they seem to have been the exception rather than the rule, as the frequent changes of land ownership during this period attest, other examples of successful landholders can be found. Among them was the prominent planter, businessman, and politician Domingo Elías. A member of an established Ica family, Elías first acquired properties in the area through inheritance and marriage. In the 1830s he began adding to his holdings, so that within twenty years he owned much of the Pisco, Ica, Nazca, Palpa, and Chincha valleys. He concentrated on the production of grapes, foodstuffs, and especially cotton, quickly establishing himself as the foremost cotton producer in the country.[9]

However, even successful planters such as Elías had to deal with a problem that commanded the attention of virtually every Peruvian landholder, whether large or small, owner or renter, successful or unsuccessful, as well as the attention of those commenting on the agrarian scene. That problem was the shortage of agricultural labor. Contemporary observers insisted that the country suffered from a lack of workers, particularly on the coast. Ricketts referred to a general "deficiency of hands" and a particular shortage in the sugar industry, and he proposed some reasons for that deficiency. "A want of population," he wrote, "necessarily causes an excessive scarcity and dearness of labour; the disposition of the people is feeble and inert; they are most ignorant; and the comforts and even the decencies of life are generally unknown." Moreover, alternative workers could not be recruited, even from the heavily populated highlands. In Ricketts's words, "It has been found impossible heretofore to induce the natives to leave the mountainous districts for the purpose of working as labourers in the low lands." It was a view shared by Peruvians. A newspaper article in 1830 claimed that the numbers of whites and mestizos on the coast were inadequate for its agricultural needs, and *serranos* could not be lured from their Andean homes because they were unable to cope with the coastal heat and were needed to work in the sierra.[10]

Ricketts and the anonymous newspaper writer were either ignoring deliberately or unaware of the significant contribution that *serranos* and free workers were making to the labor needs of the coast. Although the poor state of communications between the sierra and the coast plus the factors listed in the newspaper report limited the numbers involved, many *serranos* traveled from their sierra homes to work as temporary laborers between their own harvesting and planting seasons. In addition, Indian villages still existed along the coast, and their inhabitants (along with free blacks, mestizos, and others) were drawn into the coastal laboring population. They worked, in some cases alongside slaves, as free wage laborers, sharecroppers, and tenant farmers. A Lima newspaper claimed in 1845 that free workers such as these were responsible for the cultivation of sugarcane and the production of sugar in entire districts of Lambayeque and Camaná. In the Chancay Valley they grew much of the food that was eventually sold in Lima. The British traveler Clements R. Markham found local Indians working on estates in the Mala Valley in the early 1850s.[11] Thus, alternative workers existed, but they would not play the role in weakening Peruvian slavery that similar workers did in Cuba and in Northeast Brazil, for they were difficult to hire, located in the wrong part of the country, inadequate to meet local needs, and not totally reliable as they could leave the estates and return home whenever they wished.[12] In sum, they were not the preferred type of worker, with the result that attention continued to focus on the group who comprised the major visible sector of the coastal labor force, the slaves.

While the number of slaves was small, their importance was unquestioned. One result, in Ricketts's view, was that they could expect no further concessions from the government, since "the manumission of the slaves who are the only cultivators of the soil, would be followed by their desertion from the Estates on which they were employed, and . . . the landholders would hence be exposed to have their lands left waste." It was a view shared by others, including the 1830 newspaper writer who concluded that blacks had to be kept enslaved because they refused to work when freed.[13] The link between agricultural well-being and the size of the slave labor force would be mentioned time and again by analysts and observers trying to explain Peru's agricultural problems. Paz Soldán, the minister of government, referred to it in his address to congress in 1847. That same year an official in the province of Ica made the same points when he argued that the decline in the number of slaves had resulted in the "decadence" of valuable estates, whose output no longer covered their operating expenses or rents.[14]

The view that the labor shortage in general and the falling number of slaves in particular were responsible for Peru's agricultural problems was not totally inaccurate, but it was simplistic and failed to take into account other important factors. The complexities of the issue had not been lost on Ricketts who, in his evaluation of the causes of the agricultural crisis, listed (in addition to the shortage of workers) the limited consumption of rural products resulting from the general poverty and local political problems of the country, the distances involved, and the poor state of communications and transportation.[15] However, more Peruvians shared the view of the Ica official. They were convinced that the country's agricultural production was dependent upon an adequate supply of slave labor, and, consequently, they opposed any measures to abolish or even to weaken slavery.

This commitment was reinforced by the belief that slaves were cheap workers. With the agrarian sector and the economy in general in a depressed state, employers wanted the cheapest workers available, and (according to Pablo Macera, who has examined the relative costs of slaves, wage labor, and Chinese coolies during the postindependence period) slaves were by far the least expensive. Whether employers made this type of calculation is unknown, but many of them believed it to be the case. The 1830 newspaper article cited above argued that slaves were cheap because they were accustomed to living on very little: They could be satisfied with beans and salt in a corn-flour soup for food, and with rough, durable wool for clothing. The writer concluded that without slave labor day-to-day necessities would not be produced, prices would rise, expensive foreign goods would flow into the country, and the poor would suffer.[16] Thus, despite their falling numbers, slaves retained their importance and continued to be used in preference to whatever other workers were available, including free wage labor. In the Chancay Valley, for example, the agrarian sector in 1848 employed 2,420 slaves and only 329 free workers.[17]

The general belief that slavery was integral to the country's well-being was reinforced daily by the concrete evidence of the slaves' employment in a variety of rural and urban occupations. In the countryside, slaves were the field workers on sugar and cotton plantations, in vineyards, and on truck farms. The average number of slaves per estate, in tandem with the slave population as a whole, may have declined following the wars of independence, yet many planters continued to own large numbers. Ricardo Palma claimed that the average was between 150 and 200, with many planters owning 300 slaves. In the 1820s seven or eight estates in the Cañete region possessed 400 slaves each; in 1829, San Javier de la Nazca and San José de la Nazca owned 328 and 149 slaves, respectively. Flora Tristán wrote that there were 900 slaves on the Lavalle estate near Lima in the early 1830s, while Pedro Félix Vicuña counted 500 on the San Pedro estate near Lurín in 1846.[18] Most of these men, women, and children would have been field workers, but the nature of the work and the need for foremen and specialists in the cultivation and processing of the commodities would have created a few divisions among them.

Some rural slaves had urban links. Muleteers in charge of their owners' trains of mules transported goods between towns or from the countryside to the urban centers and back again. Robert Proctor has left a colorful description of them. "The muleteers," he wrote, "formed the most grotesque appearance imaginable. Most of them are blacks or half castes, and remarkably tall: their dark features under the immense brimmed hats of the country, sometimes of the natural colour, white, sometimes painted black, and their long legs hanging down naked on each side of their beasts, with their huge Dutch breeches gave them a wild and ferocious appearance, the effect of which their long whips and cries of anger or encouragement to the mules tended to increase."[19] Others with rural and urban ties were the market vendors. As in the colonial period, male and female slaves were involved in the production, preparation, and sale of food in the urban markets. Proctor described Lima's markets in the early 1820s as "crowded with negroes, who cook savory dishes in the open air, and sell them. . . . Those who sell fruit and vegetables spread them on the ground beneath a huge umbrella of canvas: these commodities are conveyed by slaves from the farms and orchards in the vicinity of Lima: they are paid by their masters according to the price they can procure, and, in general, everything of the kind is extremely dear." Thirty years later, Clements Markham noted that slaves were still taking fruit and vegetables to market for sale.[20]

In the Lima region, unlike the rest of the country, most slaves were employed in urban occupations. This pattern had been evident in the late colonial period, and it continued through the early republic. One writer calculated that 80 percent of the country's "41,228 registered slaves" in 1821 were engaged in agriculture, primarily in work on sugar plantations, with the rest employed in domestic or artisanal occupations. Yet in the province of Lima, "most" of the slaves in 1792 worked in the capital. In 1828, after the Independence Wars, 4,206 slaves or about half the slave population were working in the city with the other half working on haciendas in the area. By 1839 the figure had grown to 60 percent living and working in the urban zone, a level that continued to the 1850s.[21]

In the urban centers, slaves were found in virtually any job involving artisanry, skilled, or unskilled labor. They made shoes, adobe bricks, and chocolate; they worked in bakeries and pastry shops; they were general laborers, porters, water carriers, painters, and bricklayers. Many slaves possessed a number of skills, acquired probably at the behest of their owners since this increased their value and salability. A newspaper advertisement in 1843 announcing the flight of three male slaves reported that one had worked as a bricklayer, painter, and bakery worker; another as a shoemaker and bakery worker; and the third as a master adobe brick maker, night watchman (*sereno*), and soldier.[22]

Slaves were also indispensable to the operation of many households in both the city and the countryside. As a result of his experiences, Proctor came to the conclusion that Lima women were "extremely bad housewives" who "never take the least interest in domestic concerns, which are always wretchedly managed by some favorite slave, or *majordomo*." Regardless of how they performed their tasks, slaves were responsible for purchasing the family's necessities and for seeing to all the household duties, such as cooking, cleaning, and laundering. In families with infants, the wet nurse was usually a slave.[23] Outside the house there were additional duties. Female slaves accompanied their mistresses to church, carrying the rugs on which they sat, since churches lacked pews or seats. Male slaves accompanied their owners when on business or when engaged in more leisurely activities, such as attending the theater. They drove the carriage when the family took its nightly circuit along the alameda. In the countryside their duties were much the same. Markham gives the impression that they were ubiquitous in the houses that he visited along the coast in 1852–53. At one house they attended meals, waving fans to circulate the air and to keep the flies off the food. Another of his hosts provided slaves as guides. So important were slaves as domestics that even nuns sworn to poverty took them into the convent to run errands and maintain contacts with the outside world.[24]

With the development of the guano industry in the 1840s, a new use for slaves appeared. Along with convicts, army deserters, and free wage laborers from Peru and Chile, they were the initial labor force on the guano islands. The introduction of Chinese coolies reduced their importance, but some were still employed. In September 1853, fifty slaves were working on the islands, earning 2 reals daily like the other eleven hundred guano workers.[25]

While the slaves' multifaceted role in the labor force was probably the single most important factor in the continuing commitment to slavery in Peru, other features of the system also contributed. Many Peruvians were attracted by its financial possibilities, as slaves constituted a significant investment with the potential for a high rate of return. Slaves were expensive, although average prices had declined since the colonial period, when a healthy adult male cost between 500 and 900 pesos and infants, depending on sex, sold for between 100 and 300 pesos.[26] During the early republican period an optimistic owner might demand 1,000 pesos for a slave, but this was the rare exception.[27] In Lima the more usual top price for a slave during the three decades after 1824 ranged between 300 and 400 pesos; the average price, as the following table shows, was often much lower. Outside Lima, prices tended to be slightly higher, perhaps enough to convince owners to ship slaves around the country to obtain the best price. Newspapers of the period give the names of individuals who had obtained passports for themselves and their slaves for internal travel. In some instances the slaves were probably being taken from one of their owner's residences to another; in others they were accompanying the owner on business or pleasure; but in others they either were being taken to be sold or had just been bought and were being brought back to the owner's home.[28] The table also indicates that prices increased slightly in the final years of slavery. This increase probably reflected the declining number of slaves, the growing demand for workers, the shortage of alternative sources of indigenous labor, and the high prices being demanded for *libertos*, many of whom were in their early thirties and at the peak of their value. Masters in Lima at this time were demanding between 400 and 500 pesos for a *liberto*.

Average Price of Slaves and *Libertos*
(in pesos)

|          | 1820s | 1830s | 1840s | 1850s |
|----------|-------|-------|-------|-------|
| Lima     | 197   | 229   | 211   | 296   |
| Arequipa | 309   | 255   | 182   | 202   |
| Trujillo | —     | —     | 260   | 291   |
| Estates  | 281[a]|       | 249[b]| 246[c]|
| Average  | 262   | 242   | 225   | 259   |

a Acaray-cua and Puente
b Chiclín, Retes, San Antonio, and Palpa
c Mocán and others

The prices for slaves and the numbers owned by individuals or institutions meant that slaves constituted a significant portion of the value of the estates or businesses to which they were attached. Prior to independence, slaves on a rural estate could be worth almost half the estate's value. In 1811, San José de la Nazca possessed slaves worth 46.6 percent of its value; in 1815, San Jacinto de Nepeña's slaves were worth 41.8 percent.[30] Despite the subsequent destruction of the Independence Wars and the declining number of slaves, they continued to comprise a significant percentage of the total value of the estates. The return from fourteen slaves of Monterrico Grande in 1825 amounted to two thirds of the rent paid for the estate and its slaves. The leaseholders paid 1,500 pesos in the first year of the contract, when the rental value of each slave was reckoned at 6 pesos monthly, or over 1,000 pesos annually. The ratio fell as the rent rose to 3,000 pesos by 1827, but it still amounted to one third of the estate's rent.[31] The ratio fell even further as the number of slaves continued to decline over the following decades and land values rose in response to agricultural developments. Nevertheless, slaves remained a substantial part of the value of rural properties. In 1845 the Chiclín estate near Trujillo was appraised at 39,655 pesos, including twenty-seven slaves worth 3,155 pesos, or 7.9 percent of the total. In 1847 the wine-producing estate of San Antonio de Zárate in Ica was appraised at 137,717 pesos, with fifty-six slaves worth 11,610 pesos, or 8.4 percent of the total.[32] Urban slaves constituted a much higher percentage, reflecting the lower value of the property to which they were attached. In 1849 the Lima bakery of Pablo Bocanegra was appraised at 4,565 pesos, of which 2,160 pesos or 47.3 percent was the value of the bakery's ten slaves.[33] However, even when slaves constituted a small percentage of the total value, they were still a vital component, for without their labor the enterprise's income would have been much reduced, or perhaps eliminated altogether if alternative workers could not be found. Moreover, they were a commodity that always could be sold if the need arose.

Slaves could be used to obtain money in other ways as well. Since they were property they were accepted as collateral for loans and mortgages, either by themselves or along with the estate or place of business to which they belonged.[34] At a time when capital was scarce and income uncertain, they could make the difference in securing the money their owners required. They could also earn money for their owners by being hired or rented out. Wet nurses were frequently used in this fashion. In 1827 the state, as owner of San Javier de la Nazca, received 6 pesos monthly for one of its slaves hired out as a wet nurse. Other San Javier slaves, both male and female, earned the same wage for their labor, while children received from 2 to 4 pesos per month depending on their age. Daily wages paid to slaves were usually 1 or 1.5 reals, but they could range as high as 4 reals. In 1831 the government ordered that all slaves sent by their owners to work on the island of San Lorenzo as a form of punishment were to receive 3 reals daily. The annual return on this practice was not high, but it was sufficiently attractive to maintain it. For its slaves' outside work, San Javier received 314 pesos in 1827 and 500 pesos for the period between March 1828 and September 1829; San José received 106 pesos during an eight-month period in 1828.[35] For some owners, especially those with only a few slaves, the wage or rental fee might be their sole source of income. According to Archibald Smith, poorer members of Lima society survived on the 1 real they received from their slaves' daily wage.[36]

The various money-making possibilities associated with slaves meant that slave owning was perceived to be a profitable enterprise. Although calculating the financial return on slaves is extremely difficult, and there are no precise figures for Peru, indications are that the return was high.[37] A survey into slavery conducted by the government in 1848 reckoned that a slave made 8 pesos per month.[38] Over one year, a slave could thus earn almost 100 pesos, which by itself may not have amounted to much once the expenses of both the slave and the owner had been deducted, but in those cases where fifty or more slaves were involved, the return was quite handsome.

As a result, slave owners remained convinced of the utility of slavery and were willing to meet the extra expenses that their commitment often entailed. They did not hesitate to move their valuable property from place to place when a perceived threat arose. In 1841, for example, there was a general exodus of slaves south from the Ecuadorian border following an invasion by Andrés de Santa Cruz.[39] Buyers were prepared to go long distances to obtain the slaves they needed, which became increasingly necessary as numbers shrank and sales declined.[40] In 1851, Manuel Saravia of Lima traveled to Trujillo, where he bought six slaves for 1,612 pesos in April and three for 1,200 pesos one month later.[41] Buyers also werc willing to pay a premium for the slaves they wanted, in some cases relying on middlemen. An advertisement in the Lima daily, *La Miscelánea*, in 1832 announced the establishment of an agency that would buy, sell, and rent slaves; maintain a register of slaves who were required and available; buy and sell furniture; provide respectable individuals as foremen for farms and bakeries and as shop assistants; rent houses; and locate houses for prospective renters. With regard to slaves, its fee was 2 percent of the sale price, with the cost of the paperwork split equally between vendor and buyer. For rented slaves, whose conduct it guaranteed, it demanded 1 peso per slave paid by the renter and lessee.[42] Other buyers offered cash as an inducement to find the slaves they wanted. In the 1840s, advertisements appeared in Lima newspapers offering 50 pesos and more above the price of a slave to attract sellers.[43] When money failed to provide precisely the worker they wanted, some owners turned to barter. Again, the classified advertisements in the newspapers were used as the medium. In one case an owner offered a strong and robust thirty-year-old slave suited for field work in exchange for a female slave aged between twelve and twenty; in another, an owner offered a pregnant slave in exchange for a wet nurse or other female slave.[44]

The willingness of owners to barter and to pay the costly extras that increased the price of slaves and thereby drove up labor costs counters the argument that Peruvians remained committed to slaves because they were the cheapest workers available. Some owners may have believed it, but many more seem to have viewed slaves as an irreplaceable component of the labor force and slavery as the most suitable labor system for Peru at this time. It was this wide range of benefits that ensured continuing support for slavery. In many cases the financial position and, consequently, the social and political position of many members of the elite depended upon slavery's survival. Slaves were important to them as workers, investments, security for loans, and a source of income. At the same time, slaves were perceived to be integral to the economic recovery and development of the country as a whole. Why, then, would the owners or the government seek to alter the situation? Reason dictated maintenance of the status quo. The continuing importance of slavery in early republican Peru meant that any attempt to limit the institution was certain to arouse great hostility across a wide spectrum of the population ranging from large landowners to small farmers, urban artisans, religious orders, and poverty-stricken pensioners. Indeed, even before independence had been secured, attacks on the liberators' antislavery legislation began, attacks that intensified over the following years as slaveholders and their allies sought to reestablish slavery on a firm footing and to maintain this relic from the past.

## *Notes*

1. Ricketts to Canning, 26, December 27, 1826, F.O. 61/8. The entire report is a rather pessimistic account of Peru's existing and future economic prospects. An annotated copy is included in R. A. Humphreys, ed., *British Consular Reports on the Trade and Politics of Latin America, 1824–1826* (London, 1940), chap. 6.

2. "El prefecto de este departamento, dando parte de la aprehensión de una negra María Fernandez, esclava de la hacienda de San Regis," AGN, 1826, P.L. 6-222; "Expediente sobre inventario de las haciendas nombradas San José y la Ventilla del valle de Nazca actuado al tiempo que las recibió el Presbítero D. Manuel Barreto de D. Juan Bautista Mesa," AGN, 1828, P.L. 8-22; Wilfredo Kapsoli E., *Sublevaciones de esclavos en el Perú, s. XVIII* (Lima, 1975), 149–53; Luis Valencia Avara, *Bernardo O'Higgins: el "buen genio" de América* (Santiago de Chile, 1980), 433; Carlos Aguirre, "Cimarronaje, bandolerismo y desintegración esclavista: Lima, 1821–1854," in *Bandoleros, abigeos y montoneros: criminalidad y violencia en el Perú, siglos xviii–xx*, ed. Carlos Aguirre and Charles Walker (Lima, 1990), 145.

3. "Cuentas correspondientes a la administración de la hacienda San Javier de la Nazca, siendo interventor de ella Dn. Francisco Iglesias y corren desde el 18 de agosto 1819 hasta el 3 de 1825," AGN, Temporalidades, Legajo (hereafter cited as Leg.) 70, Cuaderno (hereafter cited as Cuad.) 106; "Cuentas que rindió al supremo gobierno Dn. Miguel Bernales, administrador de la hacienda San Javier de la Nazca, y corresponde a los años de 1826–1828," AGN, Temporalidades, Leg. 70, Cuad. 110; "Cuenta de cargo y data que rindió al supremo gobierno en el despacho de hacienda Dn. José Félix Hurtado, administrador de la hacienda San Javier, y de su anexo San Pablo y corre desde el 5 de marzo de 1828 hasta el 21 de setiembre de 1829," AGN, Temporalidades, Leg. 70, Cuad. 113; "Cuenta que rindió al supremo gobierno D. Juan Bautista Mesa, administrador de la hacienda San José de la Nazca, propia del estado; y corresponde a los años de 1824–1831," AGN, Temporalidades, Leg. 97, Cuad. 83.

4. José Rufino Echenique, *Memorias para la historia del Perú (1808–1878)*, prologue by Jorge Basadre, notes by Félix Denegri Luna (Lima, 1952), 1:103; P. Campbell Scarlett, *South America and the Pacific: Comprising a Journey across the Pampas and the Andes, from Buenos Ayres to Valparaiso, Lima, and Panama; with Remarks upon the Isthmus* (London, 1838), 2:83; Pedro Félix Vicuña, *Ocho meses de destierro o cartas sobre el Perú* (Valparaíso, 1847), 20–21, 27.

5. *El Peruano*, September 4, 1847.

6. Dancuart, *Anales* 4:149–50.

7. Juan Rolf Engelsen, "Social Aspects of Agricultural Expansion in Coastal Peru, 1828–1878" (Ph.D. diss., University of California, Los Angeles, 1977), 32–40.

8. AGN, Notarial, Ignacio Ayllón Salazar, 1825, Protocolo (hereafter cited as Prot.) 41, February 16, 1825; Archivo Arzobispal de Lima (hereafter cited as AAL), Augustinos, Leg. 22, Expediente (hereafter cited as Exp.) 12, October 6, 1834; AAL, Augustinos, Leg. 22, Exp. 40, April 27, 1836; AAL, Augustinos, 1850–1859, No. 25, June 22, 1854; Swayne Reid and Company to John Barton, November 29, 1843, F.O. 177/27; *El Comercio*, November 30, 1843, August 28, 1848; Bill Albert, *An Essay on the Peruvian Sugar Industry, 1880–1920, and the Letters of Ronald Gordon, Administrator of the British Sugar Company in Cañete, 1914–1920* (Norwich, 1976), 219a; Engelsen, "Social Aspects," 312–13, 476–82, 496.

9. Engelsen, "Social Aspects," 427–75; W. S. Bell, *An Essay on the Peruvian Cotton Industry, 1825–1920*, Centre for Latin American Studies Working Paper 6 (Liverpool, 1985), 11.

10. Ricketts to Canning, 24, December 19, 1826, 26, December 27, 1826, F.O. 61/8; *La Miscelánea*, June 26, 1830.

11. Engelsen, "Social Aspects," 22–25; Flores Galindo, *Aristocracia*, 192; Michael J. Gonzales, *Plantation Agriculture and Social Control in Northern Peru, 1875–1933* (Austin, 1985), 120; Macera, "Las plantaciones azucareras," 171–72; *El Comercio*, April 22, 1845; Clements R. Markham, *Cuzco: A Journey to the Ancient Capital of Peru; with an Account of the History, Language, Literature, and Antiquities of the Incas. And Lima: A Visit to the Capital and Provinces of Modern Peru; with a Sketch of the Viceregal Government, History of the Republic, and a Review of the Literature and Society of Peru* (London, 1856), 22.

12. Engelsen, "Social Aspects," 23, 29. For the developments in Northeast Brazil and Cuba see J. H. Galloway, "The Last Years of Slavery on the Sugar Plantations of Northeast Brazil," *HAHR* 51 (1971): 599–602; and Scott, *Slave Emancipation*, chap. 4.

13. Ricketts to Canning, 24, December 19, 1826, 26, December 27, 1826, F.O. 61/8; *La Miscelánea*, June 26, 1830.

14. *El Comercio*, May 29, 1847.

15. Ricketts to Canning, 26, December 27, 1826, F.O. 61/8; Dancuart, *Anales* 2:28, 3:32.

16. Macera, "Las plantaciones azucareras," 164, 167–68; *La Miscelánea*, June 26, 1830.

17. "Cuadro que manifiesta la población indígena y de castas; la agricultura y el comercio y el sistema tributario de la provincia de Chancay," Lima, January 12, 1848, BN D1964.

18. Palma, *Tradiciones* 18:188; AGN, Temporalidades, Leg. 52, San Javier de Nazca 1786–1830; Ricketts to Canning, 26, December 27, 1826, F.O. 61/8; Flora Tristán, *Peregrinaciones de una paria*, trans. Emilia Romero (Lima, 1946), 414; Vicuña, *Ocho meses*, 22. Around Lima, with its numerous small estates producing food for the local market, the tendency was to have fewer slaves, up to twenty on average. See Carlos Aguirre, "Agentes de su propia emancipación: manumisión de esclavos en Lima, 1821–1854" (Unpublished paper, 1991), 10.

19. Robert Proctor, *Narrative of a Journey across the Cordillera of the Andes, and of a Residence in Lima, and Other Parts of Peru, in the Years 1823 and 1824* (London, 1825), 113.

20. Ibid., 125; Markham, *Cuzco and Lima*, 42. See also Léonce Angrand, *Imagen del Perú en el siglo XIX* (Lima, 1972), 151, which contains many pictures of Lima's black population in its various occupations.

21. Macera, "Las plantaciones azucareras," 54; Palma, *Tradiciones* 18:188; Dobyns and Doughty, *Peru*, 124; Alfonso W. Quiroz Norris, "La consolidación de la deuda interna peruana, 1850–58: los efectos sociales de una medida financiera estatal" (Bachiller en humanidades, Pontificia Universidad Católica del Perú, 1980), 17; Aguirre, "Agentes," 7; *La Prensa Peruana*, September 13, 1828.

22. *El Comercio*, February 18, 1843.

23. Macera argues that slave wet nurses were required because white mothers were inadequate as a result of "insufficient alimentation." See Macera, "Las plantaciones azucareras," 267. This argument is not entirely convincing, since it seems unlikely that slaves enjoyed a better diet than their owners.

24. Proctor, *Narrative*, 227–28, 247; Tristán, *Peregrinaciones*, chap. 11; Clements R. Markham, "Travels in Peru in 1853" (Manuscript in the Library of the Wellcome Institute for the History of Medicine, London), 1:47, 72. An edited version of Markham's work can be found in *Markham in Peru: The Travels of Clements R. Markham, 1852–1853*, ed. Peter Blanchard (Austin, 1991).

25. Basadre, *Historia* 3:160; *El Peruano*, January 4, 11, 1854. One real was equal to one eighth of one peso.

26. Nicholas P. Cushner, *Lords of the Land: Sugar, Wine, and Jesuit Estates of Coastal Peru, 1600–1767* (Albany, 1980), 199 n. 33.

27. See *El Telégrafo de Lima*, January 20, 1832.

28. These figures were computed from the total number of slaves taken from the sources below. The number for each decade varies, and there has been no attempt to make an exact comparison between slaves. Such a comparison is virtually impossible because of the large number of variables involved and the limited information contained in the records. Sources: AGN, Notarial, Ignacio Ayllón Salazar, 1825, Prot. 41, 1829, Prot. 48; Eduardo Huerta, 1834–35, Prot. 267, 1844–45, Prot. 274, 1849–50, Prot. 278; José Antonio Menéndez, 1839, Prot. 422; Jerónimo de Villafuerte, 1842–1845, Prot. 1025, 1848–1851, Prot. 1027; Lucas de la Lama, 1845–1855, Prot. 333; Remigio Deustua, 1854–55, Prot. 1092; AGN, Expedientes Judiciales, Causas Civiles (hereafter cited as CCiv), 1850, Leg. 159; Archivo Departamental de Arequipa (hereafter cited as AD-A), Notarial, Rafael Hurtado, 1824, Leg. 674, 1825, Leg. 675; Francisco de Linares, 1829–1831, Leg. 678, 1834–35, Prot. 681; Toribio de Linares, 1839–40, Prot. 707, 1844–1846, Prot. 709, 1848–51, Prot. 710; Juan N. Pastor, 1854–55, Prot. 775; Manuel A. Zegarra, 1854–55, Prot. 918; Archivo Departamental de La Libertad (hereafter cited as AD-LL), División Notarial, Escrituras, José V. Aguilar, 1845, Leg. 408, 1846–47, Leg. 409, 1850–51, Leg. 411, 1850–1852, Leg. 412, 1852–53, Leg. 413, 1854–55, Leg. 414; Juan de la Cruz Ortega, 1850–51, Leg. 454, 1852–53, Leg. 455; AAL, CCiv, 1852–1855, Leg. 236; "Hacienda de San Antonio de Zárate, en el valle de Cóndor, provincia de Ica, departamento de Lima,"

July 12, 1847, BN D11995; Engelsen, "Social Aspects," 64, 342. Aguirre has arrived at similar figures for Lima slaves in the 1840s and 1850s from a much broader sample. See Aguirre, "Agentes," 30, table 8.

29. *El Comercio*, March 12, 26, 1840.

30. Kapsoli, *Sublevaciones de esclavos*, 32; Quiroz Norris, "La consolidación," 179.

31. AGN, Notarial, Ignacio Ayllón Salazar, 1825, Prot. 41, February 16, 1825.

32. AD-LL, División Notarial, Escrituras, José V. Aguilar, 1845, Leg. 408; "Hacienda de San Antonio de Zárate," BN D11995.

33. AGN, Notarial, Eduardo Huerta, 1849–50, Prot. 278.

34. See "Dn. José Faustino de las Casas con Dn. Pascal Bieytes, sobre la entrega de una esclava," Lima, July 31, 1839, BN D12426; AGN, Notarial, Ignacio Ayllón Salazar, 1825, Prot. 41; *El Comercio*, February 4, 1846; *Mercurio Peruano*, May 23, 1832.

35. Archibald Smith, *Peru As It Is: A Residence in Lima, and Other Parts of the Peruvian Republic, Comprising an Account of the Social and Physical Features of that Country* (London, 1839), 1:110; "Cuentas que rindió al supremo gobierno Dn. Miguel Bernales, administrador de la hacienda San Javier de la Nazca, y corresponde a los años de 1826–1828," AGN, Temporalidades, Leg. 70, Cuad. 110; "Cuentas de Dn. José Félix Hurtado 1828–29," AGN, Temporalidades, Leg. 70, Cuad. 113; "Cuenta documentada que rindió al supremo gobierno el administrador de la hacienda San José de la Nazca y corre desde el 24 de noviembre de 1827 hasta el 30 de noviembre de 1828," AGN, Temporalidades, Leg. 97, Cuad. 82; *El Conciliador*, January 12, 1831. Renting slaves was common in other Latin American countries. See Magnus Mörner, *Historia social latinoamericana (nuevos enfoques)* (Caracas, 1979), 252–53.

36. Smith, *Peru As It Is* 1:110. One real was the price of a newspaper at this time.

37. Macera has argued that because it is impossible to calculate the slaves' expenses, it is impossible to calculate the return on slaves. See Macera, "Las plantaciones azucareras," 70–73. Mörner has written that the profitability of slaves in all of Latin America ranged between 5 and 10 percent. He, too, notes the difficulties in calculating a precise figure because of the numerous variables involved, including productivity, price of the slave, life expectancy, and maintenance costs. See Mörner, *Historia social*, 245.

38. *El Peruano*, August 23, 1848. Noted in Juan de Arona, *La inmigración en el Perú* (Lima, 1891), 85.

39. *El Comercio*, June 5, 1841.

40. As early as 1827 the state refused to sell two of its San Javier de la Nazca slaves on the grounds that it needed all its slaves "for service on its properties." See "El prefecto de este departamento acompaña con la nota del intendente de Ica, la solicitud de Da. Juana Maúrtua, sobre le venden dos esclavos de la hacienda de San Javier de la Nazca," AGN, 1827, P.L. 7–428.

41. AD-LL, División Notarial, Escrituras, Juan de la Cruz Ortega, 1850–51, Leg. 454. For another example involving the sale of slaves in Trujillo to a buyer from Lima see AD-LL, División Notarial, Escrituras, José V. Aguilar, 1850–51, Leg. 411.

42. *La Miscelánea*, February 20, 1832.

43. See *El Comercio*, November 20, 1843, January 23, 1844. In both cases a Señor Echegoyen was the advertiser.

44. *El Comercio*, December 13, 1844, January 10, 1851. See also *El Heraldo de Lima*, February 15, March 9, 1854.

# 3
# The Slaveholders' Counterattack

While slavery's continuing importance helped ensure that it survived for thirty years after Peru's independence, also crucial to the institution's survival was the pressure of the slaveholders.[1] As soon as San Martín issued his antislavery decrees they responded, launching a counterattack to preserve slavery and their property. Their response may have been disorganized; it may have lacked any formal structure; but it was wide-ranging, multifaceted, vigorously pursued, and very effective. In speeches, letters, articles, and books, proponents justified the continued existence of slavery; they attacked anyone perceived as an opponent; and they demanded the passage of new laws to protect their rights as slaveholders and the repeal of old laws that infringed upon those rights. Their aims were simple: to maintain slavery and, if possible, the size of the slave population. To these ends some of slavery's defenders set their sights on what at first glance may have seemed an unrealizable, even absurd, goal: the reopening of the slave trade. That they, like their Argentine counterparts at virtually the same time, enjoyed a great deal of success, even managing to reestablish the slave trade briefly, was a measure of their influence and their commitment.[2] They also benefited from the developments of the period, which frequently came to their aid and assisted them in preserving slavery.

One of the reasons for the slaveholders' success was the political chaos that marked Peru's first three decades as an independent republic. International conflicts, civil wars, coups d'état, and rebellions were the order of the day. This was the age of caudillos, when a succession of military men, most of them veterans of the wars of independence, competed for political dominance. Historians have tried to differentiate among these "men on horseback" on the basis of ideology, but the depth of their ideological commitment is open to question, since most of them seemed willing to modify or even reverse their views to satisfy political aspirations. Power was their ultimate motivation, whether local, regional, provincial, or national, and the result was years of political turmoil.[3] This, however, worked to the advantage of the slave owners. As Paul Gootenberg has shown, early republican Peru was a Lima-dominated state with a local elite of large and small landholders, urban financiers and retailers, wealthier artisans, and heroes of the Independence Wars in firm control. The sierra was little more than an economic dependency of Lima, and separatist elements centered in Arequipa lacked the resources to mount a serious challenge to the capital. Regional leaders and regional interests existed, but their influence remained localized. Even those regional caudillos who achieved national power quickly genuflected to the wishes and interests of the Lima elite rather than impose their local concerns.[4] One of those interests was the preservation of slavery, and in a situation where political support was uncertain and competition fierce, few caudillos were prepared to alienate the slaveholders. As a result, the latter enjoyed political influence regardless of who occupied the presidency. Although many of them chose to participate directly in the political system, they had no real need to do so, for government leaders turned to them for advice and support, if only to prevent them from establishing alliances with some ambitious rival.[5]

Economic factors reinforced these trends. The financial distress of the late colonial and independence periods extended into the republic, even after the beginning of the guano boom in the 1840s. A chronic revenue shortage forced governments to seek loans from private citizens, many of whom were estate owners and slaveholders, men such as Isidro Aramburu, José María Sotomayor, and Domingo Elías.[6] In this situation, governments could hardly be expected to implement existing antislavery legislation, nor could they ignore the pressure for other changes demanded by the slaveholders.[7] Yet, while political and economic developments such as these benefited the slaveholders, they could not be certain that these alone would ensure slavery's survival. The situation demanded direct intervention, and the slaveholders' response was a spirited public campaign in defense of slavery.

The slaveholders' first concern was to justify the institution. To that end they delivered speeches, wrote newspaper articles, and published pamphlets and books that advanced their views. Their most common ploy was to link slavery with the survival and restoration of Peru's agricultural sector. Abolition, they argued, would lead to its ruin and, by extension, the ruin of the national economy. Adopting some of the language and ideas of the Enlightenment, they claimed that Peruvians had a "natural right" to own slaves. They extended the concept of "rights" to include the right of owners to punish their slaves in the same way that parents had the right to discipline their children. They argued that denying those rights would lead to "abuses, miseries, and vice." Similar conclusions were voiced by those who argued that slavery had to be maintained because blacks were a brutalized sector of the population who lacked the veneer of "civilization" and, therefore, needed to be kept under strict paternalistic control. The subject of social control and fears that the country's security and tranquility would be menaced by sudden emancipation aroused trepidation even among antislavery commentators. One, writing in 1830, believed that abolition was part of "our liberal principles, our religion, and our naturally sensitive character," while slavery was an undesirable colonial inheritance. Nevertheless, he contended that slavery had to be maintained because freed blacks would not know what to do, except for those "of a ferocious spirit, of which this caste is replete," who would turn to pillage and murder to satisfy their needs.[8]

Racism lay at the heart of this argument, for it was also applied to *libertos*. Their transition to complete freedom should be delayed, it was argued, to ensure that they were fully "civilized" beforehand, or, as a writer who described his aims as "humanitarian" argued, to teach them the habits of work and sobriety and to make them worthy citizens and useful members of the community. He recommended that an indemnity of 200 pesos be paid before freeing any *liberto* over the age of twelve and that smaller amounts be set for those younger and less skilled. At the age of majority, if the indemnity had not been paid, the *libertos* should not be permitted to leave their masters, and even those who were freed should remain with their parents until the age of majority, receiving

4 pesos per month plus food and medical care from the master.[9]

Another regular component of the proslavery propaganda was the contention that Peruvian slavery was comparatively benevolent. In the words of one defender, "Slavery does not present here the horrible evils that accompany it at other points on the globe. In Peru, slavery is a tranquil domesticity, directed through kindliness. The slave is paid and is satisfied, perhaps more than the free worker." Supporters could point to individual slave owners such as Bernardo O'Higgins, whose efforts to improve the lives of their slaves were well known.[10] They could refer also to the writings of foreign travelers who left the impression that conditions were humane and the work load was light.[11]

In 1833 the various proslavery arguments appeared together in an influential book written by the conservative aristocrat and former finance minister José María de Pando.[12] Finding his proof in both history and the Bible, Pando composed an imaginative discourse that sought to justify the continuation of slavery. Pointing to countries such as Haiti, where abolition had led to chaos that had hurt both owners and slaves, he charged that blacks were completely anarchic when controls were removed. *Libertos*, because they no longer had the controlling hand of the master, fomented "vice, danger, and disorder." Abolition, he believed, also would have serious economic repercussions. Pointing to the deterioration of Peruvian agriculture and the inability of hacendados to meet their interest payments and religious obligations, Pando claimed that since independence no group had suffered more than Peru's hacendados. Thus, any action against them, such as the abolition of slavery, would be "unjust." Why, he asked, should present slave owners be penalized for the sins of their fathers, who had been responsible for the original enslavement? Slaveholders were being penalized already by the laws that deprived them of their *libertos* who had reached the age of majority, just as they were becoming a productive commodity instead of an expense. Pando argued that the state should be compensating masters for this financial loss. It should also be protecting slave owners' property rights as recognized by the 1828 constitution. His solution went beyond merely calling for the maintenance of the status quo: He urged that the slave trade with the other American republics be restored and that *libertos* be compelled to remain with their masters until they reached the age of twenty-four.[13]

Similar exhortations in defense of slavery would be repeated by slaveholders and their allies over the following years, while they simultaneously launched attacks against anyone they perceived to be an opponent of slavery. A frequent target was the independence hero José de San Martín. The animosity that emerged in the 1820s toward the Argentine may have been the result of a growing sense of Peruvian nationalism and embarrassment that the country's liberation had been secured by foreigners. It may have been part of the general Peruvian xenophobia that marked the first decades after independence.[14] It may have been an anti-independence response from conservatives who were alienated by the instability and hardships that followed San Martín's arrival. Or, the attacks may have reflected proslavery sentiments, with San Martín's liberal legislation seen as the root of Peru's present economic difficulties. Whatever the reason, the Argentine liberator was vilified in the press, while his antislavery laws were labeled "regrettable" and an "insult." Critics noted that elsewhere similar laws had involved long negotiations, but in Peru they had been introduced without any benefit to the cause of independence, had been imposed by "despotic means," and had condemned the land to sterility at the hands of "vicious fugitives and *libertos*." A writer in 1835 charged that San Martín's legislation had virtually guaranteed the "total extermination" of agriculture, provoked the flight of capital and capitalists, left slave "owners in the most straitened circumstances," and caused the "ruin of the masters and the demoralization and neglect of the blacks," since the former were no longer capable of attending to even their own needs, while the latter, instead of being "the most industrious and productive class," supplied with clothes, food, and an education by their masters, had abandoned themselves to idleness, misery, and crime.[15]

Another target of slaveholder ire, and one who attracted more attention than San Martín by the 1840s, was the *defensor de menores*, a legal official appointed to protect the interests of slaves as well as those of children and mental incompetents. Arousing particular animosity were those who took the job seriously and tried to help their clients to the limits allowed by the law, which included emancipation. Opponents accused them of encouraging slaves to flee or to resist their owners in other ways, thereby undermining the latter's authority. One *defensor*, Manuel Rueda, was viewed with suspicion because slaves were constantly at his home. He was charged with using his office in an "abusive and arbitrary manner"; being "an active agent in slave unrest"; promoting idleness, theft, and agricultural decline by securing the freedom of slaves; and violating the owners' property rights by assisting slaves in getting reductions in their values, which facilitated self-purchase. To the owners' way of thinking, a slave's price should rise unless he or she became infirm or suffered some physical disability.[16]

Slaveholders tried to counter San Martín's decrees and the actions of the slave protectors by pressing for legislation to maintain slavery intact and to recognize their control over their property. The laws of the period relating to slaves were often a part of broader legislation aimed at controlling society as a whole, a response to the unsettled conditions of the time, the high crime rates in both urban centers and the countryside, and the belief that blacks in general and slaves in particular were contributing to that instability. Over the years the same or similar laws were passed again and again, indicating that successive legislators had consistent views where slaves were concerned and that the existing legislation was not working satisfactorily. In general, the laws sought to reinforce the owners' control while limiting the slaves' actions, reducing vagrancy, and preventing flight. One control mechanism was the identity card or *boleto*. Enabling legislation was much like Bolívar's 1825 decree, directing owners to supply the authorities with the names of their slaves and compelling slaves to carry a *boleto*. Without one, a black person could be considered a fugitive or arrested as a vagrant or disruptive element. Employers had to verify the *boleto* before offering a job to ensure that they were not hiring a fugitive. Failure to do so could result in a fine or a payment to the slave's owner of twice the wages that had been paid to the worker. In addition, to ensure order and security, slaves were prohibited from riding horses in and around Lima, and rural slaves could not leave their estates on workdays without a pass from their owner.[17]

Most owners probably approved of the *boleto*. However, having to renew them with each new law and replace them every time they were lost must have been tiresome and could prove costly. In 1834 the prefect of Lima began charging a fee of .5 real per *boleto*. Suspicious, the slaveholders calculated that he stood to make over 400 pesos from the fee and complained that this charge, plus the 4-peso fine levied whenever one of their slaves was arrested without a *boleto*, meant that they and agriculture in general were being forced to shoulder an excessive financial burden. They recommended that slaves without *boletos* should receive a dozen lashes. Their pressure had some effect, for early the following year *boletos* were issued free of charge again and the recommendation concerning whipping was implemented.[18]

The whip, that "grand badge of slavery," was the commonly accepted means for controlling slaves.[19] It was approved of by owners and sanctioned by the state. One of the most extensive pieces of legislation affecting slaves, the Lima police regulations of November 1839, like its predecessor, Bolívar's rural regulations, accepted the use of the lash and specified when and how severely slaves could be whipped. Failing to carry a *boleto* could result in a dozen lashes; so, too, could being caught absent from an estate on a workday without permission. Runaways could be whipped six times if they were caught within four days; twelve times for eight; and twenty-four for two to four months, with the added punishment of being sold fifty leagues from the city. If apprehended in the company of thieves, the slave would be held for trial. Owners also might be punished, although not by whipping, if they failed to keep their slaves under control or tried to hire runaways. There was a fine of 4 pesos for not furnishing a slave with a *boleto* and of 5 pesos for not informing the police of a runaway. Employing blacks who could not prove that they were free could result in a fine of 20 pesos, and hiring a fugitive slave could lead to a fine of twice the slave's wages or even to imprisonment. When a fugitive was apprehended, the owner had to pay 6 pesos if the slave was caught in the city, 12 in the countryside.[20]

As they pressed for laws such as these, the slaveholders also actively opposed other legislation that they considered inimical to their interests. In 1831 they successfully challenged a legislative proposal, introduced in response to charges that the internal slave trade was causing hardships to both agriculture and urban labor, that would have established a maximum price of 500 pesos for slaves, prohibited owners from raising prices to prevent slaves from purchasing their freedom, and permitted slaves who were invalided as a result of their work or scarred by excessive whipping to seek a reduction in their price through the courts. Opponents charged that the proposal attacked property rights by setting a maximum price for slaves. The senate supported them, as did the minister of government and foreign relations, who contended that the first two articles were inconsistent since one established a set price for slaves while the second allowed a variable price.[21]

The year 1831 also saw the revocation of Bolívar's 1824 order that allowed slaves to change owners on their own prerogative. During its brief lifetime this order had aroused frequent criticism. According to one opponent, it had "introduced the greatest disorder amongst the slaves." Those who composed the rescinding law claimed that slaves were changing owners arbitrarily and capriciously, resulting in grave abuses that had hurt the nation's agriculture and domestic service.[22]

While the slaveholders as a group pressed the government to make certain that the state remained committed to slavery, they also were acting privately to ensure that their slaves remained firmly under their personal control and that, consequently, slavery remained a vibrant and viable institution. Here, again, they scored notable successes. One of their major concerns was to see that the number of slaves did not decline. Thus, in the years immediately after the wars of independence, they resisted the demands for freedom from those slaves who had fought in the revolutionary armies.[23] Subsequently they expended their energies in a number of directions. For example, they challenged wills that freed slaves. In one case the son of the conde de Monte Mar y de Monteblanco retained control of a slave named Jovita, who claimed she had been given her freedom in the count's will. According to Jovita's mother, she had been whipped, imprisoned, and shackled in the same stocks as men. The mother demanded Jovita's freedom plus compensation for what had been an assault on a free person. A court ordered her freed, but the son refused, questioned the legitimacy of the will, and managed to delay a final decision for more than two years. He justified his actions by saying that the case was not clear and that any surrender would demoralize the rest of his slaves.[24]

Slaveholders also resisted attempts by their slaves to get reductions in their valuations. This had the double advantage of making self-purchase by the slaves very difficult, if not impossible, and protecting the owner's investment and possible income from a future sale. Therefore they refused the requests from their slaves and from the *defensor de menores*, who usually became involved in cases of this sort, for a reevaluation. The owner of Mariana Lavalle, a slave on the Villa estate, refused her request for a reevaluation on the grounds that it constituted an attack on his property rights. He maintained that she was worth at least 500 pesos since she was young, healthy, and robust. Either he was unsure of her identity or he was deliberately lying, for in the ensuing trial three court-ordered evaluators decided she was worth much less. The owner's evaluator set a figure of 400 pesos, while the two chosen by the *defensor de menores* believed that 290 pesos were sufficient since she was over forty and suffered from a variety of physical disabilities. The owner objected, arguing that the *defensor*'s evaluators were unqualified to judge the value of a field hand because they were bakers, that Mariana had faked her illnesses, and that 290 pesos was a "joke." The *defensor* replied that the bakers were eminently qualified to judge Mariana since they had frequently bought and sold field workers. The court agreed and ordered a new evaluation.[25]

In other instances the owners had more success. Carmen Zerpa resisted her slave's attempt to have his value reduced by 100 pesos so that he could purchase his freedom. The ensuing trial cost her 27 pesos in lost income, as the slave was placed in a deposit for over two months while the trial lasted, plus 37 pesos in court costs. However, the court decided in her favor, and she may have recovered her expenses, for she demanded compensation.[26]

The owner was also successful in an 1854 trial involving a *liberta* whose employer wanted to purchase her but was not willing to pay 400 pesos. The Civil Code of 1852 permitted slaves and *libertos* to change masters on their own initiative once again, but the employer wanted a lower price and went to court, where he offered 300 pesos on the basis of her numerous physical defects. He claimed that her left arm was virtually useless, she suffered abdominal pains that could have been the result of excessive work or working while she was menstruating, she had a prolapsed uterus, and she was ill each month during the waxing of the moon. The trustee of La Molina estate, to which the *liberta* was attached, was suspicious, wondering why there was interest in what was apparently a useless worker. He refused any reduction, pointing out that menstruating women were accustomed to working. A doctor testified that the *liberta* did not have a prolapsed uterus or dead arm; in fact, she was strong and robust.[27]

Examples such as these show that slaveholders were prepared to expend time, energy, and money in ensuring that their property rights over their slaves were recognized. To the same end, they had their *libertos* baptized to establish a record of their existence. More important but also more time-consuming and expensive were their efforts to regain control of their fugitive slaves. In many cases, the runaways were nearby, hiding on a neighboring estate. The repeated decrees and regulations imposing fines and other punishments for hiring fugitives, and the numerous court cases in which owners demanded the return of their slaves, indicate that hiring known runaways was common. Individuals were accused of luring slaves by offering them presents or the promise of an annual reduction in their price. Ceferino Elguera accused a neighbor of stealing his slaves by attracting the women, who then urged their husbands and children to join them. Elguera used his local influence to mobilize troops, who helped him round up seventeen slaves from the accused's property.[28] Slaveholders flouted other laws as well in an attempt to retain their slaves. In one case an owner sought to conceal the fact that one of his slaves had killed another in a drunken brawl on Christmas Day by promising fifty lashes to any informer. His attempt to protect his property by silencing the witnesses failed, however, for this, like the previous case, found its way to the courts.[29]

Owners paid little attention to the passage of time when they were determined to regain control of their property. In 1839, Francisco Benavides claimed ownership of a slave left to him in his brother's will twenty years earlier. During that time the slave had been sold by the lessor of the deceased's estate, a not-uncommon occurrence when slaves were rented along with an estate. She had also had four children, a fact probably at the root of Benavides's desire to reestablish his legal rights, for he would also gain control over these *libertos*.[30]

As indicated by the cases above, slaveholders employed the services of a variety of intermediaries to confirm ownership of their slaves. The courts, the police, and the army were the most usual; occasionally vigilantes were hired to recapture missing slaves.[31] To facilitate identification of the fugitives, owners ran advertisements in newspapers that listed in minute detail the slaves' physical characteristics, their clothing when last seen, their profession or professions, any known contacts, and a reward that usually ranged from half an ounce to three ounces of gold or from 12 to 50 pesos, but which might rise as high as 100 pesos. Most advertisements included the warning that anyone hiding the fugitive would be held responsible for double the slave's wages and any expenses incurred. An 1842 advertisement announced a reward of 60 pesos for the return of Juan Infantas, a light *zambo* who was tall and clean-shaven, with a round face, chestnut eyes, pug nose, thick eyebrows, a fat lower lip, smooth *zambo*-like hair, small feet, thin shins, broad shoulders, a pot belly, and a stammer. He was wearing a pair of breeches, good shoes, a black-and-white striped alpaca poncho, very dirty white trousers torn at the cuff, and a striped shirt. Placed on board a ship bound for Pisco, he had taken advantage of a delay in sailing and a reduced and sleeping crew to disembark at Bocanegra.[32]

Another advertisement described four fugitives. Manuel de los Reyes was a dark coppery *zambo*, around twenty, of average height and weight, with somnolent eyes, slow almost effeminate speech, a full face, pug nose, and a smiling appearance with dimples when he laughed. A guitar player, singer, and dancer, he had worked as a bricklayer, painter, and bakery worker. His mother was a stout *zamba*, the wife of a barber who worked near La Merced. Cayetano (alias Dulce or el Diablo Mayor de San Lázaro), a former servant of the Catalans of Abajo del Puente, was short, slight, black in color, and clean-shaven, with a hoarse voice. He was a shoemaker and bakery worker and was married to an obstinate *negra*, a wet nurse called Silvestra, who was the daughter of Tomás Muñoz, a master paver who lived on the left side of Ormeño street in a house known as Vargas's. Mariano Camanejo or Carabello was a tall, thin, bombastic, light-coppery *pardo* of around forty-five. He had a full beard, small somnolent eyes, an unhealthy hue, and a hoarse voice, and he suffered from a hernia. He sang Indian songs and always carried a bag of stamps around his neck. A master adobe maker, he had worked on many farms near the town and had been a night watchman and soldier. Many took him to be free. Dolores, a light *china* of around twenty-six, was in the habit of changing her name. She was whitish, freckled, cross-eyed, short, slight, and full-breasted, with hair to her shoulders and a scar on her face. She carried herself in a haughty manner and was considered quite smart. She had been arrested following a slashing incident but released from jail on Christmas Eve. The owner believed that some of these fugitives might be found enrolled in the army. He offered a reward of three ounces of gold for Manuel and Cayetano, and one for Mariano and Dolores.[33]

Prepared to go to almost any lengths to retain possession of their slaves, owners were not so blinded by their commitment that they accepted without question whatever was available when buying one. If they discovered that their purchase suffered from some illness or physical disability or proved to be a malingerer, thief, or fugitive, they went to the courts to demand their money back. They were legally protected, for the typical contract clearly stated that the slave lacked "vices, flaws, defects, or hidden or apparent illnesses."[34] Thus, Manuel Cáceres felt justified in demanding his money back for a slave who, he claimed, was a thief and a drunkard, had a reputation as a runaway, and was unable to do the laundry, even though she had been advertised as a laundress and as having no vices. In a similar case, Manuel Oyague demanded that his money be refunded when he discovered that his new slave was a drunkard and a thief and was demoralizing his other slaves, who were refusing to do laundry or wash dishes. The former owner insisted that the slave had never displayed these vices when she was in his possession.[35] In cases of this sort the new owners could not delay in claiming restitution. One who waited six months before deciding that he had purchased "damaged" goods was denied redress by the court because too much time had passed.[36]

The slaveholders' efforts to preserve slavery were crowned with notable successes, especially from the mid-1830s as the liberal trends of the previous decade were diverted or sabotaged and government leaders showed themselves to be more openly responsive to slaveholder demands.[37] Their efforts succeeded in part because their interests meshed with those of the government, which was still a slaveholder itself and was determined to restore Peru's moribund agricultural sector. Many government leaders seemed to believe that this could be accomplished only with slave labor; the problem was that the number of slaves was insufficient. From this line of thinking came the demand that the slave trade be reestablished, as José María de Pando had recommended and as many owners wanted. It was a demand that became increasingly forceful as the need for workers and the slaveholders' self-confidence grew through the 1830s.

One political leader who was fully in tune with these views was the youthful and erratic Felipe Santiago de Salaverry. A conservative who had been influenced by aristocrats such as Pando, Salaverry seized the presidency in February 1835. On March 10 he issued a decree allowing the duty-free importation of slaves from other American nations. His stated reasons were the backwardness of the country's agriculture, which he blamed on the lack of workers, and the "invincible force of custom" that blocked the employment of free workers in the rural sector. To permit the rural estates to deteriorate would be "unjust" and harmful to the nation, he argued, while trading slaves within the Americas was acceptable since it would neither increase the slave trade nor aggravate the condition of existing slaves.[38] As a further sop to the hacendados, he freed them from paying any property tax for five years.[39]

This decree was the kind of support the slaveholders wanted, but Salaverry was not in power long enough to ensure that it was implemented. His irrational and authoritarian acts antagonized both friends and enemies. For instance, in August he instituted compulsory military service for all males between the ages of fifteen and forty, including urban slaves and rural free blacks. Any slave who failed to enroll or any owner who hid his slaves faced execution.[40] Numerous slaves belonging to coastal estates in the north, where opposition to Salaverry was centered, were forcibly conscripted into his army.[41] They failed, however, to provide him with sufficient military strength to keep him in power. In February 1836 his army was defeated by the combined armies of the president he had overthrown, Luis José de Orbegoso, and the president of Bolivia, Andrés de Santa Cruz. Salaverry was captured, tried, condemned, and executed.[42]

Santa Cruz now assumed direction of Peru as head of the Peru-Bolivia Confederation. Although he was a more liberal figure, he was not prepared to alienate Peru's slaveholders. He ordered that rural slaves who had served in Salaverry's army be returned to their owners, and, although he did not implement Salaverry's decree reopening the slave trade, he did not expunge it from the record.[43] His sensitivity to the slaveholders' concerns was probably a result of his less-than-firm hold over the country. He was resented by nationalistic Peruvians, both liberals and conservatives, and his confederation was feared and opposed by its southern neighbor,

Chile. In 1838 an army of Chileans and Peruvians invaded Peru. In January 1839 it defeated Santa Cruz's army at the Battle of Yungay. Santa Cruz was forced to flee, his confederation was destroyed, and Agustín Gamarra, a conservative who had held power between 1829 and 1833, reassumed the presidency.[44]

In Gamarra the slaveholders again had an individual who was attuned to their wishes. Their efforts to preserve slavery now intensified, leading to some notable successes over the next eight years. On November 10, 1839, a new constitution paved the way for reopening the slave trade. It allowed only free-born persons to become Peruvian citizens, eliminating the proviso of its predecessors that enslaved persons brought into Peru were free upon reaching Peruvian soil. The reactionary intent of the changes was confirmed subsequently by the minister of foreign affairs who, in response to an inquiry about the status of fugitive Ecuadorian slaves entering Peru, replied that since the constitution no longer covered this situation, the status of an enslaved person did not change upon entering the country.[45] The reply referred to Ecuador, but Peruvian attention was really focused on New Granada and Brazil with their far more substantial supplies of slaves.

The constitution may have removed any legal impediment to reopening the slave trade, yet it had not created a single worker to satisfy the country's labor needs. This deficiency was met in part by such rules as the Lima police regulations of November 1839, which compelled slaves to work. Then, on December 24, Gamarra introduced a more significant piece of legislation, one that directly addressed the labor question while simultaneously claiming to attack a commonly perceived cause of Peru's social problems. Focusing on the *liberto* population, the law declared that *libertos* were now to remain under the patronage and control of their parents' owners until the age of fifty. The stated reason for the extension of the period of control was that agriculture required it; so, too, did the *libertos* themselves, since they, upon leaving their masters, had formed a part of society that was "entirely devoid of virtues," for they commonly entered into a life of vagrancy without any means of support. The passage from "domestic dependency to a state for which they were not prepared" threatened to reduce them to "a state of disorder that corrupts public morals and exposes them to unfortunate disasters." Patronage, on the other hand, provided them with "freedom," legal protection, and the care of a master, so that they remained a useful part of society. It provided their children with educational opportunities, saving them from the ignorance and misery that usually followed upon leaving the master. The decree listed other supposed advantages for the *libertos*: Rural *libertos* were to receive the same benefits as rural slaves plus 1 peso weekly as a wage when they reached the age of twenty-five, urban *libertos* were to receive half the wages of domestic servants, and masters were to pay for the education and training of their *libertos'* children. Masters had the benefit of being able to transfer or sell the patronage of their *libertos* if they wished.[46]

The decree's declared aims may have been to help solve the country's perennial labor shortage and to reduce social unrest, but its real effect was to reduce the *libertos* to a state little different from that of slaves. It allowed slaveholders to control the children of their slaves for their effective working lives and then to release them when their usefulness and value began to decline. Masters gained a new source of income, for they could sell their *libertos* in the same manner as slaves. The only real difference between the two systems was that there was a finite termination point for the servile status of the *libertos*. However, as this decree clearly indicated, that termination date could be changed whenever the government wished.

The commitment to servile and semiservile forms of labor, especially black labor, remained, but the government and the slaveholders still had to find an adequate supply. Prolonging the patronage of the *libertos* was only a partial solution, as it could neither meet the growing labor needs of the country nor replace slaves who were dying or being emancipated by themselves or their owners. Reopening the trade with Africa seemed a pipe dream because of the distance involved, the intensity of the British antislave trade campaign (which included Peru within its orbit), and the opposition to the trade within the country among members of the executive council of state that advised the president.[47] Nevertheless, in August 1841, Francisco Javier Calvo, a Lima merchant operating out of Havana, together with several others petitioned the council to permit the importation of slaves from Africa for agricultural work. The situation was propitious for Calvo and the slaveholders, as the council of state was presently led by Manuel Menéndez, a slave owner who was keen to reestablish the slave trade, according to the British consul.

The council, however, citing San Martín's legislation, rejected the proposal, calling it "illegal and unjust."[48]

Further action was interrupted by political developments in the country. In November, Gamarra was killed while leading an invasion of Bolivia. A new period of political anarchy that was extreme even by Peruvian standards followed. Rebellion was the order of the day, and the presidency became a revolving door, with several prominent figures holding power briefly. During this period of instability the slaveholders received some welcome news. On June 22, 1843, New Granada passed a law permitting the export of slaves to its neighbors. The only limitations were that families could not be separated and that children of slaves were to be considered free.[49] The Peruvian government, led by the conservative Manuel Ignacio Vivanco, determined to take advantage of the opportunity. On August 12 it issued a decree that reiterated Gamarra's constitutional proviso that the condition of slaves entering Peru did not change. It was, according to Lord Aberdeen, the British foreign secretary, an obvious attempt "to encourage and to protect the revival" of the slave trade.[50]

Political events intervened once again, however. A new round of rebellion and civil war flared until another veteran of the Independence Wars, Ramón Castilla, assumed the presidency in 1844. Castilla would be the dominant figure in Peruvian politics for the next twenty-three years, until his death in 1867. His accession to power marked the beginning of what was to be a comparatively stable period for Peru, although political loyalties in the first years were still uncertain and Castilla's hold over the country was anything but assured.

With the political situation stabilized, attention could return to the issue of the slave trade. Slavery's proponents may have experienced some trepidation, for the new president was a mestizo and a reputed liberal, and when Calvo's proposal permitting the restoration of the slave trade with Africa was reintroduced in 1845, it once more encountered intense opposition in the council of state.[51] Nevertheless, the slaveholders were not disheartened. Confident of their ability to influence events, they turned their attention to the senate, the traditional representative of property rights, and found an ally. On July 29 the upper legislative body approved a project that permitted the importation of slaves from other American republics.[52] The chamber of deputies and the press immediately castigated the senators while the proslavery forces jumped to their defense, reasserting many of the old arguments. Only those slaves who were acculturated to local social customs and who could speak Spanish would be imported, they claimed; foreign slaves would be coming to a better life; the lack of workers, the result of past abolitionist legislation, had so undermined the hacienda system that the rent for lands worth 40,000 pesos was a paltry 600 pesos per annum, a return of only 1.5 percent; only those haciendas that still had slaves were prospering; alternative workers were unavailable or unsuitable, as *serranos* would not come from the interior, whites refused rural work because of the low wages, and free workers were expensive, unreliable, and worked only half the day; and slaves, on the other hand, were better workers than *serranos* and could work in the hot sun. The defenders admitted that abolition was inevitable, "But it is not yet time!"[53] Manuel Suárez Fernández and fifty-three other hacendados added their support in yet another petition that urged the importation of American slaves because of the "lamentable decadence" of Peru's coastal agriculture. Other proponents claimed that even Great Britain was not opposed to a trade in American slaves, as a recent treaty with Ecuador had not ruled out such commerce.[54]

The proslave trade pressure was sufficient to overcome the opposition. Late in the year the council of state bowed to the slaveholders' wishes and accepted the senate's proposal. On December 16 it declared that "provided every precaution is taken by the supreme authority . . . to prevent fraud and to protect the slaves and their offspring, the introduction of slaves from the other states of the continent, as now requested, may be permitted on a trial basis and as a present measure to help the ruined coastal property." Amendments were added to ensure protection for the slaves: The government was to provide them with moral and religious education, they were to be allowed to hold private property, laws regarding hours of work in the fields were to be carefully observed, and the government was to do all in its power to stimulate immigration in order to obtain alternative agricultural workers. However, past legislation protecting slaves had been notable for its ineffectiveness. Moreover, a further amendment setting a specific date in the near future for abolition was withdrawn because of the opposition of one council member, General José Rufino Echenique.[55] When the minister of foreign affairs accepted the ruling on January 14, 1846, the importation of slaves from neighboring American states became legal for a trial period of six years.

The reopening of the slave trade might be taken as a reflection of the political realities of the time. It indicated the continuing strength of the slaveholders and planters and their influence at the centers of power. It also indicated the uncertain position of the president in 1845. Castilla had not played a particularly prominent role in the debate and seems to have either supported the initiative or bowed to the wishes of the dominant group. Perhaps he was more actively involved than the evidence suggests, for the law might be seen as a transitional piece of legislation leading away from slavery. The specific trial period, the state's involvement in the slaves' education and its control over their working conditions, the recognition of the slaves' property rights, and the emphasis upon stimulating immigration might give some credence to the view that the law in the long run would assist the slaves and help end slavery.

This interpretation, however, seems overly generous. Stripped to its essentials, the law, as many critics pointed out, was a retrograde step, contrary to the aims of San Martín, an affront to abolitionists everywhere, and a blot on the history of Peru and the career of Castilla. Even the law's framers seemed to be aware of this, for they felt compelled to envelop it in a mantle of high-sounding phrases and moralistic statements justifying their actions. Even though their law indicated the exact opposite, they declared that they were not "nor shall we ever be authors or accomplices in so repugnant and odious a crime against nature, Christianity, and philosophy" as "the barbarous and impious commerce in human flesh." They emphasized their liberal and humane antecedents: Since independence, Peru had joined in the opposition to the slave trade, the country condemned the enslavement of one by another as unchristian, and by law no one could be born a slave in Peru. However, agriculture was in ruins because of a shortage of workers, and it required restoration. They preferred immigrants, but efforts to attract them had been unsuccessful because of Peru's political turmoil, lack of financial support, and limited colonization schemes. Thus, the government had to turn to a solution that was repugnant and of debatable effectiveness, but easy and immediate.

The framers questioned whether San Martín and his abolitionist successors objected to every plan to import slaves. They believed that their solution was acceptable and would

cause little opposition because it did not involve the enslavement of free men; rather, it involved people who were already
enslaved. They even claimed that these were not slaves but
rather "workers" who had been slaves for some time and
whose position might now improve in Peru. Furthermore, the
proposed trade might improve relations with neighboring
republics, neighbors who were described as "family."[56] Recent
history indicated that "family" relations were anything but
amicable, and the real aim of the terminology seems to have
been nothing less than an attempt to disguise the international
nature of the trade.

When Great Britain attacked the law, the minister of
foreign affairs, José Gregorio Paz Soldán, responded with a
similar litany of self-serving phrases. He wrote that his
country's constitutions had long opposed slavery but that a
lack of workers was undermining coastal agriculture. *Serranos*
feared to come to the coast because of various factors such as
susceptibility to disease, which he blamed on their consumption of fruit and alcohol; free wage labor was expensive and
limited; and European immigrants had failed to materialize.
He argued that Peruvian slavery did not deserve to be condemned, because local conditions were not harsh: Some Lima
slaves, such as water sellers, porters, cooks, and laundresses,
earned good wages, up to 2 pesos daily, while field slaves had
a set amount of work and received the wages of free workers
for anything extra. During rest periods they cut firewood,
which they could sell locally, or completed other tasks that
earned them cash. Thus, slaves had money that they could
use to buy their freedom, but, according to Paz Soldán, they
wasted it on clothes and liquor, like the lower classes everywhere. Lima's slaves, he noted, were internationally notorious
for the sumptuousness of their clothing.

He adopted a line of attack that was common to slavery's
defenders everywhere: He compared Peru's slaves with workers in industrialized nations, arguing that with their fiestas
and good food Peru's slaves were better off than England's
factory workers and, as a result, many refused their freedom
when it was offered.[57] With the law in place he expected that
slaves would be imported from Brazil and New Granada,
where conditions were far worse than in Peru. In New
Granada, he claimed, slaves received only ten or twelve
bananas per day for food. He also furnished statistics to show
how an influx of new slaves would benefit the country economically: One thousand slaves could operate five sugar

estates and produce an annual income of 30,000 pesos for each estate, four thousand slaves could produce an income of 600,000 pesos, and twenty thousand slaves 1,200,000 pesos.[58] Like most of his response, these statistics are far from convincing. What Paz Soldán had really shown with his letter was that the government in 1846 was determined to acquire more slaves.

In a narrow sense the law might be seen as merely legalizing a trade that existed already. According to reports in the Lima press and complaints by the consul general of New Granada, perhaps as many as one hundred slaves had been imported into the northern part of Peru since Vivanco's decree in 1843. The consul was concerned because the reports indicated that many of the slaves were children, a contravention of the New Granada law that allowed the export of slaves only as long as families were not separated and children were not enslaved. British inquiries verified the rumors. Information from the north of Peru claimed that owners in the Chocó and Buenaventura areas of New Granada were selling the children of slaves in Paita and other centers on the Peruvian coast. A British merchant in Paita described the trade as "considerable": Ships sailing between the two areas were accustomed to carrying three to five slaves. In one case José Agustín Alegría, a native of Caracas, outfitted a small vessel at Paita in February 1844 and sailed to the Chocó where he obtained ten slaves, seven of them males, of whom three were adolescents. He returned to Peru and sold them at Casma for 3,600 pesos. In July 1846 the consul demanded that the importation and enslavement of children from New Granada be halted. However, he could expect little from the Peruvian authorities, who were now committed to opening the trade and who, in the past, following reports that slaves were being smuggled from New Granada, had limited themselves to publishing a newspaper advertisement that advised the contraband slaves to demand their freedom.[59]

This trickle of slaves into northern Peru was hardly what the country needed to satisfy its labor needs, but with a law in place a full-scale trade could be mounted. Prospects seemed good, for owners in New Granada were willing to sell because of internal political problems, a decline in domestic slave prices, and slave unrest in the Cauca Valley.[60] Two shipments of note followed. In August 1846, the Peruvian brigantine, *Tres Amigos*, embarked with 180 blacks, 140 of them *libertos* from Panama. They had been bought by José Antolín

Rodulfo, one of the principal speculators in the trade. The governor of Panama freed 25 of them, and an equal number escaped, so that only 130 slaves and *libertos* were carried to Lambayeque, where the slaves were sold and the *libertos*, according to reports, were freed.[61]

The second expedition involved another Peruvian ship, the *María de los Angeles*, which set sail from Buenaventura on April 20, 1847, with a load of 126 slaves and their 111 children.[62] Instructions were issued to frontier officials not to interfere, and the ship docked at Ancón on June 18. The Peruvian middlemen, Rodulfo, Pablo del Solar, and Felipe Revoredo, then completed the deals they had made for the slaves. The majority, 87 slaves (41 men and 46 women) and 116 *libertos* (55 males, 54 females, and 7 babies), were bought by the Pisco hacendados Domingo Elías, José María Sotomayor, and Francisco Sagastaveytia, who paid 54,888 pesos to buy the slaves and to cover the expenses of the *libertos*.[63]

The trade now came to an abrupt halt. On April 27, one week after the *María de los Angeles* set sail, the government of New Granada issued a law prohibiting the export of slaves and demanding that dealers who had sold slaves abroad ensure their return within four months. New Granada, which had raised the hopes of Peru's slaveholders, now effectively torpedoed the Peruvian law and ended definitively any opportunity for importing American slaves. The numbers involved had been small, around four hundred to five hundred slaves.[64] Nevertheless, at least one commentator believed that the trade had been a success. He contended that the imports, together with the existing workers, demonstrated how the value of hacienda land could be increased. He recognized, however, that with the slave trade now terminated, the government would have to bring in European immigrants.[65]

The slaveholders had suffered a major setback. It was to all intents and purposes a fatal blow, since slaves could no longer be imported to replenish the diminishing supply. Yet their commitment to slavery remained firm, and they continued to defend their interests with the energy they had displayed over the past thirty years. They still enjoyed significant influence at the centers of power, as governments continued to respond to their concerns by issuing and reissuing regulations controlling the movements of slaves, requiring slaves to carry proper identification, maintaining whipping as a punishment, and refusing to consider complete abolition.[66] The owners opposed any move to weaken slavery or to lighten the load of their slaves. When the government recognized slaves' legal rights and provided other protections in its 1852 Civil Code, they attacked with all their old vigor, in this instance arguing that property rights in slaves were still constitutionally recognized.[67] They continued to see slaves as important for labor and investment purposes. Many may still have wanted to own another human being for the prestige value or for the sense of power it conveyed. Others, by continuing to purchase slaves, may have wanted to underline that this right still existed. Perhaps that explains why, in 1852, Manuel Atanasio Fuentes of Lima bought two *libertos* and a slave in Trujillo. The *libertos* were in their twenties; the slave was a woman of eighty-seven.[68]

Whatever their motivations, the slaveholders had managed to frustrate the intentions of the liberators. In their efforts to preserve slavery they had revealed their substantial and continuing influence, their determined resistance to abolition, and their enthusiasm for the ways of the past. They had benefited from the fact that Peru's governments had either sympathized with their objectives or been frightened by their power. The intensity of their counterattack reflected their commitment to slavery, their opposition to the liberators' aims, and their response to those who were actively pressing for abolition during these years. Confronting the slaveholders was a substantial group of people who wanted to destroy a system they found exploitative, inhumane, and irrational, a system they believed should be abolished regardless of what the defenders might think and argue. The opponents of slavery may not have enjoyed the same influence as the slaveholders—they lacked the unity and intensity of a group who saw their whole style of life challenged—but their numbers were far greater, for they included sections of the white population, foreign abolitionists, and the slaves themselves. They found common ground in their hostility to this institution which, despite the claims of the slaveholders and their supporters, exhibited the same dehumanizing characteristics that were common to slavery systems everywhere. However, while they found much to abhor and many reasons to urge slavery's destruction, they had to operate in an environment where the slaveholders were dominant. As time passed, the numbers of the latter may have declined and their influence may finally have begun to wane, but by then they had left an indelible imprint on the face of early republican developments and had determined the shape of Peru for many years to come.

## Notes

1. The composition of the slaveholding group and the number of slaveholders during these years have yet to be studied in any detail.

2. For the Argentine campaign see Andrews, *Afro-Argentines*, 49–56.

3. For more on caudillismo and the caudillos see Lynch, *Spanish American Revolutions*, 344–47; Frank Safford, "Politics, Ideology and Society," in *Spanish America after Independence, c. 1820–c. 1870*, ed. Leslie Bethell (Cambridge, 1987), 72–84; Eric R. Wolf and Edward C. Hansen, "*Caudillo* Politics: A Structural Analysis," *Comparative Studies in Society and History* 9 (January 1967): 168–79; and Pike, *Modern History*, chaps. 3, 4. Paul Gootenberg has argued that Peru's caudillos can be divided according to their attitudes to commercial policy. See Gootenberg, *Between Silver and Guano*, chap. 4. For Peru's postwar instability see also Julio Cotler, *Clases, estado y nación en el Perú* (Lima, 1978), 69.

4. Paul Gootenberg, "North-South: Trade Policy, Regionalism, and *Caudillismo* in Post-Independence Peru," *Journal of Latin American Studies* 23 (1991): 282–300.

5. There is some disagreement over the postindependence influence of the landholders. Jorge Basadre has written that the coastal estate owners were "politically weak" during the early republic, as indicated by their failure to protect their economic system based on slavery and to reestablish the slave trade. The facts, however, do not seem to support this conclusion. A more accurate assessment is that of Pablo Macera, who has written that after the Battle of Ayacucho Peru's hacendados were more powerful than ever before because of the removal of imperial controls. In this, they reflected the general Spanish American pattern as described by John Lynch, who has argued that following independence "the landowners were the new ruling class," and "the hacendados reached a position where they did not simply control the state, they were the state." See Jorge Basadre, *Introducción a las bases documentales para la historia de la república del Perú con algunas reflexiones* (Lima, 1971), 1:197, 309; Macera, "Las plantaciones azucareras," 76; and Lynch, *Spanish American Revolutions*, 340, 347. See also Safford, "Politics, Ideology and Society," 82–84.

6. Quiroz Norris, "La consolidación," tables 2, 14, 15.

7. During this period, estate owners benefited in other ways, as laws were passed reducing their rents, duties, taxes, and interest payments on loans and levying high tariffs on such imported raw materials as sugar. See Dancuart, *Anales* 1:60, 2:85; *El Peruano*, November 30, 1839, May 20, 1843; *Telégrafo de Lima*, January 31, 1835; and Ricketts to Canning, 26, December 27, 1826, F.O. 61/8.

8. *La Miscelánea*, June 26, 1830, May 17, 1831. See also *El Comercio*, October 5, 1849.

9. *Miscelánea*, December 31, 1833.

10. *La Verdad*, July 16, 1833. See also *El Peruano*, January 31, 1846. Concerning O'Higgins see Basadre, *Historia* 2:214; and Valencia Avara, *Bernardo O'Higgins*, 433.

11. See Chapter 4 in this volume.

12. For more on Pando see Pike, *Modern History*, 78. Gootenberg argues that Pando was an economic liberal favoring free trade. See Gootenberg, *Between Guano and Silver*, 28–29.

13. José María de Pando, *Reclamación de los vulnerados derechos de los hacendados de las provincias litorales del departamento de Lima* (Lima, 1833). See also Basadre, *Historia* 2:301. Many of Pando's points appeared in editorials in the Lima newspaper *El Conciliador* in 1830. See, for example, the issues of April 7 and 17.

14. See Gootenberg, *Between Silver and Guano*, 53–63; W. M. Mathew, *The House of Gibbs and the Peruvian Guano Monopoly* (London, 1981), 15–16; Crompton to Palmerston, 11, February 28, 1851, F.O. 61/131.

15. Palma, *Tradiciones* 18:188; Pando, *Reclamación*, 33; *Gaceta Mercantil*, March 21, 1835; *Miscelánea*, December 31, 1833; *El Voto Nacional*, March 11, 1835.

16. *Mercurio Peruano*, January 24, 1829.

17. For examples of the laws concerning *boletos* see Perú, *Colección de leyes* 3:374–75, 457–58, 4:112–13, 6:151; *El Conciliador*, December 22, 1830; *El Heraldo de Lima*, June 14, 16, 28, 1854; *Mercurio Peruano*, July 1, 1839; *La Miscelánea*, May 18, 1832; and *Telégrafo de Lima*, March 27, 1838.

18. Perú, *Colección de leyes* 5:41; *El Voto Nacional*, December 13, 1834.

19. Quoted in Davis, *Slavery and Human Progress*, 169.

20. Perú, *Colección de leyes* 6:425–50.

21. *El Conciliador*, August 3, 1831.

22. Ibid., September 3, 1831; "Autos que sigue Rosa Gasteagudo, madre de Beatriz, con Dn. Blas Zavaleta su amo sobre que la venda," AGN, CCiv, 1834, Leg. 84.

23. See, for example, "Expediente sobre la petición presentada por Angela Zagal, para que se deja sin efecto la solicitud presentada por un esclavo de su propiedad y se le ponga bajo su dominio," Lima, May 28, 1828, BN D10936. If the slaveholders were unsuccessful, their second line of defense was to ask for compensation from the state.

24. "Sobre la libertad de una esclava, Jovita Carrillo," AGN, CCiv, 1846, Leg. 141. See also *El Comercio*, November 27, 1840, for the case of an attempt to claim ownership of a free black.

25. "Sobre la libertad de María Lavalle, esclava de Señor D. Juan Bautista Lavalle," AGN, CCiv, 1850, Leg. 161.

26. "Expediente emisiado en el juzgado de paz que despacha por Miguel Rivera por la defensoria general de menores, sobre variación de dominio de Blas Valverde, esclavo de Doña Carmen Zerpa," AGN, CCiv, 1845, Leg. 137.

27. "D. José Damian Aguilar con el sindico de La Molina sobre variación de dominio de la sierva Petronila García," AGN, CCiv, 1854, Leg. 172.

28. "Expediente seguido por D. Agustín Arismendi como apoderado de D. Joaquín de San Martín para recoger a una esclava nombrada Manuela de donde se halle," AD-A, Corte Superior de Justicia, CCiv, 1834, V, September 2, 1834; *El Comercio*, February 9, 11, 16, 1843,

January 29, 31, February 8, March 13, 1845. For an incident involving *libertos* being lured from their masters see *El Comercio*, October 28, 30, 1843.

29. "Contra Gregorio Nini para homicidio al moreno Andrés, esclavo de la Granja," AGN, Expedientes Judiciales, Causas Criminales (hereafter cited as CCrim), 1848, Leg. 594.

30. "Seguidos por Don Francisco Antonio Benavides con Don Sebastián de la Llosa sobre el derecho a una esclava nombrada Dominga y los hijos de esta," AD-A, Corte Superior de Justicia, CCiv, 1839, VII, August 10, 1839. See also AAL, Causas de Negros, 1815–1855, Leg. 36, LXII:50.

31. An advertisement in *Mercurio Peruano*, April 10, 1832, refers to such a vigilante group.

32. *El Comercio*, September 15, 1842. See also Aguirre, "Cimarronaje," 150.

33. *El Comercio*, February 18, 1843. Although the terms *zambo*, *negra*, *pardo*, and *chino* originally were used to indicate differences between individuals according to their racial mix, by this time they seemed more an indication of variations in skin color.

34. See, for example, "Sobre la venta de un esclavo negro," Huaura, April 17, 1822, BN D12653.

35. "Seguidos por el D. D. Manuel Muñoz a nombre de Don Manuel Cáceres con Doña Melchora Mendoza sobre devolución de 270 pesos valor de una esclava vendida por esta al primera," AD-A, Corte Superior de Justicia, CCiv, 1843, VII, September 29, 1843; AAL, CCiv, 1837–1843, Leg. 233. For a similar case of an owner demanding a refund because his slave was a thief see "Seguido por el abogado defendor de menores, con Dn. Andrés María Alvarez sobre de su esclava Josefa Bernales," AGN, CCiv, 1834, Leg. 84. See also AAL, Causas de Negros, 1815–1855, Leg. 36, LXVII:10, 22; AD-A, Corte Superior de Justicia, CCiv, 1834, V, October 21, 1834; and "Dn. José Faustino de las Casas con Dn. Pascual Bestes, sobre la entrega de un esclavo," Lima, July 31, 1839, BN D12426.

36. *El Comercio*, June 2, 1849.

37. In 1839 the British minister commented on the "powerful political influence" of the slaveholders. See Wilson to Palmerston, ST1, March 24, 1839, F.O. 84/294.

38. Perú, *Colección de leyes* 5:50.

39. Basadre, *Historia* 2:302.

40. Perú, *Colección de leyes* 5:162, 165–66.

41. *Redactor Peruano*, March 5, 1836.

42. Basadre, *Historia* 2:chap. 19; Pike, *Modern History*, 79–81.

43. Perú, *Colección de leyes* 5:235–36.

44. Robert N. Burr, *By Reason or Force: Chile and the Balancing of Power in South America, 1830–1905* (Berkeley, 1962), chap. 3; Pike, *Modern History*, 81–83. In 1837, amid reports of a Chilean invasion, a story appeared that the invaders planned to emancipate the slaves and carry the young ones back to Chile in order to destroy Peruvian agriculture. See *El Estandarte*, June 6, 1837. The story seems to have been a rather obvious attempt by Santa Cruz's people to win slaveholder and planter backing.

45. *El Peruano*, August 16, 1843. Basadre has described the 1839 constitution as "reactionary." See Basadre, *Historia* 2:199.

46. The decree was first issued at Huancayo on November 27. *El Comercio*, December 28, 1839; *El Peruano*, December 25, 1839.

47. See Chapter 8 in this volume.

48. Wilson to Palmerston, ST2, August 30, 1841, F.O. 84/375; *El Comercio*, August 27, September 4, 1841; *El Peruano*, September 8, 15, 1841, June 22, 1842.

49. *El Peruano*, July 11, 1846.

50. Aberdeen to Adams, ST1, May 25, 1844, F.O. 84/537.

51. See Chapter 7 in this volume.

52. For these developments see Basadre, *Historia* 3:188–90.

53. *El Comercio*, August 7, 12, 1845.

54. Perú, *Colección de leyes* 10:350–54.

55. Adams to Aberdeen, ST10, December 30, 1845, F.O. 84/595.

56. Perú, *Colección de leyes* 10:350–54.

57. American slaveholders made much the same argument about the living conditions of their slaves. See Genovese, *Roll, Jordan, Roll*, 58–64.

58. *El Peruano*, January 31, 1846. Paz Soldán was not a disinterested observer: His brother, Pedro, owned the San Juan de Arona estate, which employed slave labor.

59. O'Leary to Aberdeen, ST6, September 30, 1844, F.O. 84/537; enclosure with Adams to Aberdeen, ST4, August 4, 1845, F.O. 84/595; *El Comercio*, October 21, 1844, January 3, 1845, July 13, 1846; *El Peruano*, July 11, 1846.

60. James Ferguson King, "The Latin-American Republics and the Suppression of the Slave Trade," *HAHR* 24 (1944): 405; Michael T. Taussig, *The Devil and Commodity Fetishism in South America* (Chapel Hill, 1980), 48.

61. Perry to Aberdeen, ST1, August 20, 1846, F.O. 84/645; Perry to Palmerston, ST2, September 20, 1846, F.O. 84/645; O'Leary to Palmerston, ST3, October 6, 1846, F.O. 84/645; Perry to Palmerston, ST1, January 6, 1847, F.O. 84/649.

62. Some reports list 116 *libertos*. The difference may be a result of accounting errors or births en route.

63. *El Peruano*, June 26, 1847; Arona, *La inmigración*, 92–93; Perú, *Colección de leyes* 10:411; "Promovido por el Señor D. Domingo Elías con la testamenta de Don Felipe Revoredo para que le descuentera una cantidad de pesos," AGN, CCiv, 1852, Leg. 168.

64. See, for example, Tavara, *Abolición*, x, 21. Ricardo Palma has given a figure of eight hundred slaves imported from the Chocó after 1839. See Palma, *Tradiciones* 18:189.

65. *El Comercio*, February 7, 1848; *El Peruano*, June 16, 1847.

66. See, for example, *El Comercio*, March 20, 1847, February 13, 1849; and *El Heraldo de Lima*, June 14, 16, 28, 1854.

67. *El Comercio*, June 25, 28, 1852.

68. AD-LL, División Notarial, Escrituras, José V. Aguilar, 1852–53, Leg. 413.

# 4
# Slave Life

In the first years following independence, Peru's slaves found themselves in as confusing a situation as that confronting the nation as a whole. The liberators' antislavery legislation followed by the slaveholders' countermeasures left a great deal of uncertainty as to whether slavery was going to die a quick death or whether its demise was to be a long, drawn-out affair. Subsequent initiatives on both sides did not resolve the issue. A similar sense of confusion about Peruvian slavery emerges from the historical record. From contemporary observers one gets the impression that it was little more than a system of domestic servitude. The same conclusion might be reached based on an examination of the legal protections enjoyed by the slaves, the opportunities they had for ameliorating their condition and securing their freedom, and the nature of their everyday existence, which seemed to differ little from that of other sectors of society. This evaluation, however, ignores the realities experienced by the majority of Peru's slaves. While they may have had advantages not shared by slaves in neighboring countries, they were still property and still subject to the whims of their owners. They had very little control over their lives, uncertainty pervaded their existence, abuse and exploitation were their everyday companions, and the freedom promised by the liberators remained an unfulfilled dream.

The impression that Peruvian slavery was a more humane system than that found elsewhere in the hemisphere was largely the creation of contemporary observers. British travelers such as Archibald Smith, Robert Proctor, and Clements Markham have left a picture of a happy people and a light work load. Proctor noted how domestic slaves amused themselves when the family was absent, dancing, singing, and playing blindman's buff. He concluded that "the slaves certainly lead a very happy life in Lima. There are generally a great many of them in every house, with little else to do than for one sex to loll on the back of their mistresses' chairs during meals, and the other to do needlework." Smith noted that rural slaves could work as they wished and earn wages like free laborers once their assigned tasks were done. Markham wrote that slaves in the Cañete Valley "appear a happy and contented race, and though their labour is forced, they receive clothing, food, and lodging, and escape the capitation tax of the oppressed Indians of the Sierra." The Swiss scientist J. J. Von Tschudi came to the same conclusion. He wrote that "the treatment of slaves in Lima, especially by the Creoles, is exceedingly mild, and generally much on the same footing as the treatment of servants in Europe," adding that the treatment was so good that blacks preferred to remain enslaved because of the food, clothing, and lodging the owners provided.[1] Another British observer made the same points:

> The slave is, generally speaking, both well fed and well treated—his labour is not excessive: he generally receives a small allowance in money: and has the means of accumulating the sum necessary for purchasing his freedom, but seldom avails himself of this privilege, at least not openly, because by becoming legally free he becomes exposed to the levies for the army: he, more frequently pays his own price to the Master, leaving his name on the Register of Slaves, and no instance is known of this confidence having been abused.[2]

Descriptions such as these can be dismissed as the inaccurate observations of individuals who had limited knowledge or preconceived notions of slavery in general, had only superficial contact with Peru's slaves, and were unwilling to criticize the people who had been their hosts. But there may have been a grain of truth in what they wrote: Peruvian slavery may have been less harsh than that elsewhere in the hemisphere. If so, this was the result of years, perhaps centuries, of resistance and accommodation by the slaves, producing what had become "Peruvian slavery." Such a development was common to slavery systems. Although the slaves were property and subject to their owners' wishes, they had some latitude of action which permitted them an opportunity to establish their own lives. In the words of James C. Scott, slaves retained "considerable autonomy to construct a life and a culture not entirely controlled by the dominant class."

Eugene Genovese has shown that this was certainly true of the United States.[3] In the case of Peru, the result may have been the "humane" system described by foreign travelers, and it might explain, in part, why it differed in many ways from what might be termed "classical slavery."[4]

The impression of a benevolent system can be derived as well from an examination of the nation's legal system and the various laws that seemed to favor the slaves. Legislation introduced in the first months after independence appeared to indicate that Peru and Peruvians were committed to an early end to the institution and that slaves could easily change their legal status. Today's slave would be tomorrow's freedman. Other laws seemed to protect the slaves. Bolívar's 1825 regulation of coastal haciendas limited their workday to ten hours, so that, although starting hours might vary according to the season, work had to end at 6 P.M. In addition, owners had to supply daily rations of one pound of flour and one pound of beans, as well as an annual clothing allowance of two pairs of shorts, two shirts, and a poncho for men, and two shirts, two fustians, two petticoats, and a mantilla for women, with a blanket and two sheepskins for both.[5] Attempts were made to see that the directive was implemented. In 1827 the provincial intendant instructed the administrator of the state-owned estate of San Javier de la Nazca to begin the work day at 5 A.M. in the summer and 6 A.M. in the winter, and he detailed what was to be the clothing allowance, the weekly ration of meat (from two to four pounds depending on the difficulty of the work), and the allocation of seed corn (to be distributed during the harvest season according to the work done). Children and elderly slaves were to care for the infants of working mothers, pregnant women were not to do any shoveling but could be used in easier jobs, and postpartum mothers were to receive chicken for the first two days after delivery and mutton for the next six. The instructions permitted whipping, but only for the most severe crimes and no more than twelve lashes. Finally, although the workday began early, not all of it was devoted to estate labor: the instructions specified that on the completion of their tasks the slaves were permitted to till their own land and to tend to their animals. Any savings could be applied toward their purchase price, which the slaves knew because they had to be evaluated regularly.[6]

Cognizant of their rights, slaves were not afraid to take their owners to court to defend them, although this may have been more common in the early years of the republic when San Martín's liberal legislation was still fresh, the concept of freedom was a cherished principle, and liberation was an apparently tangible goal. One petitioner, Isabel Verano, was a twenty-two-year-old slave owned by the mayor of Huaura. In 1825 she demanded a new owner because the mayor had been mistreating her, even though she had been born, educated, and married in his house. She pointed out to the court, "We are now constituted in republics with everyone enjoying freedom, and it is not right for you to deny the miserable slave the only freedom [to change owners] the law permits him." She was obviously not intimidated by either her owner or the court, as she threatened to appeal directly to the government if the court refused to act.[7]

The decisions of the courts were another indication that the system was not rigidly set against the slaves. Courts heard cases involving slaves who had been mistreated by being punished unjustly, forced to work excessively, and denied adequate food and clothing. They could decide in favor of the slaves by reducing their value, compelling their sale, or freeing them.[8] Although in most instances they may have been concerned about protecting property rights and so decided against the slaves, they did not differentiate between slave and free in criminal cases, nor did they forego their customarily thorough investigation just because the complainant was a slave. When José Miranda (or Mejía) demanded his freedom through the courts, numerous witnesses were called for both sides. José claimed, first, he should be freed because his former owner had freed him in her will, even though she had sold him before the will was executed. Second, he should be freed because his sales contract had been violated: It stipulated that he could not be sold for more than 140 pesos, yet he had been sold for 206. Witnesses explained that the larger amount was because José was a thief and one of his owners, Gregorio Basallo, had sold him for 140 pesos plus 66 pesos, the value of the goods he had stolen. To arguments that his labor, not his person, had been sold, José replied that if his labor had been for sale, he should have received the wages. Calculating a rate of 8 pesos per month for the more than three years he had worked, he reckoned he had made enough to obtain his freedom. He was accused by some witnesses of having fled from his present owner, stolen a horse, and lured another slave to flee with him, while others claimed that Basallo had threatened to kill him. Eventually a document was found supporting José's original claim. He derived no benefit from it, however, for the court discovered that his old owner was still alive, which meant that her will could not be executed and José, despite his imaginative defense, was still a slave.[9]

The courts also played a role in weakening and even reversing some of the laws that negatively affected the slaves, especially the 1839 decree extending the period of patronal control over *libertos*. Questions were raised concerning the applicability of the law and even its validity. Did the law apply to all *libertos*, or only to those born after the decree? Lawyers argued that in the case of the former interpretation, the decree was being applied retroactively and was thus unconstitutional. In 1846 a court agreed, finding that a *liberta* who had been born in 1823 had been held illegally by her master after she reached the age of twenty-one, and ordered her freed. Other courts concurred, freeing more *libertos* and perhaps giving hope to those born after 1839 that further loopholes might be found to invalidate the law completely.[10]

Freedom was the principal goal of Peru's slaves, despite the contrary belief of foreign observers, and various ways existed for them to become free, providing further evidence of a humane system and a society that was not unalterably committed to the preservation of slavery. Peruvians were willing to free their slaves in repayment for years of faithful service. Manumission might come unexpectedly in a will or be offered as an inducement, as in the case of María Trinidad, an Arequipa slave who after nine months' service was promised her freedom on her owner's death if she continued to serve him with the loyalty she had shown thus far.[11] Many infants were freed on being baptised, perhaps in recognition of the mother's past service.[12] Some of these gestures may have been hollow. María Trinidad's owner may have been in his prime, while the babies may have been sickly and expected to die. Nevertheless, slaves were being freed—and in increasing numbers after 1840—while others were being offered freedom in the not-too-distant future.[13] An Arequipa slave was bought with the condition that she would be a slave for only four more years, until she became twenty-five. A newspaper advertisement in 1840 appealed for a female slave to work outside Lima, offering freedom in return for two years' service. Another offered a woman and her infant daughter for sale, but with the conditions that the woman was to be used as a wet nurse and was to be freed on the completion of her duties. Wet nurses as a group seem to have been particularly successful in obtaining their unconditional freedom after completing their obligations.[14]

If slaves could not depend on a humane or liberal owner to free them or an aged one to show a degree of generosity in his or her will, they had the option of purchasing their own freedom. They had been doing so since the early sixteenth century, and the practice had become institutionalized by the mid-1600s.[15] In the early republic it seems to have occurred far more frequently than owners freeing them.[16] Slaves had the legal right to buy their freedom if they had the necessary funds, and many did. Urban slaves retained some of the wages that they received for their work. Rural slaves earned wages too. Those in the Ica area received the same wage as free laborers, 6 reals per day, when they worked on Sundays and feast days. On the estates of San José and San Javier some slaves received wages instead of rations. Rural slaves also could sell the produce of their individual plots in the local towns or to the estate itself, as happened on the state-owned estates that purchased corn, beans, and other vegetables for distribution as rations. On the Chavalina estate, Clements Markham found that

> all the married slaves and workmen are allowed a piece of ground rent free, where they grow vegetables and breed pigs and poultry, while their children may be seen driving donkey loads of provision towards the town, and sitting before their heaps of fruit and vegetables in the market place of Yca. They are thus enabled to earn money and live in comparative comfort. One old slave at Chavalina had made several hundred dollars by lending money on usury; and, unable to write, he kept his accounts by notches on a stick.[17]

If slaves could not earn money, they might obtain it by other means such as gambling, stealing, or even through inheritance. When María Fuentepacheco, a free *morena*, died in 1844 she left all her possessions to her husband, a slave.[18] They might receive the required funds from a third party, whom they then served for a set period to pay off the debt. The relationship was formalized by a contract and seems to have involved primarily domestic slaves who had few other means to obtain money.[19]

The accumulation of funds may have been a long and arduous task, with numerous temptations for spending it elsewhere, but many slaves demonstrated a remarkable self-discipline and managed to save enough to purchase either their own freedom or that of family members, or the *patronato* of *libertos*. The records list numerous examples of husbands purchasing wives, wives husbands, parents children, children parents, and other interfamilial combinations. Catalina Colo's daughter paid 250 pesos for her mother's freedom in 1854; María de la Cruz Salazar purchased the *patronato* of her daughter for 150 pesos in 1850.[20] In the late 1820s the state seemed particularly willing to permit its slaves to buy their freedom, in recognition perhaps of the liberators' abolitionist legislation, although more likely in response to its desperate need for cash and a desire to get rid of an unprofitable slave population. Whatever the reason, several slaves managed to free themselves. In 1827 a foreman on the estate of San José paid 500 pesos, a formidable saving, for his own freedom and for that of his daughter. Manuel de los Inocentes, a freedman, paid 100 pesos in 1828 for one of his daughters and 200 pesos the following year for a second. Manuel Sacramento paid 100 pesos for his niece; Agueda Josefa Funés paid 200 pesos for her daughter.[21]

The savings involved so great a sacrifice by the slaves or their families that they were not prepared to have their efforts frustrated. In the 1830s, Melchora Valverde, a free woman, paid 500 pesos to free her husband, a master carpenter. However, he had only just begun to enjoy his new status when the owner of the Palpa estate had him abducted off the street, claiming he had fled the estate two years earlier. Melchora determined to secure his release, even though it might involve "the sacrifice of all my fortune and the product of my work and the work of my husband." She appealed to the courts and eventually obtained a favorable decision, only to learn that her husband had been put in shackles and sent to Palpa. Once again she appealed to the courts, this time to secure his unconditional freedom.[22]

Slaves without the full amount to purchase their freedom had other options open to them. They could arrange to amortize their price over a period of time, paying off a certain amount each month until the full price had been met. Slaves on being sold could pay part of their purchase price to their new owner, thereby reducing their value and the amount they needed to save for their eventual freedom.[23] To improve the possibility of self-purchase, they tried to have their values reduced by appealing either directly to their owners or, if this failed, to the courts.[24] In July 1827 all the slaves of the San José and San Javier estates demanded new evaluations based on their present skills and medical state. Many sought reductions on the grounds of ill health, citing venereal disease, bleeding from the mouth (probably consumption), rheumatism, or simply "chronic illness." The usual reduction requested seems to have been 50 pesos, as was the case with one San José slave who had her value reduced from 250 to 200 pesos because of venereal disease, eye problems, advanced age, and habitual sickness. But the reduction was sometimes more. In 1828 a San Javier slave secured a reduction of 100 pesos because of her poor physical condition, permitting her to buy her freedom.[25] When a claim of poor health was not possible, slaves sought reductions on the grounds of long years of service, injuries suffered while working for their owners, or, in the case of women, their reproductive record. Atanasia de la Cruz, another San José slave, had her price reduced by 50 pesos in recognition of long years of service and the production of six children.[26]

Slaves also benefited from owners setting a maximum sale price for their property and including the figure in sales contracts and other legal documents. This meant that, although a slave's value might increase and his or her owner change, the sale price could not rise. Moreover, since the amount was contractually set, the slaves knew exactly how much they had to save to buy their freedom.[27] A common accompanying condition was that they could not be sold outside the city. In these cases the owners may have wanted to save slaves that they knew from the hard work of a plantation or to prevent the division of families. Whatever the rationale, the courts recognized the condition even though it contributed to the rural labor shortage.[28]

If slaves were unable to obtain the necessary money to purchase their freedom, they had the alternative of changing owners, or masters in the case of *libertos*. They enjoyed this right first under Bolívar's order and later under the 1852 Civil Code. During the earlier period, at least one slave appealed directly to Bolívar himself, demanding a change because his owner had failed to provide the necessities required by law. When Patricia Sayán sought a new owner, she specified one who would appreciate her weak and sickly state which, she claimed, was a result of pulmonary problems brought on by her present owner's insistence that she work in the fields, even though she had been bought for housework.[29]

The slaves' struggle for change and improvement was part of a day-to-day existence that, in the opinion of many foreign commentators, differed little from that experienced by other sectors of Peruvian society. Neither urban nor rural slaves were confined to their homes or their place of work. They mixed openly with fellow slaves, free blacks, Indians, mulattoes, and other members of the community. They were probably as law-abiding as anyone else, although the records tend to focus on their deviance from the norms set by the white community and leave the impression that they were an antisocial and immoral sector of society. Gambling seems to have been popular among them, and they did not always use their winnings to purchase their freedom, spending it instead on alcohol, entertainment, their notoriously sumptuous clothing, and other goods. Lima residents complained in 1853 that slaves and servants congregated on the street corner of Rifa and San Antonio from six in the morning to six at night, gambling with dice, bothering pedestrians, blocking the sidewalk, and corrupting the students at a nearby school with their example and obscene language.[30]

In their life cycle Peru's slaves closely followed established norms. The church strongly influenced their lives, which may help to explain why they were more successful in preserving their family structure than were slaves elsewhere.[31] Although cohabitation and consensual relationships were common, they seem to have made some effort to legalize their relationships, choosing either free persons or other slaves to marry. Their willingness to marry indicates a confidence that family ties would be respected by their owners. Their willingness also could prove costly. The estate accounts of San Javier and San José for the late 1820s record a fee of 12 pesos for a wedding. The owners—recognizing that family ties served as a means of social control—might have paid the fee, but in many instances the slaves themselves were forced to provide the money from their hard-earned savings.[32] Before marrying, they had to have their owner's permission and provide two witnesses to attest to their unmarried state. Female slaves had to swear that they had not made a vow of chastity or entered a convent, and had no hidden illnesses or defects. Males had to swear to their chastity with regard to certain relatives of the bride. In 1850, Hipólito Moncada, a free black, had to swear that he neither was related to his bride, a slave, nor had had sexual relations with her sister.[33]

When a child was born to slaves, the parents seem to have made an effort to have it baptized. This was true even when the child was illegitimate and the father "unknown" according to the records. In some instances, the father may have been the slave's owner, as was probably the case of two illegitimate baby girls born in the Lima parish of Santa Ana in 1824, whose fathers were listed as Don Agustín Bustamente and Don Ramón Echenique.[34] Baptism was relatively cheap— 1 peso at San Javier and San José—yet owners and masters of *libertos* insisted that the mother pay, even though baptism provided written proof of the existence of the offspring. Owners complained that they had already been deprived of their slave's labor for two months or more and now had to feed and clothe a child who was almost free.[35] Slaves were willing to pay for a baptism because it not only satisfied their religious concerns but also provided an opportunity to record any conditions affecting the status of their child. Some slaves used the occasion simply to make the point that the child was free according to San Martín's 1821 decree.[36] That freedom was still circumscribed, but they at least had made a gesture toward securing a better future for their children in both this life and the hereafter.

Death brought with it one final expense for the slave, the cost of the funeral. In the countryside the fee was 6 pesos, 6 reals for adults and 4 pesos, 4 reals for children.[37] Death may have relieved the slaves of their earthly obligations and ended their suffering, but some of the discriminatory distinctions that had accompanied them during their lives pursued them to the grave. The racial terminology that had developed during the colonial period continued to be applied, for death notices still differentiated among them as blacks, *morenos*, *pardos*, mulattoes, and the like.[38]

These divisions indicate that much of the colonial past had survived the Independence Wars, that Peru's black population still had to contend with widespread racism, and that the favorable picture of slavery presented by foreign observers should be viewed with some skepticism. While examples like the above might suggest that Peru's slaves enjoyed an almost normal existence or, at least, were experiencing some improvements in their daily lives, the reality was quite different. Despite the freedoms and perquisites provided to many of Peru's slaves, despite their various legal rights— which leave the impression that Peruvian slavery had deteriorated so that it was nothing more than the "contractual arrangement between the master and his bondsman," as described by Frank Tannenbaum—slavery in Peru was still extremely exploitative, like chattel slavery elsewhere.[39] Peruvian slaves were harshly treated, they had to overcome enormous obstacles in their struggle for freedom, and they could not guarantee that their legal rights would be recognized by their owners or the state. *Libertos* may have been technically free, but their lives were still circumscribed, and they were considered inferior by many whites. The views of one lawyer, who objected to educating young *libertos* because "*libertos* are not children of a class who need grand comprehensive principles to direct their actions but those that are in keeping with their condition and state," were not atypical.[40]

The interrelationship of color and prejudice was evident in the harassment suffered by all Peruvian blacks, even those who had never been slaves. Free blacks were often arrested and held as runaways. In some instances this may have been a simple case of mistaken identity, but the details from numerous court cases suggest that more often the action was deliberate. Blacks were hounded by individuals who saw them as a means to make money or to obtain workers and who were confident that their illegal actions would succeed. For the blacks, a trial to right this wrong might mean years of litigation and heavy costs. Isabel Urrutia, a freedwoman, was involved in a case that lasted six years. In 1825 her owner promised that in recognition of the past service of her mother she would be freed when she either married or became twenty-one, and she was subsequently freed. However, in 1851 a court decided that she had been legally sold in 1832 and turned her and her two children over to the person claiming to be her owner. Isabel appealed the decision through the *defensor de menores*, charging that the 1832 sale was of another person and that the birth certificate submitted as evidence had been a fake. An appellate court agreed and ordered her freed. The *defensor*, however, was still not completely satisfied and sought a court document for Isabel and her children to prevent further harassment. Another case involved an ex-slave named Francisco Venegas who had been freed in 1822 and who subsequently worked in the congress, earning 15 pesos per month. In 1850 he was abducted by Juan Venegas, who claimed that he had just bought Francisco. The latter appealed through the *defensor*, who demanded that criminal charges be brought against Juan for participating in the sale of a free man. This may have been another case of mistaken identity, but the *defensor* believed that someone was deliberately lying in order to make some money. The court decided in favor of Francisco and ordered that he be paid the wages he had earned while being held in a bakery. His position remained uncertain, however, for Venegas appealed the decision.[41]

Thus, all of Peru's blacks were condemned by the color of their skin and by the nation's continuing commitment to slavery, but those who suffered most were the slaves. They remained property and had little control over their lives. They could be seized and moved to a new owner with no warning or explanation except that some previous sale had not been legal.[42] Many of them existed in an unclear legal position because of the conditions placed on their status. A slave who was promised her freedom when she married but was placed in the charge of another before this occurred seemed to be neither slave, *liberto*, nor free, according to the person who was trying to sell her.[43]

Adding to the uncertainty was the courts' inconsistent interpretation of the laws. Frequently, they found in the owners' favor, protecting property rights and preserving slavery. Some courts, for example, interpreted Gamarra's 1839 decree strictly, insisting that *libertos* remain with their masters until they reached the age of fifty, and even applying it to the children of *libertos*, known as *ingenuos*. In 1843, Inés Salazar sought the court's intercession to secure her own freedom and that of her two-year-old daughter. Inés, a *liberta* who had been born in October 1821, argued that the decree could not be applied retroactively. The court decided, however, that her argument applied only to *libertos* who had reached the age of twenty-one before 1839; others were not affected. The court then took the decree one step further, applying it to her daughter, an *ingenua*, and declaring that she had to remain with the master until she, too, was fifty. Other courts supported this interpretation, adding only the limitations that *ingenuos* could not be sold and that the master had to provide for their education. According to newspaper reports, this interpretation opened *libertos* and their children to illegally extended periods of domination, as masters altered their recorded ages.[44] Slaveholders also followed the time-honored tradition of ignoring legislation. Routinely ignored were the laws that permitted parents to demand a new master or complete freedom for their *liberto* children if a master failed to provide food, clothing, education, and medical assistance. Even when brought to court, owners refused to comply.[45]

With the courts and the laws of questionable use, the slaves had to try other means to alter their status, but these often proved to be equally ineffective. Many slaves who were promised freedom in return for loyal service found the promises hollow. For example, in 1825 a woman commenced a legal action on the grounds that her daughter had been freed in a will that had subsequently been ignored by the dead slaveholder's heirs; she was still in the courts eight years later. In 1854 a slave claimed that she had been promised her freedom in return for eight years of service and that despite mistreatment she had completed the eight years. Now she sought her freedom through the courts but faced one delay after another; eventually, quite likely out of frustration, she took matters into her own hands and fled. Toribio Elmes also turned to the courts to seek compliance with a promise of freedom. He claimed that upon his purchase in August 1853 he had been promised his freedom in one year, plus a wage of 4 pesos per week, but he had received only 2 pesos per week during his ten months in service. He wanted his back pay (amounting to 90 pesos) and, on the basis of calculations that his value had depreciated over the year so that he was now worth only 33 pesos, 2.5 reals, he offered to buy his freedom. Instead, he found himself in a bakery in irons while his owner explained that his slaves could not make public pronouncements without his consent. The court found in Toribio's favor, but he had to turn to it again one month later, as he was still being held and was still without his back pay of 34 pesos. Once more the court decided in his favor, and finally he was freed.[46]

Slaves also found their chances for freedom limited because they were unable to obtain reductions in their value—even if they could prove poor health—or because a reduction left their price still too high. In 1828 a seventy-five-year-old San José de la Nazca slave was valued at 120 pesos. He managed to produce the funds to buy his freedom, but many others did not. One Lima slave who in 1843 had her value of 350 pesos reduced by 150 pesos—100 pesos for a payment to her owner and 50 pesos for years of good service and the production of four children—was unable to accumulate the remaining 200 pesos in the twelve years before abolition.[47]

Sometimes money was available, but the anticipated reward was snatched from the poor slave's grasp. In 1827 a judge set up a voluntary subscription fund to purchase the freedom of a slave valued at 150 pesos. When 200 pesos were collected, the slave, "dancing with joy," went to secure his manumission, only to be told that the money had been spent. Confronting the judge, he was insulted and then informed that the money was going to be returned to the donors because he was "an insolent scoundrel." Theft of funds also kept two slaves, whose uncle had paid 600 pesos to a middleman, in bondage. Instead of buying their freedom the agent took the money, and the slaves ended up being sold to a new owner. Some of those slaves who obtained loans to purchase their freedom found the interest payments so high that they were unable to pay off the loan, forcing them to work for the creditor for the rest of their lives, with little real change in their status. Furthermore, owners might simply refuse to accept the money, although this was illegal. Josefa Dionisio offered her owner 400 pesos, which was 50 pesos more than a court-imposed valuation, but he refused it, demanding to know where she got the money. Courts, too, ignored the law, returning slaves who had the necessary funds to buy their freedom to their owners. Even an apparently legally completed purchase could prove illusory. In 1850 a court ordered a *liberta* to remain with her master despite the fact that her mother had paid her value. Although a higher court overruled the decision, the case emphasized once again that Peru's slaves could be certain of virtually nothing.[48]

Attempts by slaves to change owners could be equally unsuccessful, regardless of the law in their favor. In 1854, María Henríquez, complaining of bad treatment and fearful that she was going to be returned to a hacienda, sought a new owner. She found a possible buyer who deposited her purchase price, but her owner, Irene Aria de Henríquez, refused, stating that slaves had no right to alter their dominion on their own, as it set a bad example. She also denied the charge of mistreatment, explaining that she once had sent María to a hacienda for twelve days because of insolence, "licentious living," and misconduct, and as punishment for striking her son, but that otherwise she had treated her "like a daughter." She was backed by the hacendado, who testified that María had been sent to the farm after being arrested for "sleeping in the street," for which her owner had been fined. María denied that she had hit anyone, insisted that she had been at the farm for a month, but agreed that her owner had been caring. The court decided against her and returned her to Irene.[49] Other slaves were equally unsuccessful despite pressure from officials, the courts, and even relatives of slave owners.[50]

Denied opportunities to change their legal position or their owners, slaves had to cope with the harsh realities of their daily existence. Rural slaves faced especially difficult conditions, as the depressed state of agriculture and the limited returns meant that planters sought to make economies, often at their slaves' expense. In some cases the situation was so desperate that even whites felt compelled to comment. In 1845, Cañete Valley residents complained that "the hacienda blacks are wretched; as a result of their very slave state they lack many necessities."[51] Housing was primitive. Proctor noted that plantation slaves lived in cane huts. They were probably clustered "in villages . . . round a plaza generally with a cross in the centre," as Markham found the slave *galpón* or quarters in the Cañete Valley in the 1850s. He added that the "villages are surrounded by high walls, and all must be within by a certain hour." He did not comment on the condition of this accommodation, but elsewhere found at least one hacienda in a dilapidated state, a description that probably applied to the slave quarters as well.[52]

Little money seems to have been spent on food for the slaves. Pablo Macera has written that Peru's slaves were better fed than either the Chinese coolies, who were imported later in the century, or other groups in Peru and elsewhere, but this does not prove that they were eating well.[53] Legislation specified the rations that were to be provided, and the records indicate that owners purchased meat, beans, chickpeas, grapes, and *aguardiente* for their slaves. However, laws were ignored. In 1824 each slave on an estate whose slave population had recently declined from one thousand to four hundred was receiving what observers described as "small" quantities of corn and beans, amounting to less than one liter of each.[54] In 1828, when slaves on San Javier de la Nazca were reported to be searching for food "in the street" because of shortages on the estate, the subprefect had to intervene and increase their rations. Slaves on the sister estate of San José did receive weekly food rations, but not the clothing, tobacco, and medical treatment that they were promised.[55]

The minimal amount spent on slaves was reflected in the estates' maintenance figures. The costs, including food, rented mules, and clothing, totaled 1142.5 pesos for San Javier in 1824 and only 90 pesos for the period from November 1827 to February 1828. On San José the estate paid 426 pesos, 1 real for slave maintenance in 1825 but only 251 pesos the following year. In that same period the slave population remained constant, while total estate expenses rose from 1753.7 pesos to 2997.3 pesos.[56] Providing slaves with a plot of land to grow their own food enabled owners to reduce their costs and avoid their obligations concerning rations. Whether the slaves could grow enough on their plots to meet all their needs is unclear. Some were evidently unsuccessful, as they fled their estates owing to the shortage of food and other basic essentials. In 1836 seven slaves fled the Nepén estate, complaining that they had received no food or clothing, been assigned excessive work, and been punished without cause. They were willing to return to the estate, "for they knew that they were obliged to do so because they were slaves," but they wanted the administrator to be replaced. In court, the owner's widow denied the complaints, stating that each slave received land to cultivate and that rations were distributed each Sunday. The court accepted her version and ordered the slaves returned, but it was not completely convinced, for it directed that the slaves should not be punished for their appeal to the court and absence from the estate.[57]

Because of poor rations, inadequate housing, limited health care, and mistreatment, illness among the slaves seems to have been common. Comparative statistics are not available, and since the coast of Peru was a notoriously unhealthy place all sectors of the population may have been suffering equally. Yet the frequent claims for price reductions on the basis of illness suggest that slaves were a disease-prone group. One of the few sources that examines slave illnesses deals with the state's Nazca holdings. In 1828, 39 (of whom 23 were women) of San Javier's 300 slaves, and 17 of San José's 130 slaves, were listed as having various illnesses. The most common were "blood from the mouth" (probably consumption) and venereal disease, usually syphilis. Other physical complaints included pulmonary typhoid, scabies, leprosy, flatulent colic, piles, gout, hernias, buboes, ruptures, rheumatic pain, loss of limbs, sunken chest, eye inflammation, hysteria, weeping sores from branding, and sore throats. On both estates medicines and medical treatment were lacking, which probably translated into high mortality rates, although the lack of statistics makes it impossible to prove this was the case.[58]

Deficiencies in health care, food, clothing, and accommodation, along with excessive labor demands, were all part of the abuse and exploitation that both urban and rural slaves had to face daily.[59] In addition many were physically confined, as owners tried to control their movements and prevent flight. José Aguirre was kept chained by his owner, who claimed this was a condition of his purchase since José had a reputation for being a fugitive and a pickpocket. This owner may have had some justification for his actions, but others did not. A former San Javier de la Nazca slave accused her new owners of mistreating her by threatening to whip her, tying her to a staircase, chaining her even though she was in the final stages of pregnancy, feeding her badly after the birth, and forcing her to return to work three days after parturition. She wanted to return to San Javier, where she had been born and where her family still lived. A more celebrated case involved the infamous Manuela Pando, a member of Lima's elite who had acquired notoriety for her marriages, her relationship with a priest after the death of her last husband, her role in the separation of her daughter and son-in-law, and her alleged involvement in the poisoning death of her grandson. In 1854, at the age of seventy-three, she was at the center of a new controversy, this time involving a male slave and two young *libertas* whom she was reported to have kept locked away in her house, which she guarded with two loaded pistols. One of the girls, who was fourteen or fifteen, had no idea how long she had been in the house, while the other, a nine-year-old, had been there for four or five months. Locked in their separate rooms and fed either every second day or "once a day badly," they had never met. The slave claimed that he had suffered for two years. A further charge was leveled subsequently, that another slave had fled the house after two years of "incarceration" and had died shortly thereafter. Manuela denied any wrongdoing, but an investigation was begun. While it proceeded, the girls were sent to a convent and the slave was moved out of the house.[60]

Slaves also faced incarceration by the state. With a reputation for criminal behavior, blacks could expect close attention from the authorities for any misdemeanors.[61] However, the frequency of the arrests, the flimsiness of the charges, and the treatment of those detained suggest that goals other than punishing criminals and preventing crime were involved. Slaves were arrested for not having their *boletos* and then accused of being runaways, for being out at night, and for drunkenness, gambling, and making merry in the streets. The real purpose behind the arrests may have been financial, for owners usually had to pay a fine for the release of their slaves. In 1843 the owners of thirty slaves who were arrested for gambling and drinking had to pay 2 pesos for each one. Alternatively, the authorities may have been seeking some unpaid workers, for arrested slaves often were assigned the task of cleaning the barracks while they awaited their owners to claim them.[62]

The prospect of unprovoked arrest must have been worrisome, but a far greater fear of the slaves was to be sold and thus separated from home, family, and familiar surroundings. Many slaves seem to have experienced no stability at all, being sold time and again. Some may have been responsible for their plight, being habitual criminals or fugitives or having some other perceived defect.[63] In other instances, however, the reasons are less clear. One slave, sold in 1829 by a nun who gave the money to her "sisters" and other poor religious, was resold seven more times in the next four years. Another was sold seventeen times between 1826 and 1849, including three times in a ten-day period. A third, who was seven when she was sold in April 1817, was resold nine times by November 1846, and a fourth was sold six times between October 1837 and January 1847.[64]

The sale of a slave not only disrupted his or her life but also could result in the division and separation of families. Husbands lost their wives, parents their children. In the process, the roots of family life were undermined. Children were frequently sold, as newspaper advertisements reveal. They were also given away, often as soon as they were born, to members of the owner's family. A marriage in the owner's family might have the same divisive effect, as slaves and *libertos* were a normal part of dowries. So, too, did the death of an owner, as the slaves would be distributed among the heirs or sold.[65] Thus, separation was a fact of life that afflicted many slaves, and its frequency challenges the image of a harmonious family life among Peru's slave population.

Parents tried to prevent the divisions, but with little success. Rosa Gasteagudo appealed to the court to try to stop the sale of her daughter, Beatriz, to a hacienda distant from

Lima on the grounds that Beatriz's bill of sale contained the conditions that she had to remain in Lima and could change owners as she wished. Rosa also claimed that Beatriz suffered from a chest condition and monthly "fatal weaknesses," and asked that her value be reduced from 330 pesos. In reply, the owners noted that the bill of sale contained no such conditions, Beatriz was perfectly healthy, and hacienda air would be good for her. The court agreed, upholding the right of property in slaves and the right of the owner to sell his property.[66]

Most of the cases of this sort involved the separation of *liberto,* and thus technically free, children from their mothers. The separation might take place years after the child's birth, as in the case of Ursula Fuentes; her former owner demanded her eight-year-old son since Ursula had been her slave when the boy had been born, which meant that he was her *liberto.* Manuel La Rosa was a twelve-year-old boy who was taken from his mother and the house where they had lived for nine years by the heirs of his mother's former owner.[67] Cases such as these raise questions about the degree of freedom permitted *libertos.* With the decline in the number of slaves and the continuing shortage of labor, the reasons why individuals were prepared to go to virtually any extreme to claim *libertos* years after their parents had been sold or freed are obvious.

Competing demands could leave the mother with a choice that would have tried the wisdom of Solomon. Feliciana was a slave who sought the court's help in returning to her former owner, with whom she had left her two infant children. She claimed her present owner was planning to sell her away from Lima. She was assisted by the *defensor de menores,* who called on the court to respect maternal love. Her owner denied that he intended to sell her, although his defense that there was no law requiring families to remain together raised some doubts. He then offered to buy the *patronato* of the children. Although it would have united the family, Feliciana refused because she thought that the children's present master was a better guardian than her owner.[68]

Following the promulgation of the Civil Code in 1852, with its proviso that slave families were to remain together, slaves were afforded somewhat better protection, as the case of Juliana Rojas indicates. She had been a slave on La Molina estate where, she claimed, she had suffered from hunger, lack of clothing, cruel and unjust punishment, and work beyond her capabilities. Nevertheless, she had managed to save enough to buy her freedom, and for the past four years had been working on a neighboring estate, supporting herself and her four children. Now the renter of La Molina, Juan Pedro Lostaunau, claimed the children as his *libertos*. Juliana argued that, since the estate had neither fed, clothed, nor educated them for over three years, they were legally free. Lostaunau replied that he had provided pabulum after the birth of the two youngest children, as well as food and money for clothing. In 1853 a court agreed that he had not abandoned them; however, it was not prepared to separate minors from their parents and decided that the *patronato* should be sold to a person of the parents' choosing. Lostaunau objected, calling the order prejudicial to his interests and arguing that by law children had to remain with their parents only for their first three years. Juliana and her husband objected, too. They demanded that the children be freed on the grounds of the laws of nature and humanity that prevented the division of families. Their case was still being decided in September 1854.[69]

Not every case ended unhappily for the slaves. Manuela and her two-year-old son, Timoteo, were sold to the subprefect of Caylloma in 1841. Two years later she and her ten-month-old daughter were sold back to Manuela's former owner, but Timoteo remained with the subprefect. Five months later mother and daughter were sold again, but the following day the new owner also purchased Timoteo, reuniting mother and children.[70] This comparatively happy denouement seems to have been one of the few exceptions to the generally tragic rule.

The fate of their children weighed heavily on mothers. While charges that neglect by slave mothers resulted in the death of three quarters of the children born to them were probably exaggerated, abortion and infanticide were not unknown, as slaves sought to save themselves the heartache of separation or worse. Flora Tristán heard from one owner that the incidence of abortion among slaves was high, and she met two slaves who were in jail for starving their children to death. Face to face with them, she speculated that they preferred to have their children dead rather than enslaved. Another observer claimed that slaves suffocated their children rather than see them be victims of cruelty. He added that, on seeing their children whipped, mothers cursed their wombs and the hour they were born.[71]

In addition to the death, loss, and punishment of their children, female slaves had to contend with the sexual demands of their owners. The law tried to prevent this form of exploitation by granting freedom to any slave who could prove it, but only a few of those abused seem to have appealed to the courts. In 1830, Rafacla Marín charged that her owner, who had bought her the previous year for 100 pesos, had promised to free her in return for sexual favors and had forced her to work as a prostitute while continuing to sleep with her. They had even been caught in flagrante delicto by his wife. The court accepted her charge of abuse and ordered her freed.

In another case, Remijia Nuñes had been promised her freedom in her owner's will on her twenty-fifth birthday if she was married; if not, she was to remain the slave of his sister. In 1847, when she was twenty-nine, she sought her freedom but was unsuccessful because she was still single. She appealed through the *defensor de menores*, who testified that at the age of twenty she had been engaged to marry Maximo Rojas but that he had been jailed to prevent the marriage. She then had been raped by her new owner's husband and had borne his child. Nevertheless, Maximo had still been willing to marry her, but again he was jailed to prevent the marriage that would have secured her freedom. The husband denied the charge of rape and accused Remijia of having abandoned herself to "sensual pleasures" at an early age, engaged in prostitution, and been a runaway. However, he did not deny fathering the child, probably because the affair had been common knowledge and the reason why his wife had tried to sell Remijia on one occasion. The court ordered her freed on the grounds of sexual exploitation.[72]

The men involved in cases such as these usually denied the charge of sexual abuse, but occasionally the women could counter with evidence that was the product of the exploiters' actions. Vicenta Urrutia, the slave of Father Manuel Palma, had three children during the nine years she was his slave, one of whom was given to Palma's parents. Obtaining her freedom, Vicenta sought to free her son, claiming he was Palma's illegitimate child, even though his birth certificate stated he was the legitimate child of Vicenta and her husband. Palma denied the charges as "unjust and malicious." Vicenta, however, pointed out that the boy was a *samba obscura* while her husband was a *negro tinto*, so that the boy's father had to be white. Palma continued to deny any paternal relationship, charging that the adultery had occurred "only in the imagination of this unhappy colored woman."[73]

With family life unstable, relations between spouses were bound to suffer. Disempowered by the system, slaves turned to violence as a release for their frustrations. Domestic assaults were numerous and in some cases resulted in death. The slavery system may not have been responsible in every instance, but it and the accompanying tensions were at the root of some cases at least. Was it responsible, for example, for undermining the eleven-year marriage of Luis Castro and his wife? In 1823 he accused her of attacking him once with a machete and twice with a knife before leaving him for another man, who had also attacked him with a knife and had insulted him. He blamed the lover and his wife's owner for the troubles. Less clear are cases such as that of Juan Espejo, a fifty-year-old water seller, who hit his partner on the head after she said she wanted to end their relationship. The injuries were not severe, but Espejo was sentenced to be sold fifty leagues from Lima within a month. Toribio Elmes, a bakery worker, planned to kill his wife, whom he accused of having an affair with another slave, but his attack went astray and he slashed a free black woman who seemed to be trying to protect his wife. The injured woman demanded 34 pesos in compensation for her medical treatment. Petronila Vasquez was arrested for slashing her lover, a slave, but was released after testifying that she had only been defending herself against him when he began hitting her in a drunken stupor.[74]

This same lack of power may help to explain why some slaves resorted to rape. The records may or may not reflect the reality of the situation, but the instances seem to have been few. In 1845, Mateo Ugarte, a shoemaker, was charged with raping a six-year-old orphan. According to the court record, Ugarte threw the girl on a bed and tried to have intercourse with her but failed because of her size. He then sexually assaulted her with his hand, breaking her hymen and leaving her pubis bruised. The court decided that since intercourse had not occurred there had been no crime, but at the same time it found that the girl had been corrupted "in a certain sense" and so levied a fine of 30 pesos, which Ugarte was to pay off by working in a bakery. His owner decided that this was enough to render him valueless and indicated his intention to sell Mateo after the fine was paid.[75]

While the day-to-day existence of Peru's slaves might be seen as a form of punishment in itself, those convicted of crimes were subject to special abuse. Like freedmen they might be fined, jailed, or conscripted into the army. They could also be "exiled" from their homes if the court ordered them sold to some distant spot, a punishment owners resisted since it meant losing their property.[76] A more common form of punishment was to be imprisoned in a bakery and compelled to work. Many bakeries contained holding cells of some sort, along with shackles and chains. Slaves being held for trial might also be deposited in a bakery, with their wages paid to their owner. Archibald Smith described the use of bakeries as the "ordinary mode of punishment." Von Tschudi echoed this observation, adding that corporal punishment was uncommon. Rather, if a slave "requires punishment, he is sent into the *Panaderia* . . . to knead the dough and bake the bread, which work they perform under the supervision of a mayordomo, who is usually a hard task-master. Owing to the heat of the climate, working in the *Panaderia* is more feared by the slaves than any other kind of punishment."[77] Yet, in the eyes of the law, bakery work was not the most severe punishment. A sentence of hard labor in a bakery could be increased to a term in prison, and slaves could be condemned to death.[78]

However, the most common form of punishment for slaves, according to the records and contrary to the views of Von Tschudi and others, was whipping.[79] It was permitted by law and administered by both officials and owners. In the latter case, owners usually justified their actions by claiming that the slaves were lazy and could be compelled to work only with the lash.[80] It was used quite arbitrarily: Slaves were whipped for "grossly" insulting officials, "shameless public conduct," and throwing stones in the street—but not in every case, for the courts might fine the owner a few pesos instead.[81] The severity of this form of punishment was circumscribed by law: The maximum was twelve lashes, blood could not be drawn, certain individuals were exempt, and the owner had to be present at the whipping. Failing to have the owner present could create problems for the person who carried out the whipping. In 1849 the Lima police intendant found himself the target of a congressional inquiry after whipping a slave of José María Lizarzaburu four times. Lizarzaburu was a member of the chamber of deputies, and he sought the chamber's assistance in punishing those responsible. The

justice committee complied, deciding that the slave was protected by the constitution "because a slave is also a man, also
a member, although a passive one, of society and humanity."
It also condemned the police for their actions and for considering themselves "the lash of God."[82]

Despite interventions of this sort, the laws regarding
whipping, like other laws, were commonly ignored. Neither
sex nor age spared slaves from the lash: Children, pregnant
women, and the aged were whipped. Some beatings were so
savage that slaves died or had to be hospitalized, sometimes
with the expectation that they would not survive. In one case
a minor had to be taken to the hospital after he was "cruelly
punished" by his owner. On the Pedreros estate an elderly
man who was whipped by the majordomo for having stolen
some sheep required hospitalization, as his wounds became
gangrenous and maggoty. Another slave on the same estate,
an aged woman, complained that she had been whipped
despite having two daughters and ten grandchildren. She
demanded her freedom on the grounds of mistreatment and
old age. Another female slave had been whipped more than
thirty times. Two female slaves on the San Nicolás estate
were reported to have been whipped far more than twelve
times, as their wounds still had not healed after twenty days.
They were also imprisoned and held incommunicado, all for
having demanded that their *liberto* children not be treated as
slaves.[83]

*Libertos*, most of whom were children, were subject to the
same punishment. Andrés Castro, whose master accused
him of attempting to murder him, was whipped over fifty
times and confined in stocks. The whipping produced wounds
on his buttocks that were half an inch in depth and took over
a month to heal. A *liberta*, a girl of ten or eleven years, had
scars on her body from whippings administered by her
master's wife. A seventeen-year-old *liberta* from the San Pedro
estate was whipped twenty times by the estate foreman for
failing to carry out his orders and for associating with known
highwaymen. She was accused of being the concubine of the
notorious robber Juan de Mata Duanes, a San Pedro slave.
She insisted that she had been kidnapped by Duanes and
was unable to escape because she was ignorant of the roads.[84]

In cases of excessive whipping, slaves could demand their
freedom from the courts. Gerónimo Jauregui, one of the first
slaves to use the services of the *defensor de menores*, demanded even more when he complained to a court in 1830

about the punishment meted out to his family. His wife had been whipped twice for fleeing, while his son had received anywhere between six and twenty-five lashes—the evidence differed—for leaving a door open that permitted a *"zambito"* to carry on affairs with other slaves. A doctor testified that the scars from the whipping were still visible in the boy's buttocks a month later. Gerónimo wanted a new owner, as well as his present owner, Juan Pedro Lostaunau, to be considered an enemy of the fatherland since his actions were contrary to the law. Lostaunau's defense was not to deny the whippings but rather to try to discredit the *defensor* and his evidence. His lawyer accused the *defensor* of "seducing" the slave witnesses and causing other slaves to flee and make excessive demands.[85]

These and many other cases show that Peruvian slavery was not the mild institution that contemporary observers claimed. Peru's slaves were an abused and exploited sector of the population. Opportunities for enjoying what might be called a normal life may have existed for some of them, but the vast majority faced uncertainties, frustrations, and tensions that denied any possibility of normalcy. The effects of the abuse, exploitation, and uncertainties were mixed. Many slaves responded by accepting the situation or accommodating themselves to it, waiting for improvements or even emancipation to occur. Some were so completely indoctrinated that they came to accept the dominant sector's attitudes toward slaves and slavery. This may explain the actions of one slave who tried to sell another, claiming to be his owner.[86] The vast majority, however, took advantage of any opportunity that might arise to secure some minimal benefits for themselves and, at the same time, to chip away at the system that kept them in chains. Peru's slaves may have been exploited, but they were not passive. They confronted their owners and the state in various ways, some more violent than others, and in the process proved to be the most effective of the abolitionist forces that were slowly but surely undermining Peruvian slavery.

## Notes

1. Markham, *Cuzco and Lima*, 27; Proctor, *Narrative*, 232–34; Smith, *Peru As It Is* 1:110–11; J. J. Von Tschudi, *Travels in Peru, during the Years*

*1838–1842, on the Coast, in the Sierra, across the Cordilleras and the Andes, into the Primeval Forests*, trans. Thomasina Ross (London, 1847), 107–8.

2. Enclosure with Adams to Aberdeen, ST5, August 4, 1845, F.O. 84/595. The fear of military conscription prompted some free blacks to obtain slave *boletos*. See *El Comercio*, February 1, 1842, December 13, 1843.

3. James C. Scott, *Weapons of the Weak: Everyday Forms of Peasant Resistance* (New Haven, 1985), 280, 328; Genovese, *Roll, Jordan, Roll*.

4. Manuel Burga has approached this point of view from a different perspective, arguing that by the late colonial period the mode of production in Peru had progressed from a slave mode to more of a feudal mode, so that "classical slavery" did not exist. See Manuel Burga, "La hacienda en el Perú, 1850–1930: evidencias y método," *Tierra y Sociedad* 1 (1978): 17–23.

5. Sales de Bohigas, *Sobre esclavos*, 123–27.

6. "Ordenes e instrucciones dadas por la comandancia general e intendencia de Ica a Dn. Miguel Bernales, administrador de las haciendas San Javier y San Pablo de la Nazca," AGN, Temporalidades, San Javier de la Nazca, 1819–1828, Leg. 70, Cuad. 109.

7. "Expediente sobre los autos seguidos por la esclava Isabel Verano, para cambiar de amo," Huaura, October 17, 1825, BN D12586.

8. Enclosure with Adams to Aberdeen, ST5, August 4, 1845, F.O. 84/595.

9. AAL, Causas de Negros, 1815–1855, Leg. 36, LXII:59. For another case illustrating the care taken by a court, in this instance deciding whether a woman was a slave or a *liberta*, see "Promovido por el sindico procurador con la testamentaria del D. D. José Pando, sobre la libertad de la sierva Petronila Pando," June 11, 1853, AGN, CCiv, 1852–53, Leg. 169. The case covers 150 numbered folio pages.

10. *El Comercio*, July 18, 1846, October 5, 1849, January 27, 1855.

11. AD-A, Notarial, Francisco de Linares, 1829–1831, Leg. 678, January 10, 1831.

12. See, for example, AAL, Bautismos de Indios, Esclavos, Mestizos, 1819–1825, Parroquia de San Sebastián, Leg. 11, October 1, 1824.

13. Engelsen, "Social Aspects," 81, table 4.

14. AD-A, Notarial, Toribio de Linares, 1844–1846, Prot. 709, April 3, 1845; *El Comercio*, April 10, 1840, April 20, 1849. For more examples see Aguirre, "Agentes," 46–49.

15. Bowser, *African Slave*, 278–82.

16. A survey of Lima slaves in the last fifteen years of slavery shows that close to three quarters of them were freed through self-purchase. See Aguirre, "Agentes," 14.

17. "Información que el prefecto del departamento de Ica mandó levantar en el valle de la Nazca con el fin de pesquisar la conducta del pbro. Dn. Manuel Barreto, administrador de la hacienda San José de la Nazca y tierras anexas, en orden a la recta administración de los dichos fundos," AGN, Temporalidades, Leg. 97, Cuad. 84; "Cuentas de Don Miguel Bernales," AGN, Temporalidades, Leg. 70, Cuad. 111-A; Markham, *Cuzco and Lima*, 42; John Thomas, *Diario de viáje del General O'Higgins en la campaña de Ayacucho*, trans. Carlos Vicuña Mackenna (Santiago de

Chile, 1917), 220. See also Markham, "Travels" 1:133–35. Foreign observers used the terms *dollars* and *pesos* interchangeably.

18. AGN, Notarial, Eduardo Huerta, 1844–45, Prot. 274, October 19, 1844.

19. Aguirre, "Agentes," 40–42.

20. For these and similar purchases of slaves and *libertos* see AGN, Notarial, Lucas de la Lama, 1854–55, Prot. 333; AAL, Causas de Negros, 1815–1855, Leg. 36, LXVII:33; AD-A, Notarial, Francisco de Linares, 1834–35, Prot. 681.

21. "El prefecto de departamento acompaña el expediente sobre la libertad del esclavo Matías propio de la hacienda de San José de la Nazca," AGN, 1827, P.L. 7-229B; "El prefecto de este departamento participa haber dirigido a los administradores del tesoro público, un libramiento de 382 pesos, 4 reales girado contra la administración de correos de esta capital, cuya suma han recibido por su libertad, Manuel Sacramento y Nolberta, esclavos que fueron de la hacienda de San José de la Nazca," AGN, 1827, P.L. 7-335; "El prefecto de esta capital dando parte de haber entregado a Manuel de los Inocentes, esclavo que fue de la hacienda San José de la Nazca, al sub-prefecto de Ica 150 pesos por la libertad de su hija, Norberta de Jesús," AGN, 1828, P.L. 8-597; "El prefecto de este departamento acompañando el expediente promovido por Agueda Josefa Funés, sobre la libertad de su hija, Isabel, esclava de la hacienda de San Javier de la Nazca," AGN, 1828, P.L. 8-670; "El prefecto de esta capital sobre la libertad de Gregoria, esclava de la hacienda de San José de la Nazca, y entrega de 100 pesos que ha hecho al sub-prefecto de Ica," AGN, 1828, P.L. 8-714. See also Aguirre, "Agentes," 12–31.

22. "Expediente promovido por Melchora Valverde sobre la libertad de su marido, José Antonio Rivadeneyra," AGN, CCiv, 1834, Leg. 84.

23. Aguirre, "Agentes," 36–37.

24. For cases of this sort in La Libertad see *El Peruano*, October 28, December 30, 1826.

25. "El prefecto de este departamento acompaña la nota que le ha remitido el intendente de la provincia de Ica, sobre el reclamo que hace la esclavatura de la hacienda de San José de la Nazca, por el excesivo valor en que ha sido tasado," AGN, 1827, P.L. 7-229C; "El prefecto del departamento de Lima acompaña la solicitud de Inocente, Manuel, y otros esclavos de la hacienda de San José de la Nazca sobre que se les dé su carta de libertad, previo el entero que ofrecen de su tasación," AGN, 1827, P.L. 7-425; "El prefecto de esta capital acompañando representación de María Natividad, esclava de la hacienda de San Javier, sobre que se haga de ella nuevo avaluo," 1828, AGN, P.L. 8-715. See also "El prefecto del departamento de Lima acompaña la nota del sub-prefecto de la provincia de Ica sobre la solicitud de la liberta María Libonia, esclava que fue de la hacienda de San Javier de la Nazca sobre su nueva tasación por los motivos que expresa," AGN, 1829, P.L. 9-227; "Gertrudis Atela, esclava de la hacienda de San José de la Nazca, solicitandose el justo precio para reclamar su libertad," AGN, 1829, P.L. 9-31; and "El prefecto del departamento de Lima acompaña el expediente promovido por María del Carmen Valdez sobre la libertad de su hijo, Casimiro," AGN, 1829, P.L. 9-444.

26. See "El prefecto de este departamento acompaña el expediente relativo a la libertad de Narciso y Simón de los Santos, esclavos de la hacienda de San Javier de la Nazca," AGN, 1827, P.L. 7-143; and "El prefecto de este departamento acompaña la representación de Atanacia de la Cruz, esclava de la hacienda de San José de la Nazca, en que solicita su libertad y rebaja del importe de su tasación," AGN, 1827, P.L. 7-193.

27. AAL, Causas de Negros, 1815–1855, Leg. 36, LXVII:1.

28. *Mercurio Peruano*, November 13, 1827.

29. "Petición presentada por la esclava, Patricia Sayán, para que se proceda a su tasación," Huacho, January 19, 1828, BN D12551; AAL, Causas de Negros, 1815–1855, Leg. 36, LXII:32. For an example of a *liberto* seeking a new master see "Seguidos por sindico D. Francisco Garfias con D. Nicolás Prunedas sobre la libertad de Juan Bautista," AGN, CCrim, 1854, Leg. 612.

30. *El Comercio*, July 21, 1853. See also "Seguidos contra los reos Francisco Olavid, N. Sambrano, José Alforno Cabillas y otro por la muerte alevosa executada en la persona del teniente conductor, Don Ambrosio Rojas," AGN, CCrim, 1830, Leg. 529; "Criminales contra Agustín Palacios, Jacinto Muñoz y Bernardo Pino para homicidio Ylavio Mendoza," AGN, CCrim, 1840, Leg. 576; and "Expediente sobre las averiguaciones acerca de la muerte de un criado negro," Huaura, March 16, 1824, BN D12591.

31. Macera, "Las plantaciones azucareras," 62.

32. "El Dr. D. Silvestre Peñaranda, cura del Ingenio en Ica, solicitando el pago de las pensiones que a su favor gravan sobre la hacienda de San José y San Javier de la Nazca, además de los derechos de obenciones que le corresponden por la esclavatura," AGN, 1828, P.L. 8-32; AGN, Temporalidades, Leg. 70, San Javier de la Nazca, 1819–1828, Cuad. A.

33. "Peticiones presentadas por varios negros para que se les expide licencias para que pueden contraer matrimonio," Lima, November 4, 1828, BN D10859; "Expediente sobre la petición presentada por el Gral. de Brigada José María Lizarzaburu para que se expide el decreto de matrimonio de una esclava a su servicio con un mozo libre," Lima, July 1, 1850, BN D9508. See also AAL, Matrimonios, Indios, Negros, Parroquia de San Marcelo, 1789–1838, Leg. 4; and AAL, Matrimonios, Indios, Negros, Parroquia de Santa Ana, 1795–1824, Leg. 3.

34. AAL, Bautismos de Negros y Pardos de la Parroquia de Santa Ana, 1820–1825, Leg. 10. See also AAL, Bautismos de Indios, Esclavos, Mestizos, Parroquia de San Sebastián, 1819–1825, Leg. 11; and AAL, Bautismos de Indios, Mulatos, Negros, Parroquia de San Marcelo, 1810–1828, Leg. 14.

35. *Mercurio Peruano*, July 17, 1828. For baptismal fees see "El Dr. D. Silvestre Peñaranda . . . ," AGN, 1828, P.L. 8-32.

36. See the case of María de Jesús, AAL, Bautismos de Indios, Mulatos, Negros, Parroquia de San Marcelo, 1810–1828, Leg. 14.

37. "El Dr. D. Silvestre Peñaranda . . . ," AGN, 1828, P.L. 8-32.

38. See, for example, AAL, Defunciones, Parroquia de San Lazaro, 1821–1830, Leg. 11; and AAL, Defunciones, Parroquia de San Lazaro, 1831–1843, Leg. 12.

39. Tannenbaum, *Slave and Citizen*, 55.

40. "Doña Manuela Aguirre sobre el deposito de Isabel Urrutia y sus dos hijos menores," AGN, CCiv, 1851, Leg. 162.

41. Ibid.; "Seguidos por el defensor general de menores contra Don Juan Bautista Venegas sobre la libertad de Juan Antonio Iglesias," AGN, CCiv, 1850, Leg. 158.

42. See, for example, AAL, Causas de Negros, 1815–1855, Leg. 36, LXII:2.

43. "D. José Ascona con Doña Manuela Nuyn sobre la libertad de Matea Martel," AGN, CCiv, 1851, Leg. 162.

44. *El Comercio*, October 3, 1843, August 4, 7, 1852; *El Peruano*, September 28, 1850.

45. For examples of court cases see "Seguidos por Juliana Rojas con Don Juan Pedro Lostaunau y el sindico de La Molina sobre la libertad de sus hijos, 1852," AGN, CCiv, 1854, Leg. 172; and AAL, Causas de Negros, 1815–1855, Leg. 36, LXVI:38.

46. "Autos seguidos por Doña Carmen Loayza con su esclava María Jesús Flores sobre su libertad," AGN, CCiv, 1825, Leg. 20; "Seguidos por Josefa Chunga con Doña María Estebes sobre su libertad," AGN, CCiv, 1854, Leg. 172; "Causa de libertad de Toribio Elmes, esclavo del Doctor D. Luis Ponce,"AGN, CCrim, 1854, Leg. 614.

47. "El prefecto del departamento de Lima hace presente la consulta del sub-prefecto de Ica sobre la cuota que presenta Carmen Valdez por la libertad de su hijo, esclavo de la hacienda de San José de la Nazca," AGN, 1828, P.L. 8-454; "El prefecto de esta capital comunicando haber entregado al esclavo de la hacienda de San José de la Nazca, José Ugalde, al subprefecto de Ica los 120 p. valor de su tasación," AGN, 1828, P.L. 8-531; "El prefecto del departamento de Lima acompaña el expediente promovido por María del Carmen Valdez sobre la libertad de su hijo Casimiro," AGN, 1829, P.L. 9-444; "D. Rafael Vilsa—dos esclavos," Archivo de la Cámara de Diputados, Lima (hereafter cited as ACD), 1856/1857, Convención Nacional, Leg. 21-25, Junta de Manumisión, 81.

48. *El Comercio*, January 23, February 5, November 14, 1846, January 27, 1854; *Mercurio Peruano*, November 3, 1827; "Seguidos por el abogado defensor general de menores con Doña Concepción Malpartida sobre nombramiento de curador de la menor, Petronila Voto," AGN, CCiv, 1850, Leg. 160.

49. "D. Luis Monsante, como defensor de la esclava María Henríquez con su ama, Doña Irene Aria de Henríquez sobre variación de dominio," AGN, CCiv, 1854, Leg. 172. See also *Telégrafo de Lima*, July 27, 1833.

50. For an example see *Telégrafo de Lima*, July 27, 1833.

51. *El Comercio*, June 9, 1845.

52. Markham, "Travels," 1:42–43, 46–47, 75; Proctor, *Narrative*, 303.

53. Macera, "Las plantaciones azucareras," 253–54, 270–75.

54. Thomas, *Diario*, 220.

55. "Cuenta de cargo y data que rindió al supremo gobierno en el despacho de hacienda Dn. José Félix Hurtado, administrador de la hacienda San Javier y de su anexa San Pablo, y corre desde el 5 de marzo de 1828 hasta el 21 de setiembre de 1829," AGN, Temporalidades, Leg. 70, Cuad. 113; "Cuenta documenada que rindió al supremo gobierno el administrador de la hacienda San José de la Nazca y corre desde el 24 de noviembre de 1827 hasta el 30 de noviembre de 1828," AGN, Temporalidades, Leg. 97, Cuad. 82; "Información que el prefecto del departamento de Ica mandó levantar en el valle de la Nazca con el fin de pesquisar la conducta del pbro. Dn. Manuel Barreto, administrador de la

hacienda San José de la Nazca y tierras anexas, en orden a la recta administración de los dichos fundos," AGN, Temporalidades, Leg. 97, Cuad. 84.

56. "Cuentas de Don Francisco Iglesias," AGN, Temporalidades, Leg. 70, San Javier de la Nazca, 1819–1828, Cuad. 6, 7; "Cuentas de Don Miguel Bernales," AGN, Temporalidades, Leg. 70, Cuad. 110-C; "Cuenta que rindió al supremo gobierno D. Juan Bautista Mesa, administrador de la hacienda San José de la Nazca, propia del estado, y corresponde a los años de 1824–1831," AGN, Temporalidades, Leg. 97, Cuad. 83.

57. AD-LL, División Judicial, Prefectura, CCrim, 1828–1886, Leg. 613, Exp. 117.

58. "El prefecto del departamento de Lima acompaña las diligencias obradas al reconocimiento de la esclavatura de las haciendas de San José y San Javier de la Nazca encomendado al juez de letras de la provincia de Ica," AGN, 1828, P.L. 8-725. For a thorough examination of the issue of slave diseases see Karasch, *Slave Life*, chap. 6.

59. For an example of a slave complaining about overwork see "Defensa de esclavo," *Revista del Archivo Histórico del Cuzco* 3 (1952): 356–58.

60. "D. José Reynoso sobre servicia en su esclavo José Aguirre, 1852," AGN, CCiv, 1852–53, Leg. 169; "El prefecto de este departamento acompaña la representación hecha por Don Manuel Carbajal, en que pide se le revalide la venta de dos esclavos de la hacienda de San Javier de la Nazca, propias del Estado," AGN, 1827, P.L. 7-70; *El Comercio*, April 1, 5, 8, 11, October 4, 1854; *El Heraldo de Lima*, March 31, April 6, 1854.

61. The reasons for this reputation are unclear and a lack of data prevents comparisons with other groups.

62. For examples see *El Comercio*, May 4, 8, 11, 15, 22, June 22, July 5, August 13, 26, September 2, 3, 23, 25, October 3, 22, December 11, 13, 1839, September 2, 6, 12, October 13, 1843; *Gaceta Mercantil*, July 9, 1834, February 17, 18, 1835; and AD-A, Corte Superior de Justicia, CCrim, 1842, (II), September 23, 1842.

63. Francisco Zamudio was sold six times between April 1826 and June 1827 and was finally given to the navy for being a thief and fugitive. See "D. Francisco Sánchez, acompaña la boleta de un esclavo de su propiedad y lo cede a favor del estado," AGN, 1827, P.L. 7-239.

64. AAL, Causas de Negros, 1815–1855, Leg. 36, LXVII:1; "D. Lorenzo Figueroa a nombre de Da. Joaquina Uribe, reclamando el pago del valor de una esclava," ACD, 1855, 1856, 1857, Leg. 15, Expedientes de particulares pasados a la Comisión de Memoriales, 1857, 26; "Da. Isabel Mendoza—dos esclavos," ACD, 1856/1857, Convención Nacional, Leg. 21-25, Junta de Manumisión, 78; "D. Rafael Vilsa—dos esclavos," ACD 1856/1857, Convención Nacional, Leg. 21-25, Junta de Manumisión, 81.

65. The dowry of Manuel Ravajo y Avellafuentes totaled over 64,916 pesos and included two slaves worth 500 pesos, a boy of ten and a girl of seventeen. See AGN, Notarial, Ignacio Ayllón Salazar, 1825, Prot. 41. See also AAL, Bautismos de Indios, Esclavos, Mestizos, 1819–1825, Parroquia de San Sebastián, Leg. 11; and AD-LL, División Notarial, Escrituras, José V. Aguilar, Leg. 408, August 6, 1845, Leg. 409, 1846–47, May 12 and 13, 1846, 24–27.

66. "Autos que sigue Rosa Gasteagudo, madre de Beatriz, con Dn. Blas Zavaleta su amo sobre que la venta," AGN, CCiv, 1834, Leg. 84.

67. AAL, Causas de Negros, 1815–1855, Leg. 36, LXII:24; "Expediente sobre la petición presentada por José García Moreyra, para que se deje libre al liberto Manuel La Rosa, a quien retiene Manuel Lorenzo Casas, pretendiendo ser esclavo," Lima, January 28, 1853, BN D12749.

68. "Promovido por el defensor general de menores con D. Gerónimo Sanchez sobre la variación de dominio de la esclava Feliciana," AGN, CCiv, 1846, Leg. 141.

69. "Seguidos por Juliana Rojas con Don Juan Pedro Lostaunau y el sindico de La Molina sobre la libertad de sus hijos, 1852," AGN, CCiv, 1854, Leg. 172.

70. AD-A, Notarial, Toribio de Linares, 1844–1846, Prot. 709, May 1, 2, 1844.

71. Tristán, *Peregrinaciones*, 414, 421; *El Comercio*, August 5, 1852.

72. "Expediente sobre la petición presentada por Rafaela Marín, esclava, para que su amo compla con la promesa de darle libertad," Huaura, February 1, 1830, BN D12785; "Sobre la libertad de una esclava, Remijia Nuñes," AGN, CCiv, 1847, Leg. 149.

73. AAL, Causas de Negros, 1815–1855, Leg. 36, LXVII:50.

74. AAL, Causas de Negros, 1815–1855, Leg. 36, LXI:100; "Contra Juan Espejo por heridas," AGN, CCrim, 1840, Leg. 577; "Seguidos contra Toribio Elmes por heridas inferidas a María del Rosario Zapata," AGN, CCrim, 1840, Leg. 574; "Criminales contra Petronila Vasquez," AGN, CCrim, 1843, Leg. 584. See also "Contra Dolores Argote por heridas," AGN, CCrim, 1842, Leg. 581; and *El Comercio*, September 9, 1851. For examples of murders see *El Comercio*, June 11, 12, 1841, January 2, 1845, June 20, 1851.

75. "Criminales contra Mateo Ugarte por estupro," AGN, CCrim, 1845, Leg. 586; "Homicidio de Manuel Champas," AGN, CCrim, 1851, Leg. 665. For another case of rape, this one involving an estate slave who was hunted down and killed after a second assault, see *El Comercio*, January 2, 1845. A slave participating in a manhunt where the fugitive was another slave could find himself in an impossible situation, unable to refuse his owner but subject to prosecution for his actions. In 1834 a slave helped his owner capture a slave who had stolen some pigs, but injured the thief in the process and was the one charged when the case came to trial. See *Gaceta Mercantil*, January 29, 1835.

76. For examples see "El prefecto de este departamento acompañando un expediente seguido en el juzgado de derecho de Ica, sobre la necesidad de enajenar al esclavo, Manuel Dionisio, perteneciente a la hacienda San José de la Nazca," AGN, 1828, P.L. 8-145; and "Criminales contra Bernardo Aliaga y José Luis Ulloa, José Cambiaso, y Pedro Pablo Baca a Dn. Pedro Puccio," AGN, CCrim, 1843, Leg. 583. For the punishments meted out to Brazilian slaves at this time see Karasch, *Slave Life*, 113–25.

77. Smith, *Peru As It Is* 1:108; Von Tschudi, *Travels in Peru*, 107.

78. AAL, Causas de Negros, 1816–1855, Leg. 36, LXII:63; "Criminales seguido contra Pedro Nolasco y Pablo Bosa por robo a Don Pablo Alzamora, 1843," AGN, CCrim, 1844, Leg. 585.

79. Proctor wrote that he never saw a whip or a single slave punished. See Proctor, *Narrative*, 234.

80. Tristán, *Peregrinaciones*, 415.

81. *El Comercio*, June 5, 1839, February 4, April 4, May 8, 1840.

82. *El Comercio*, September 4, December 13, 1849; "Mandando someter a juicio a los que cooperara a la vapulación de un esclavo," ACD, 1849–50, Leg. 2, Asuntos Generales Resueltos por esta Cámara, 24.

83. *El Comercio*, May 20, 1843, March 14, May 30, June 2, 1846, June 18, 1853; *La Miscelánea*, July 23, 1831; "El defensor general de menores en representación de la esclava Dolores Vivanco con su ama Doña Josefa Briseño sobre su libertad," AGN, CCiv, 1846, Leg. 141; AD-A, Corte Superior de Justicia, CCrim, 1842, (II), October 20, 1842; AAL, Causas de Negros, 1815–1855, Leg. 36, LXVII:39; AAL, CCiv, 1848–1851, Leg. 235.

84. *El Comercio*, February 22, 23, 1853; "La defensoria de menores con D. Pablo Huapaya sobre variación de dominio de la liberta Andrea Ortis," AGN, CCiv, 1850, Leg. 160; "Seguido por el sindico procurador D. Francisco Garfias con D. Manuel Gonzales sobre flagelación al liberto, Andrés Castro," AGN, CCrim, 1853, Leg. 609; "Seguido contra Mauricio Zabala y otros por salteadores," AGN, CCrim, 1854, Leg. 614.

85. "El defensor general de menores en representación de Gerónimo y Sebastián Jauregui, esclavos, con Don Juan Lostanau, sobre su venta," AGN, CCiv, 1830, Leg. 59.

86. *El Comercio*, November 15, 1844.

# 5

# Slave Resistance

In the worldwide struggle for abolition the slaves' own actions have often played a crucial role. The most dramatic example of this is Haiti, where in the late eighteenth century, after years of extreme exploitation and abuse, the slave population rose and destroyed both the slaveholding class and the slavery system. In Brazil they played a similar role, according to Robert Brent Toplin, although on a much smaller scale. Through their increasingly violent agitation, slaves in the São Paulo region raised fears of imminent racial warfare and forced the authorities and the white population as a whole to accept the idea of total emancipation.[1]

Resistance, however, does not have to involve violence. In fact, violence tended to be the exception rather than the rule. Slaves in the United States found that, instead of challenging the system openly, they could operate within it to create their own world and ease their troubled lot.[2] According to James Scott and others, this response was not restricted solely to slaves, for it was common to the weak, the underprivileged, and the downtrodden everywhere.[3] These writers contend that "everyday" or "routine" forms of resistance have been more common and perhaps more effective than the revolts and rebellions that caught the attention of contemporary observers and, consequently, present-day historians. Everyday resistance was individual, localized, less threatening, "informal, often covert, and concerned largely with immediate, de facto gains."[4] It involved responses such as foot-dragging, dissimulation, evasion, deception, denial, feigned ignorance and incompetence, and false compliance. And it was successful. The dominant class concluded on the basis of responses such as these that those below were not only weak but also ignorant, incompetent, unproductive, and not worth their constant attention. Even complying with norms set by the oppressors could be a form of resistance. According to Scott, compliance "clothed" resistance; by accepting the demands of those above them, the weak secured some leeway to do what they wished and to hurt their oppressors in some fashion, providing personal satisfaction if nothing else.[5] Did the weak intend the results of their actions? Was their resistance an attempt to strike back at their oppressors or to improve their own lives? Was their goal to modify or even to overthrow the system that oppressed them, or was it more immediate and self-interested? The answers to these questions are not always clear, and the issue of intent remains a contentious one.[6] Nonetheless, regardless of whether they intended it or not, the impact of resistance was the same: It challenged the oppressor and was an accomplishment for the oppressed.

Slaves throughout Latin America engaged in these everyday forms of resistance. In the case of Cuba, they proved integral to emancipation.[7] However, care has to be taken in applying the terminology that has been developed from a peasant context and applying it to a slavery system. Actions that were routine for peasants and other oppressed groups could be extremely risky for slaves. The difference rested on the fact that slaves were property, legally owned by others and lacking the most basic of human rights. Thus, running away may have been an act of "avoidance protest"[8] for peasants; for slaves it was an open challenge to the owner and the system. Slaves could be subjected to much harsher penalties than other oppressed people. Realizing this, they prepared their actions with great care and conscious effort. What was an everyday protest act for a peasant was one of deliberate disobedience for the slave. Moreover, by the nineteenth century, as slavery crumbled everywhere, slaves more clearly saw the consequences of their actions. As a result, while the principal aim of their resistance may have remained to make a better life for themselves, they were conscious of the system disintegrating around them and keen to assist in its fall.

In Peru, as in Brazil, Cuba, and elsewhere, slaves engaged in both routine and violent forms of resistance.[9] If the Peruvian system was in fact as mild as foreign observers contended, then Peru's slaves may have had greater latitude to resist than slaves operating under more restrictive and authoritarian systems. Some of their responses have been examined already in the context of their daily lives. Most, such as gambling, drinking, swearing, working unproductively, changing owners, and appealing to the courts for reductions in their value, were everyday forms that had the aim of either establishing a degree of normalcy in their day-to-day existence or improving it. The preferred form of resistance, and probably the most effective, was self-purchase, which definitively removed them from the ranks of the enslaved.[10] By reducing the number of slaves left in bondage, this act was also a direct attack upon the slavery system. It was openly confrontational, as were other actions such as appealing to the courts, wearing sumptuous clothing, abortion, and infanticide. So, too, were the continued practice of African customs, criminal acts, assaults on owners and overseers, and flight. Some of these indicated that Peru's slaves were prepared to resort to more violent forms of resistance. Further proof of this can be found in the actions of those runaways who banded together to rob highway travelers and raid estates. At times of political unrest some of these bands, now known as *montoneros*, adopted a political role. Claiming to support one caudillo or another, they acted as a guerrilla army and added to the political turmoil. On a few occasions slaves chose the most extreme option and engaged in open rebellion.

Thus, Peru's slaves were willing to challenge the system. In the first decades after independence, they were incapable of forcing the slaveholders and the government to accept complete abolition on their own, but their pressure constituted the heaviest of the straws that were gradually breaking the back of the Peruvian system. By reducing the number of those still in bondage and by confronting their owners through various means, they aroused anxieties among whites, stimulated abolitionist feelings, revealed many of the disadvantages of slavery, and slowly but surely convinced more and more Peruvians that it was an unjustified and inhumane anachronism that had no place in their country.

As Peruvians began reorganizing their lives following the collapse of Spanish rule, the slave community signaled that it had no intention of accepting its position at the bottom of the social order. This may have marked a shift from earlier patterns, for a study of Peru's Jesuit estates has indicated that slaves in the late colonial period tended to be conservative and cowed.[11] However, a different picture emerges from other surveys of this period. They reveal that slaves were fleeing their masters, setting up fugitive communities or *palenques*, and even rebelling.[12] As a result of independence and the liberators' antislavery legislation, many slaves may have been willing to accept the situation and quietly await the expected emancipation. Others, however, were determined to maintain their pressure on the system, a result, perhaps, of the destabilizing effects of the recent wars. By the late 1820s the unfulfilled hopes of emancipation provided a renewed stimulus for slave agitation. One contemporary commentator argued that slaves had been demoralized since independence, a result of the initial call for freedom that prompted slaves to take up arms against their owners, followed by the liberal legislation. Since the slaves still believed in the concept of "independence" and opposed their owners' rights, they, like the Haitian slaves, possessed a "revolutionary" potential to secure their own freedom; the writer concluded that there was "no slave today who is restrained by the limits of his obligations" and that all of them were waiting to "avenge themselves on their owners."[13] The weakening of the big estate, one of the pillars of slavery, was another factor blamed for the postwar unruliness of the slaves. Severely damaged during the wars, the big estates remained weak for many years afterward and could not control the slaves as they had in the past. The demoralization, corruption, and criminal behavior of the San José de la Nazca slaves, for example, was linked to this fact. Absentee ownership may have intensified the problem. It was mentioned by Clements Markham in 1852 in explaining the difficulties experienced by the Villa estate, where the slaves' "bad character" was notorious.[14]

Whatever the reason, permeating the slave community was an almost palpable sense of alienation that was not hidden from contemporary observers. In 1826, following an abortive attempt to assassinate Bolívar, the British consul reported that had it succeeded there would have been an uprising and the slaves would have "seized the opportunity of plundering and of massacring without feelings of remorse those who resisted them." Flora Tristán commented upon the animosity of Arequipa slaves eight years later, which had been brought to a head by the defeat of local forces during a rebellion. The slaveholders were terrified, while the slaves rejoiced and refused to obey any orders unless threatened with physical punishment.[15]

During the first decades after independence the slaves manifested their hostility and their desire for change in a variety of ways, many of them similar to what had been done in the past. One form of resistance that was especially popular was the practice of African customs. It maintained the slaves' racial heritage, indicated their differences from the locals, and gave obvious affront to the dominant group. A traveler in 1845 noted that Islam was still practiced by Peruvian blacks, who also prayed to foreign gods in their original languages and modified Christianity and Christian ceremonies. They participated in the Quasimodo procession after Easter disguised as devils and giants, the latter based on African models. Dressed in elaborate costumes topped by masks, they danced through the streets to a cacophony of harps, guitars, violins, and other noisemakers, gesticulating and making what were described as "obscene movements." The Spanish celebration of "Moors and Christians" that took place in Lima's cemeteries in May was almost completely controlled by the city's black water carriers, who were accused of turning it into a drunken orgy, or at least what was described as an "odious and repugnant spectacle." Some African precedent may also explain why blacks set off rockets in the doors of Lima's churches, although the roots may have been more malicious than sacred. On at least one occasion the fireworks caused the horses drawing a carriage to bolt with its load of worshippers and could have had serious repercussions. The authorities tried banning the practice on the grounds that it seemed to have nothing to do with religion, but their efforts had little effect, as the subsequent reissuance of the ban indicated.[16]

Some slaves seem to have been deliberatively disruptive, a factor, perhaps, in explaining the blacks' reputation for drunkenness and riotous behavior.[17] Particularly insolent and intransigent were the water carriers, a profession almost monopolized by urban slaves. Responsible for carrying water to businesses and private homes, they annoyed the white community by their business practices. They stopped servants and others, by force if necessary, from filling pots in public fountains to prevent competition; they set their own prices and their own terms; and they led their donkeys into the courtyards of private homes to save carrying the water jugs themselves. Critics described their conduct as "unbearable" and demanded that they be employed elsewhere.[18]

While the white community was irritated by this so-called insolence, which really amounted to the slaves acting as if they were free, it was far more concerned about those slaves who engaged in criminal activity. As mentioned elsewhere, the subject of slave crime is difficult to evaluate accurately, because the motivations of the slaves are not clear. To what extent did they view their actions as an attack on or a response to the system? Did slaves steal to obtain the money needed to buy their freedom, or were they merely satisfying some spontaneous desire to meet a materialistic need? Was Mariano Peña, a rural slave who stole from local farmers, a rebel against the system that kept him in bondage or an incorrigible thief, as his owner contended?[19] The available information tells us only part of the story, but we can assume that at least some of the crimes committed by slaves were attacks on the system, sparked by the slaves' frustrations and desires to strike back at their oppressors. Their response worried members of the white community who came to the conclusion that, rather than preventing antisocial behavior, slavery seemed to be reinforcing it. Some owners whose slaves had been found guilty of committing crimes may have questioned the logic of ownership, since a criminal record reduced the value of their property while a jail sentence deprived them of their slaves' services and income for a time. One owner, whose slave had been sentenced to two years of public work in Trujillo, sought to circumvent the law by smuggling his slave south to Pisco in order to sell him but was stopped by the authorities. Other owners, like Manuela Peña, lost their investment completely. Her slave, a water carrier, was shot and killed by the owner of a house that he was robbing.[20]

Robbery was the most common criminal activity that involved slaves. Pilfering may have abounded, but it is the more spectacular thefts that appear in the records. Asunción Aliaga, a fourteen-year-old, robbed her owner of 1,000 pesos and 2.5 ounces of gold. Her assertion that the real culprit was a neighbor's slave whom she had told about the money and supplied with a key to her owner's trunk failed to convince the court, and she was sentenced to one year of service in a hospital. Francisco Vázquez fled after stealing fifteen ounces of gold from his owner. A slave of María Pino robbed her owner of twenty-four ounces of gold but was caught and part of the money recovered.[21] Employers were a common target. Pedro Nolasco and another man stole twenty pounds of wax from Pedro's employer. He was caught and sentenced to four months of service in a bakery, which was later changed to one year in prison, then to reimbursing his employer for the wax. Some slaves robbed whoever was at hand. Bernardo Aliaga and a confederate took some knives, cups, and other goods from a store that was located in the same building as his owner's residence. He was caught and sentenced to be sold twenty-five leagues from Lima.[22]

In the countryside livestock was the preferred target because it was available, mobile, and salable either as meat or on the hoof. Toribio, a fourteen-year-old who tended his owner's cattle that grazed on the Monterrico estate, and Tomás Chavarria, the slave of an estate muleteer, together with other slaves and free workers helped steal nineteen head of Monterrico cattle. For his pains Toribio was sentenced to two years of imprisonment, while Tomás received six months. Toribio unsuccessfully appealed his sentence on the imaginative yet accurate grounds that his imprisonment deprived the industry of a necessary worker. Theft was only one problem that faced the future president, José Rufino Echenique, when he took over the San Pedro estate in 1837. He recalled in his memoirs that the majority of the slaves did only what they wished, had no respect for the foremen and other estate officials, and stole estate produce to consume or sell. Some had fled, which Echenique considered justified in the circumstances, as little attention had been paid to their needs. He wrote that he instituted a new regime of proper treatment, adequate rations and clothing, and a set workday, but he punished those who failed to comply and sold the ringleaders to distant estates.[23]

While some slaves directed their attention to the property of their oppressors, others chose to attack the person of their perceived exploiters. In 1828, Manuel Arias, a seventeen-year-old mulatto slave, killed the owner of the bakery where he worked after the latter refused to pay him for a pig he had found. He fled, taking 16 pesos and a horse, but was captured, tried, and condemned to death. Managing to escape, he evaded the authorities for a year, even serving for part of the time in the army. Recaptured, he was executed by a firing squad. Six slaves from the Acari estate, who killed the estate owner, his wife, and two children, also were shot. Francisco Herrera Palomino, a slave on the Trapiche Viejo estate, planned to murder his owner but was surprised by troops as he lay in ambush and was killed.[24] Often slaves directed their hostility toward an agent or representative of the owner, whom they perceived to be the real cause of their distress. In 1842 the slaves of La Palma bakery plotted to kill a majordomo and then escape. Slaves on the Villa estate did more than plot. As Clements Markham recalled, "Some years ago they killed the majordomo and burnt his body in an oven." In 1851, Manuel Sandoval, a slave on the Infantas estate, wounded the foreman and fled. He was apprehended, locked up, and told he was going to be sold to some distant buyer. However, he cheated the courts and his owner by hanging himself in his cell.[25]

In some instances the authority figure was also a slave. In 1847 a slave who was a foreman on La Molina estate was killed by four runaways who then fled back to their hideout on the Villa estate. Fears were voiced of a slave uprising, and the government sent thirty-four soldiers to arrest the killers and prevent further trouble. The killing, in fact, appears to have been more a personal vendetta than an uprising, for the dead man was an unpopular figure with a reputation for working slaves excessively and forcing himself on women whose husbands did not sleep in the slave quarters. His assailants certainly intended to kill him, for they stabbed him five times and then shot him. One slave was implicated in both this and the earlier killing of the Villa estate's major-domo, but although arrests were made nobody seems to have been tried for the murder. Personal differences also appear to have been involved in the killing of Bruno Lopez, a slave who was a foreman at La Palma bakery. His killer was another slave, José Francia, who was reported to have been his friend. The two had had a falling out over a debt of 4 reals. That night José hit his sleeping friend over the head with a piece of wood. He claimed during his trial that he had killed three others and had tried to kill the bakery's majordomo. He was found guilty of murder and shot.[26]

When large numbers of Chinese coolies began arriving in Peru in the 1840s, the slaves came to believe that a new group had been added to the long list of oppressors. The coolies were imported to replace the slaves, and frequently the two groups found themselves working alongside one another. The former, however, were contracted for a set length of time, and on completing their contracts many of them became petty merchants who appeared to be pocketing much of the slaves' hard-earned cash. The situation led to occasional outbursts of violence. In 1851 eight slaves from the Santa Rosa estate were arrested after a fight in which several coolies were injured, one seriously.[27] Whether this interracial hostility was fostered by the owners is unclear, but it worked in their favor by keeping the exploited groups apart and directing some of their anger toward one another, rather than at those above.

Committing a crime against one's owner or assaulting a person perceived to be an exploiter may have satisfied some slaves, but it had one obvious shortcoming: It did not improve their status. To achieve that goal, many slaves chose simply to flee. Flight provided them with the freedom they coveted, even though it might be short-lived. It was a means to join loved ones, avoid punishment, and protest bad treatment.[28] At the same time it openly challenged the system. Slaves had been fleeing their owners since the first days of African slavery in Peru. The numbers multiplied during the wars of independence as a result of the wartime chaos. Runaways knew they could survive on their own, even in Peru's narrow coastal valleys. During the colonial period they had managed to establish independent communities away from the urban centers. By the 1820s these *palenques* had become uncommon, but slaves could still live off the land if necessary. Around Lima the river valley was wide, and vegetation grew on the surrounding mountains more heavily than it does today.[29] During the dry summer months the vegetation would have disappeared, forcing the fugitives to find sustenance elsewhere. Some may have moved inland; more slaves probably remained, obtaining food from the local estates and markets. Runaways seem to have flitted easily between estates, seeking employment as free wage labor or even returning to their own estates to live undetected in the slave quarters. The shortage of labor meant that many estate owners were willing to disregard the penalties for hiring fugitives and employ anyone who claimed to be free. If slaves could not find work on an estate, they could become bandits and highwaymen, and many did. Runaways could also hide quite openly in urban centers, among other black residents or in the black barrios such as San Lázaro in Lima. Peru's coastal cities were inundated with fugitives in the first years after independence, the unclaimed property of Spaniards and royalist emigrants.[30]

The number of runaways seems to have been large. In 1828, 17 of San José de la Nazca's 132 slaves (almost 13 percent) were listed as fugitives. Even on well-run estates, such as Bernardo O'Higgins's Montalván, slaves frequently ran away.[31] Newspaper reports and advertisements, although not an accurate gauge, support the view that significant numbers of slaves fled. The same sources give the impression that over the years the incidence of flight increased. By the 1850s the number of advertisements in *El Comercio* seeking runaways well outnumbered those for buying, selling, or exchanging slaves. All ages were involved, from infants with their mothers, to children, to adults, to the aged.[32] While in most cases flight was an individual act, mass escapes were not unknown. One evening in November 1844, forty slaves from the San Pedro estate fled to an adjacent monastery. When soldiers appeared, three trying to hide fell into a well and were killed. The surviving five men and thirty women were captured and returned to the estate.[33] Three years later twenty-seven slaves from the San Nicolás estate in the Supe Valley fled to a nearby mountain and resisted attempts by soldiers to recapture them. Stones, however, were no match for firearms: Eventually the fugitives were caught, but not before at least two of them were killed. In 1852 the Santa Beatriz estate reported ten slaves missing, along with two Chinese and three Portuguese colonists.[34]

Some slaves managed to remain at large for years. Manuel Vicente had been a fugitive for six years in 1828, when he was seen working on an estate as a free laborer, married to another slave who was also passing as free. José Basurio had been a fugitive for eight years when he was arrested in 1839. Two others arrested with him had been fugitives for one year.[35] Once committed to flight and the prospect of freedom, slaves had no intention of returning peacefully to servitude. This meant resisting recapture, like the San Nicolás slaves, or like the fugitive who shot and killed a watchman who had tried to apprehend him.[36]

The problem of fugitive slaves worried the authorities, in part because of the value of the missing property and the reduction in the supply of labor, but more because of the fugitives' threat to state security. As shown by the above examples, slaves had no difficulty in obtaining weapons despite the numerous laws and decrees against their possessing arms, machetes, axes, and razors. Most weapons were probably stolen, although other avenues were open to the slaves as well. The Independence Wars and subsequent civil unrest made arms available, as did vendors who ignored the prohibitions. Even politicians were known to distribute weapons. During the 1850 presidential campaign, supporters of General Echenique supplied slaves and servants with firearms, sticks, and stones to attack the supporters of his opponent, General

Manuel Ignacio Vivanco. The ensuing riot forced a postpone-
ment of the voting and led to decrees that ordered the arrest
of anyone carrying arms and the return of slaves to the
homes of their owners.[37]

With easy access to weapons, fugitive slaves constituted
a definite threat, especially those who chose to join the ranks
of Peru's ubiquitous highwaymen. Attacking farms, robbing
travelers, and disrupting internal communications, they left
the impression that the government had little or no control
over the countryside. In 1828 depredations of rural bandits
reached such a point that landholders were abandoning their
estates. At times of rebellion and civil strife the numbers and
attacks of rural highwaymen increased even more, with the
authorities either unable or unwilling to commit the resources
needed to suppress them.[38] No one was safe, and blame often
fell on slaves.

The charges were not entirely justified, for whites, freedmen, Indians, mestizos, and other racial groups, as well as
slaves, made up the ranks of Peru's highwaymen. The racial
composition of the bands indicates that they were not necessarily an antislavery force.[39] Even some of the slaves who
engaged in this type of activity may have done so simply to
survive or for a share of the loot. Nevertheless, when they did
participate, an antislavery element was evident, for joining a
band permitted the slaves to remain at large and to strike
back at the society that had enslaved them. Moreover, most
of the attention of the authorities seemed to be directed at
those highwaymen who were black.

Among the slaves who turned to highway robbery was
José Romualdo. Operating on the Vitarte road in 1839, he
robbed a woman from Jauja of four donkeys carrying eggs
and other goods. He was arrested, and all but the donkeys
were recovered. Juan de Dios Salazar was a runaway who,
along with an army deserter, was charged with robbing
travelers in the Magdalena Valley. One of two blacks who
held up an estate majordomo on the public highway near
Lima was a slave from the Mayorazgo estate. When arrested,
he confessed, identified his colleague, and revealed the
whereabouts of the stolen goods. Slaves from La Molina,
Villa, San Juan, and Pedreros estates were especially notorious as highwaymen. Those of La Molina were accused of
being "full of vices" and thieves by profession, attacking
travelers along the Lurín road and then escaping to their
*palenques* on the Villa and San Juan estates, where the

slaves assisted them.[40] The San Pedro slaves also continued to have a reputation for being the "terror of transients," despite Echenique's efforts. In the early 1840s, for example, they assaulted an Indian and stole his horse and saddle, a loaded mule, and some money; robbed a tax collector of the money he was carrying, along with his horses and saddles; and were responsible for numerous other thefts and assaults. Their depredations produced demands that the government do something, even level the estate.[41]

The authorities were not deaf to the appeals. They tried various means to meet the perceived threat and suppress the highwaymen, including harsh punishments. In the case of the San Pedro slaves who robbed the tax collector, two were sentenced to ten years in prison. To be effective, however, sentences have to be carried out, and in many of the cases involving highwaymen the accused escaped capture. The San Pedro slaves, for example, were tried and found guilty in absentia. The authorities also passed legislation in an attempt to control the bandits. In 1828 the Lima prefect ordered all hacendados in the department to keep their slaves on their estates and threatened to treat any slaves apprehended without their *boletos* as criminals. In 1843, Lima's police intendant prohibited blacks from congregating around the Cocharcas gate and closed the gates at 8 P.M. to try to reduce thefts along the Lurín road. The law had little effect. Four years later attacks were still taking place, and slaves were still believed responsible. The intendant tried a new initiative. He informed local landholders that no slave was to be allowed to leave for Lima after prayers, that any found off the estate would be arrested, and that each estate was to keep a list of slaves to see who was missing. In 1846 the minister of government reiterated a suggestion, first made in 1833, that more secure slave quarters ought to be established. He recommended that the quarters be fenced in so that slaves could "not spend the night outside the estates surrendering themselves to vices and loose living prejudicial to the life and interests of the inhabitants and visitors of the places where the haciendas are located." But this, too, failed as slaveholders objected. They pointed out that building the recommended quarters was beyond the financial capabilities of many of them, in addition to being a wasteful use of slave labor. And was the result worth the expense and effort? Critics pointed to estates with secure quarters where slaves were still engaged in criminal activities.[42]

As new laws and harsh punishments proved ineffective in controlling the bandits, the authorities turned to illegal means. False arrest and torture probably were common throughout the period but seem to have increased when highway robbery experienced one of its periodic epidemics, such as in the early 1850s. Without any proof and with little justification, as the subsequent trials showed, soldiers and police hauled slaves out of bed and accused them of being thieves. They were chosen because they were black, had been out at night, and had (usually) a criminal record. Manuel Espiritu Santo, a runaway slave from La Molina, who had been accused once of highway robbery, was charged with being part of a band of forty armed men who had robbed five estates in the Ate Valley and assaulted their workers. The composition of the band was unclear. Some witnesses testified that all the robbers but one were black, while a mestizo who had been arrested insisted that some of his race were involved. Owners tended to deny the charges leveled against their slaves, providing them with alibis or character references. Juan Lostaunau, however, made little effort to protect Manuel, possibly because he was a runaway. His testimony that Manuel was a known robber, plus the police claim that he had been caught red-handed, the fact of his being a runaway, and the general trepidation at this time caused by the "infestation" of the countryside by malefactors were enough to convict him, even though no one had positively identified him. Sentenced to ten years in prison, Manuel appealed, claiming that all the evidence against him had been circumstantial and that he had not been caught red-handed but arrested days afterward. His argument convinced an appellate court, which dismissed the sentence and returned him to his owner.[43]

Other slaves arrested purely on suspicion had confessions beaten out of them. This seems to have been normal on the Villa and San Juan estates, where it led to the discovery of stolen goods stored in the slave quarters as well as powder, shot, clothing, jewelry, and money. However, innocent parties suffered as well. Joaquín Pardo, alias Cinco Varas, was arrested for attacks on the Chaclacayo road and beaten so severely to extract a confession that he had to be hospitalized. He, too, was a fugitive, having escaped from jail where he was serving a sentence for assault. Again, no evidence was found, and he was sentenced to complete only his original term.[44]

To end the threat posed by the highwaymen, the security forces also resorted to what seem to have been summary executions. Many highwaymen were reported to have been killed in shoot-outs with troops and police, some were executed where they were captured, while others were shot "trying to escape." The frequency of such executions suggests that officially or unofficially the forces of order had decided to eradicate once and for all those who seemed to be threatening the nation's tranquility. In October 1852, Clements Markham saw laid out in Lima's Plaza de la Inquisición the bodies of seven blacks who had been shot by a detachment of cavalry. He had encountered three of them the previous day outside the city, part of a group of five mounted blacks who, "grinning," had let him pass when he charged them with his pistols drawn. Not infrequently, executed bandits were quartered and their limbs exhibited as a warning to others. More fortunate was Ildefonso García, alias Chapín, a slave from La Molina who had been a fugitive for more than five years and was a known thief. He suffered only a saber wound on being arrested. Five of his former confederates, however, including other runaway slaves from La Molina and Villa and two Indians, were killed when they attacked the Villa estate to free some jailed slaves.[45] Bandits and highwaymen had to contend not only with soldiers and police but also with civilians who assisted the authorities in tracking them down. In 1852 workers on the Ollague farm in the Magdalena Valley pursued and killed the famous thief Soquete, a fugitive slave from the San Francisco bakery. In the sierra, Indians pursued runaways.[46]

The brutality of the response reflected the perceived seriousness of the problem, which was more than merely the disruption of economic relations and internal travel. In times of political ferment, many of the bands of highwaymen claimed to support one political leader or another and operated as guerrillas or *montoneros*. As such they constituted a significant political threat. They were also a challenge to social stability because they continued to be composed almost entirely of society's exploited groups, including slaves. They were a dangerous element in the chaos of early republican Peru. They may have been far more numerous than the records indicate, for the authorities referred to many of the gangs of *montoneros* as bandits. They preferred the latter term because it lacked the political connotations of the former.[47]

Peru's *montoneros* resembled in some ways Eric J. Hobsbawm's "social bandits." Organized in small bands, they operated in limited areas and received protection from the local society. Their leaders seem to have played an important role in their activities, and some of them acquired a notoriety that suggests they were viewed as heroes among the oppressed. To many they must have appeared as "avengers and champions."[48]

Hobsbawm's work, however, has provoked much debate, and Peru's *montoneros* differed from his model in many of those areas that have drawn his critics' attention.[49] While they may have claimed allegiance to particular political leaders and social concerns, they were still basically highwaymen and their primary motivation was the lure of booty. Few if any of the bands shared their loot with the poor. Rather, they seem to have viewed the poor as targets to be robbed like anyone else. Moreover, if their assertions of political loyalty are to be believed, their desires were to establish links with those above, not below. Hobsbawm's social bandits owed their origins to the spread of industrial capitalism, but the roots of Peru's *montoneros* can be found in indigenous political developments and regional factors, as the predominance among some of the bands of blacks from a small number of estates attests. With their self-interested motivation, they were not a revolutionary force, but those *montoneros* who were slaves possessed what might be considered a revolutionary potential. By acting as if they were free, they challenged the system. They were a model and a magnet for other slaves. Theirs was a distinctive form of resistance, with its political, social, and criminal ties. For all these reasons, they constituted a serious threat to the status quo, a threat that the authorities could not afford to ignore.

Black *montoneros* were active throughout the period, but especially during times of extreme political unrest. In the 1820s and early 1830s the Chancay region north of Lima was particularly infested, with bands claiming to support the country's first president and reputed friend of the downtrodden, José de la Riva Agüero, and enjoying the backing of local renters, sharecroppers, and small landowners. In 1829 a group of eleven well-mounted and armed *montoneros*, including slaves, were operating in the Surco Valley. Four years later soldiers destroyed a band of around forty led by a man known as Nestares; at least fifteen of them were killed, and several slaves, including two women, were captured and

returned to their owners.[50] In 1835, during the political chaos
that followed the removal of President Orbegoso and General
Salaverry's assumption of power, the number of *montoneros*
exploded, with groups expressing allegiance to one man or
another.[51] In March, a pro-Orbegoso band captured Viscount
Sartige, the French consul; Lord Edward Clinton, the son of
the duke of Newcastle; and Belford Hinton Wilson, the
English consul, who were on an ill-advised picnic in the
countryside. Robbed of everything except their trousers, the
three were lucky to escape with their lives, as the *montoneros*
attempted to shoot both Wilson and Sartige, but their blun-
derbusses misfired. This band was led by the notorious León
Escobar, who operated with impunity in the environs of the
capital. It invaded daily, exchanged shots with the militia,
and robbed and murdered at will. Backed by slaves, fugitives, free blacks, *zambos*, and mulattoes, Escobar could do
as he wished, for Salaverry had left the city virtually unpro-
tected when he departed for the south and his date with
destiny. On December 5 one band, joined by armed groups of
the lower classes, unsuccessfully attempted to "excite a general rising of the people of colour." On the 28th, Escobar and
other *montoneros* occupied Lima and began looting and killing.
Their occupation, however, was brief. After two days, General Francisco de Vidal and a force of sixty irregulars retook
the city, captured Escobar, and shot him, thereby ending his
short but eventful career.[52]

This same period saw the rise of another famous band,
that of the "celebrated" black, Pedro León. He was a slave
who had killed his owner and then turned to banditry, form-
ing a gang of robbers that operated around Lima for almost
ten years, occasionally claiming to be *montoneros*. Unlike
other bands, his was reputed to contain no slaves. Eventually, in 1842, the lure of a 1000-peso reward proved too much
for a companion and former friend, who killed León. His body
was turned over to the authorities and displayed for three
days outside the cathedral.[53]

During the Salaverry period, a group of ninety to one
hundred *montoneros* were reported to be operating in the
Cañete Valley. They were eventually defeated, and many of
them were executed. Then a new band led by a man called
Tiburcio began operating in the valley, raiding haciendas,
attacking police garrisons to obtain arms and ammunition,
freeing prisoners, and murdering, until he was wounded and
captured.[54] The political loyalties of this period were still

being used six years later to justify *montonero* activity. In December 1841 a band led by a black attacked three estates around Lima, assaulted their owners, threatened to shoot one because he was an enemy of Orbegoso, stole horses, and abducted slaves. Troops finally tracked them to the Santa Rosa estate, where they killed the leader and another man.[55]

The depredations of the highwaymen and *montoneros* and the involvement of slaves in the bands were a source of great concern to the government and to the elite in general. They clearly demonstrated the authorities' inability to maintain political stability as well as some of the social tensions that threatened further instability. Those slaves who joined the bands had gone beyond everyday forms of resistance to something far more dangerous. Their actions revealed a willingness to engage in violence against both their owners and the state. From there it was a relatively easy step to open rebellion, and some slaves took that step. The instances were few, reflecting the trepidation of the slaves, the opportunities for alternative and less dangerous forms of resistance, the continuing belief that abolition was imminent, and the obstacles to organizing such an undertaking. Rebellion required slaves to establish a common consciousness beyond a particular plantation or locale; they had to overcome the fractionalization and intragroup rivalries that the slaveholders and the state had promoted among them; and they had to accept that their actions could cost them their lives, for rebellion not only attacked the owner but also "directly challenged the power of the regime."[56] Nevertheless, despite the opposing forces, rebellions occurred, demonstrating that slaves were prepared to risk everything to change their lives and the society in which they lived.

Peru's slaveholders had always been aware of the possibility of slave rebellion. The example of Haiti lay before them, and in the late colonial period they had had to deal with a number of uprisings and with threats of others.[57] In the years immediately after independence the situation appeared less ominous, possibly because so many slaves had fled during the wars and were enjoying a degree of freedom, possibly because the prospect of complete abolition seemed very real at this time, and possibly because the conditions for organizing a rebellion were not right. As a result, except for the fears aroused in 1826 following the attempt on Bolívar's life, the few instances of unrest produced little concern. An uprising on San Javier de la Nazca in October 1827 cost 8 pesos in soldiers' expenses to settle. That same year a group headed by a black named Juan de Dios Algorta was reported to have been plotting to overthrow the government and murder whites. Two years later they were plotting again, and this time nine of them were arrested. The local press treated the conspiracy as a joke, as did the court that released those arrested.[58]

By the 1830s rebellions were still rare and largely spontaneous, but the authorities had begun showing greater concern, owing to the chronic political instability and the consequent threat posed by any unrest. An uprising in 1832 that encompassed more than one estate in the Nazca area prompted the owner of the Chocavento estate to seek help from the district governor and local citizens. A letter to the press signed by "some farmers" claimed that the countryside in the area was infested with vagrants who had corrupted slaves by their example and convinced many to flee. As a result, there were no fewer than two hundred fugitives in the area, fields were uncultivated, and livestock were being stolen. The writers mentioned uprisings on the Pastor and Pampas Libres estates and the murder of a Limatambo foreman. They predicted that unless something was done soon more tragedies similar to the racial conflicts in the Caribbean would occur.[59]

Elsewhere, slaves also were fleeing, assisting robbers, disobeying and menacing their owners, and disrupting estate discipline. Thieves, one of them a slave, robbed and tried to kill the owner of La Molina. Other slaves had more success, killing a number of landholders including the English lessor of the Huaito estate. In 1838 slaves on the San Pedro estate forced the majordomo and employees to flee, sacked the house, robbed the estate store of corn and *chancaca* (cane alcohol), and killed the livestock to eat and sell. Echenique, who had been absent at the time of the uprising, later wrote that despite the pleas of his mother and wife he returned alone to the estate to demonstrate his lack of fear of the rebels, and he found that some "good slaves," including the foreman, had remained. He announced that all could return without fear of punishment, but fugitives would be pursued to the grave. The majority returned, but he continued to have trouble, especially from the women, who scoffed at his threat to deal harshly with any insubordination. So, after two days, he armed himself with a pistol and had thirty of them punished. Subsequently, he managed to maintain control by punishing the disobedient while "treating the faithful with consideration," and he recalled his actions as having been effective. The continuing notoriety of the San Pedro slaves, however, suggests otherwise.[60]

Minor uprisings such as these continued into the 1840s. In June 1840 young slaves on the Retes estate fled and were blamed for the murder of a white man whose body was found in the area.[61] Later in the decade the killings on the Villa and La Molina estates gave further indication that slaves were prepared to engage in the more violent forms of resistance.

The rebellious outbursts may have been few, but when combined with the numerous instances of other forms of resistance that were occurring during these years they add up to a picture of slave animosity that was extensive and even growing. The slaves' alienation can be traced to the exploitative and inhumane treatment that they had to endure, the inadequate rations, the harsh living and working conditions, and the general frustration arising from the delays in the anticipated abolition. In addition, by the 1840s many plantation slaves found their conditions changing, often for the worse, as a consequence of the expansion and modernization of the agricultural sector. Estates were shifting from food production to cash crops and acquiring expensive machinery.[62] The result was an emphasis on profits that translated into increasing pressures on the slaves and new possibilities for unrest.

Yet, despite the clear indications of slave discontent, the slaveholders showed limited concern. They may have believed that they had little reason to worry because of the infrequent, short-term, and localized nature of the uprisings that had occurred so far. They may have been lulled by the changes that were taking place in the country. The gradual decline in the number of slaves, the definitive closing of the slave trade, the arrival of alternative workers in the form of Chinese coolies, the financial growth resulting from the 1840s guano boom, the relative political stability under President Castilla— all of these may have created a sense of security that pushed the slavery issue to the back of most people's minds. This could explain why the most serious slave insurrection of the early republican period came as a surprise to virtually everyone. Like its predecessors, the Chicama Valley slave rebellion of 1851 was of short duration, restricted to a particular region, and of limited impact. Nevertheless, while it may not have secured the freedom that its participants had demanded, it marked the culmination of slave resistance during this period and warned that slaves were reaching the end of their tether. Their desire for freedom had reached a point where they were ready to fight and die for it.

The accounts of the Chicama Valley rebellion are consistent largely in their inconsistencies.[63] They do agree that it was led by two tailors from Trujillo, Gregorio Tejada y Olaya and Valentín Baca. In mid-January, while selling goods at a fiesta in the nearby village of Paiján, they were approached by six to eight "unknown" blacks who sought their help in composing a petition that was to be sent to the government and to local officials. It was a radical document demanding emancipation on the basis of San Martín's postindependence decrees. As justification it listed familiar complaints: that slaves on local estates were subject to excessive work and punishment and suffered from a lack of food. During the uprising more specific complaints were made of the brutalizing conditions on the local plantations: that slaves had to live in an unventilated room with smoke-darkened walls containing a bed made of a lattice of cane and with an adobe brick for a pillow, that clothing was a coarse poncho and trousers, and that food was a ration of corn and beans. Critics charged that owners ignored the laws regulating work, noting that the work was so dangerous that most estates had slaves missing a hand or an arm. The Chicama Valley was a sugar-producing region in which the big estate had long been the dominant landholding system, but where relations of production had begun to shift in recent years with the increasing emphasis on commercial agriculture and the introduction of machinery. While conditions elsewhere were probably similar, they seem to have produced greater slave militancy in the north. Earlier that year sixty slaves on the Chiquitoy estate had been arrested after assaulting and threatening to kill its owner and majordomo.[64]

The petition indicates some prior organization and perhaps even plans for a rebellion. That the blacks approached Olaya and Baca suggests that the two tailors already had a reputation as abolitionists or that the parties were not as unknown to one another as was later claimed.[65] The tailors subsequently met with a number of slaves who then fanned out among plantations in the area, drumming up sup-port and organizing a movement that quickly spread. By January 29 it had attracted about 150 slaves, a substantial number by the standards of rebellions in the United States.[66] At this point it suddenly exploded into public view as the result of an armed confrontation on the Cajanleque estate.

According to different sources, slaves, troops, or armed civilians tried to stop the rebels, an exchange of gunfire took place, and at least two white men were killed and six wounded. Baca was captured but then freed by the rebels, whose numbers continued to grow. Some three hundred slaves from over one dozen estates were now involved, proclaiming their freedom as they advanced. On February 1 about one hundred of them, armed with farm implements, carbines, swords, and lances, marched on Trujillo.

In the departmental capital there was complete confusion. The prefect refused to offer any resistance, probably a wise decision since only twelve of the thirty-six troops usually stationed in the city remained under his command. (The rest were in the countryside hunting the rebels.) Moreover, the slaves enjoyed substantial support within the city from both urban slaves, who constituted almost 10 percent of the population, and the free inhabitants.[67] As a result, faced by a superior force and assured by the slaves that they would not commit any excesses, the prefect ordered the gates opened at 9 A.M. The slaves marched in, disarmed the garrison, raided the barracks for other arms, released slaves from the jail and other houses of correction (thereby increasing their numbers to about 150), and exercised complete control over the city. Their demands were simple: they wanted their freedom plus 350 pesos to pay their expenses while their first demand was met. The authorities and owners were in no position to quibble. They began writing out the documents of freedom, completing their task in the early hours of the following morning. Apparently satisfied, the slaves departed.

The next day they returned. According to the authorities, they intended to loot the city. The slaves later claimed that they were seeking only further guarantees for their safety. In Trujillo the situation had changed significantly from the previous day. The prefect had left, and General José María Lizarzaburu, a former deputy and a hero of the Independence Wars, had formed a city guard composed of the remaining troops and local residents who had armed themselves with whatever weapons they could find. Positioned on the flat roofs of the buildings overlooking the Plaza de Armas, they began firing as the slaves entered the square. They fired only eight to ten shots, all of which missed, but they had the desired effect. The slaves fled into the countryside, pursued by a detachment of soldiers. Over the next few days ninety-seven slaves were captured along with eleven free people and four who were accused of being the leaders: Olaya, Baca, Julián Uriarte, and Juan Rojas. All were held for trial. The letters of freedom were rescinded, the slaveholders' control was reestablished, and the rebellion was over.

There is no question that the revolt had slave emancipation as a primary goal. It involved slaves whose desperate conditions had so aroused them that they were willing to risk anything to alter their status. Olaya and Baca had channeled these tensions while providing the leadership that previous movements seem to have lacked. The two men were committed abolitionists. They later claimed that their only aim had been to free the slaves. This was why the slaves had supported them; this was why they had occupied Trujillo. Their abolitionism was based on San Martín's antislavery decrees which, they argued, had introduced the epoch of liberty. It also seemed to be rooted in religious and moral principles. They viewed themselves as "martyrs of freedom"; considered slavery as iniquitous and unsustainable on Christian, moral, and political grounds; and stated that they had responded to "humanitarian and evangelical sentiments . . . believing that this tyranny of the masters was not based on law." There was a certain naïveté to their actions. They believed that the letters of freedom obtained from the Trujillo authorities would be respected, and they had planned to go to Lima to obtain governmental approval of them. They may not have foreseen what their actions would unleash. A much smaller movement may have been planned involving one or a few estates, but local conditions caused it to snowball out of their control. This may explain the apparent spontaneity of the movement once it began as well as its sudden collapse.

Yet the 1851 rebellion was not solely a slave movement for emancipation. Evidence indicates that it had links to outside pressures and developments that affected its direction and outcome. External linkages of some sort were to be expected, for the slave community was not an isolated entity operating in a vacuum. As Eugene Genovese has noted, the slaves' "nation" was inextricably tied into a much wider "nation" that determined much of their life and affected their actions, including their resistance to slavery.[68] Their rebellions may have been as dependent upon these outside forces as the pressures within the slave community, explaining in part why they occurred as infrequently as they did.

In the case of the Chicama Valley rebellion, external linkages were evident in that neither of its leaders was a slave. Olaya was a *zambo* and Baca a mestizo. As a result they had ties beyond the slave community and could present their movement as something other than a strictly racial confrontation, even though the majority of the participants were slaves. If the support they received from various groups within Trujillo is any indication, they seem to have been successful in this regard.

The rebellion also appears to have had links with local, even national, politics. Presidential elections had been held the preceding December, with José Rufino Echenique and Domingo Elías the principal contenders. The campaign, which had ended with Echenique's election, had been a violent affair, and the animosities may have extended beyond Lima.[69] Participants in the rebellion testified that they shouted *"vivas"* not only to liberty but also to President Castilla, as well as Echenique, Elías, and Elías's local political coreligionist, José María Lizarzaburu. Elías's name appears frequently in the trial record, as does that of Lizarzaburu. Olaya, in trying to win slave support, was reported to have announced that "Elías was fighting for the freedom of all slaves" and that he had freed his own. Neither statement was true, for Elías remained one of the country's major slaveholders. He had a reputation as a "man of the people," which may account for the apparent confusion in the thinking of Olaya and the slaves. Alternatively, Olaya's statement may have been a deliberate falsehood designed to attract followers by showing that divisions existed among the country's elite.[70] Lizarzaburu was rumored to have been planning a political movement in December, and, according to reports, Baca told a priest after his arrest that the rebellion was a political movement under Lizarzaburu's orders. Lizarzaburu denied the charges, claiming they were a fabrication of the prefect, a man he dismissed as a "pygmy" who was desperate to restore his own reputation, which had been seriously compromised by the affair. The latter had disappeared from Trujillo during the occupation in rather suspicious if not farcical circumstances: He claimed that he had left to find the missing troops; his enemies charged that he had sneaked away in cowardly flight disguised as a nun.

That Lizarzaburu refused to become prefect on February 2, when offered the position, and then organized the resistance that dispersed the slaves adds some weight to his protestations of innocence. On the other hand, these may have been the opportunistic actions of someone who needed to counter the rumors and charges that were circulating and to hide the evidence of his real involvement. If the rebellion did have a political component of which most people were aware, then the leadership by free men becomes more comprehensible, as does the hesitancy of many slaves to participate, the support in Trujillo, and the general equanimity of white Trujillanos. They had fled to their houses on the slaves' invasion of the town, but it may not have been out of fear of vengeance-seeking blacks. During the occupation the slaves appear to have threatened the lives of only the prefect and the police intendant. What may have worried the inhabitants was the possibility of looting or attacks by political enemies.

A political link also helps to explain the surprisingly light penalties that were imposed after the rebellion. All those arrested were held in jail for several months while their testimony was taken. Most denied involvement or claimed they had participated unwillingly and under duress. Some, like Rojas and Uriarte, were freed after being found innocent; so, too, were many slaves freed after their owners posted bail. Only Baca and Olaya seemed prepared to admit their guilt, and they refused to implicate anyone else. Eventually they were tried for rebellion, found guilty, and sentenced to death. Execution was delayed while they appealed, and at some point congress intervened and issued an amnesty.[71] Anyone following the events might have wondered why, if this really had been a slave rebellion threatening the social relations and economic base of the area, the authorities had not imposed the exemplary punishments that had followed past incidents of slave unrest and which still were meted out on occasion in the 1850s. Why had the courts not ordered the whipping of those who had been captured and were quite obviously guilty? Other than Olaya and Baca, the only person who might be considered to have been punished was the unfortunate prefect; he was reassigned to the distant department of Puno.

The rebellion may have been short, relatively peaceful, and quickly suppressed, but it had an impact beyond the lives of those who had been directly involved. It stimulated antislavery pressures. Reporting on the events, the government newspaper *El Peruano* used the opportunity to condemn slavery as "one of the greatest violations of the laws of humanity." As long as it was permitted, Peru could not "fully avow the principles of equality and fraternity." Nevertheless, the newspaper was not hopeful of an early end to slavery. It noted that slaveholders had had plenty of time since San Martín's decrees to prepare for abolition and introduce a new labor system, yet they had limited themselves to comparing the cost of goods produced by free and slave labor. Moreover, although the government had intervened to end reported cruelties on estates and was ignoring the law of 1839, no one had raised a voice to help the slaves.[72]

In fact, one voice was raised, that of Alfonso González Pinillos, a prominent Trujillo jurist, planter, and slaveholder. In January 1852 he freed his 136 slaves, largely because of the rebellion and his resulting awareness of the slaves' distress.[73] His was now another voice among the growing antislavery chorus.

The northern revolt served as an example that others followed. In March 1851 around fifty slaves from the Casa Blanca and La Quebrada estates in the Cañete Valley rose, proclaiming "Liberty or death." They claimed to be following the lead of the Chicama Valley slaves and justified their actions with the specific complaints that a local master was exploiting *libertos* by not paying their wages and that slaves who had bought their freedom were not being liberated. This movement was quickly brought under control, and the planters resolved not to permit a repetition. Two years later, when a "bandit" tried to rouse the Casa Blanca slaves again, local hacendados armed their men, hunted him down, and executed and quartered him.[74]

The slaveholders' continuing use of terror and brutality to keep the slaves under control clearly indicated that they viewed the slaves as a very real threat. Such fears had been present, probably, since the arrival of the first African slaves in Peru, at the beginning of the colonial era. Those fears seem to have intensified in the early nineteenth century in response to the actions of slaves outside of Peru, especially in Haiti, as well as at home. The fact that untold numbers of Peruvian slaves engaged in a wide variety of forms of resistance in the decades following independence to challenge the system that kept them in bondage revealed that they were not passively awaiting their freedom. They were actively pursuing it as best they could. Their actions did not replicate what occurred in Haiti. They did not create fears of imminent racial warfare and thereby force abolition on the country. Their resistance by itself did not end Peruvian slavery. Nonetheless, the slaves' actions raised concerns and revealed the problems and dangers of maintaining the existing system. By buying their own freedom, taking their complaints to court, having conditions added to their legal status, engaging in criminal activity, running away, attacking their owners, and rebelling, they were slowly but surely undermining slavery. Their actions revealed the brutality and anachronism of the system and convinced more and more Peruvians to support abolition. Other factors were assisting the slaves by pressing in the same direction. Together they accomplished the goal that the liberators had set, the slaveholders had resisted, and the slaves had struggled to secure.

## Notes

1. C. L. R. James, *The Black Jacobins: Toussaint L'Ouverture and the San Domingo Revolution*, 2d ed. rev. (New York, 1963); Robert Brent Toplin, "Upheaval, Violence, and the Abolition of Slavery in Brazil: The Case of São Paulo," *HAHR* 49 (1969): 639–55.

2. This is one of the prominent themes in Genovese, *Roll, Jordan, Roll*.

3. Scott, *Weapons*, especially chap. 7; Michael Adas, "From Footdragging to Flight: The Evasive History of Peasant Avoidance Protest in South and South-East Asia," *Journal of Peasant Studies* 13 (1986): 64–86. (The entire January 1986 issue of this journal is devoted to the subject of peasant resistance in South and Southeast Asia.) See also Gilbert M. Joseph, "On the Trail of Latin American Bandits: A Reexamination of Peasant Resistance," *Latin American Research Review* 25 (1990): 25–33.

4. Scott, *Weapons*, 33.

5. Ibid., 278–84.

6. Adas has argued that protest must involve a "conscious and articulated intent," while Scott has pointed to the difficulties of showing intention in many acts of resistance. Adas, "From Footdragging," 69; Scott, *Weapons*, 290–91. See also Joseph, "On the Trail," 30.

7. Scott, *Slave Emancipation*.

8. The term is found in Adas, "From Footdragging."

9. For an examination of Brazilian slave resistance at approximately the same time see Karasch, *Slave Life*, chap. 10.

10. Scott discusses the self-assertive nature of slaves purchasing their own freedom in her examination of Cuban abolition. See Rebecca J. Scott, "Gradual Abolition and the Dynamics of Slave Emancipation in Cuba, 1868–86," *HAHR* 63 (1983): 471–72. Aguirre argues that this was the slaves' most important weapon in their fight against slavery. See Aguirre, "Agentes."

11. Cushner, *Lords of the Land*, 100–101.

12. Flores Galindo, *Aristocracia*, 116–20.

13. *Telégrafo de Lima*, February 11, 1835; *El Voto Nacional*, December 10, 1834.

14. "Expediente sobre inventario de las haciendas nombradas San José y Ventilla del valle de Nazca actuado al tiempo que las recibió el presbítero D. Manuel Barreto de D. Juan Bautista Mesa," AGN, 1828, P.L. 8-22; Markham, "Travels" 1:43; *El Comercio*, April 17, 1847.

15. Ricketts to Canning, 18, September 15, 1826, F.O. 61/8; Tristán, *Peregrinaciones*, 319.

16. Denys Cuche, *Poder blanco y resistencia negra en el Perú: un estudio de la condición social del negro en el Perú después de la abolición de la esclavitud* (Lima, 1975), 165; Manuel A. Fuentes, *Estadística general de Lima* (Lima, 1858), 595–96; *El Comercio*, October 1, 1849. Flora Tristán noted the participation of Arequipa slaves in the Christians-and-Moors pageant. See Tristán, *Peregrinaciones*, 173.

17. See, for example, the comments of Proctor, *Narrative*, 237–38.

18. *El Comercio*, January 4, February 21, 1854; *El Peruano*, February 18, 1854.

19. "El sindico procurador Don Francisco Garfias, con Don Francisco Antonio Alavares, sobre el siervo Mariano Peña," AGN, CCiv, 1853, Leg. 171, July 7, 1853.

20. *El Comercio*, March 1, 1847, December 22, 1851.

21. "Criminales seguidos de oficio a Asunción Aliaga y José Miguel Pruneda, acusados de hurto," AGN, CCrim, 1847, Leg. 591; *El Comercio*, July 10, 1845, August 10, 1854. See also "Seguido por el abogado defensor de menores, con Dn. Andrés María Alvarez sobre de su esclava, Josefa Bernales," AGN, CCiv, 1834, Leg. 84; *El Comercio*, October 7, 1842.

22. "Criminales seguido contra Pedro Nolasco y Pablo Bosa por robo a Don Pablo Alzamora" and "Contra Bernardo Aliaga y José Luis Ulloa, José Cambiaso, y Pedro Pablo Baca por hurto a Dn. Pedro Puccio," both in AGN, CCrim, 1843, Leg. 583. For other cases of theft, including one in which a slave helped steal over 18,000 pesos, see AD-A, Corte Superior de Justicia, CCrim, 1835, I, April 10, 1835; and *El Comercio*, August 13, December 11, 1839, August 17, 1844.

23. For these and other examples of theft in the countryside see "Criminales seguidos contra Felipe Arzola y José Villanueva por robo," AGN, CCrim, 1841, Leg. 580; "Criminales contra Marcel Contreras y otros por cuatreros y contra Manuel Guzman como comprador de unas cabezas de ganado vacuna," AGN, CCrim, 1842, Leg. 582; *Gaceta Mercantil*, January 29, 1835; *El Comercio*, August 29, 1851; and Echenique, *Memorias* 1:105–6.

24. *El Conciliador*, February 10, 1830; *El Comercio*, August 4, 1840, August 12, 1854. See also Charles Walker, "Montoneros, bandoleros, malhechores: criminalidad y política en las primeras décadas republicanas," in *Bandoleros, abigeos, y montoneros: criminalidad y violencia en el Perú, siglos xviii–xx*, ed. Carlos Aguirre and Charles Walker (Lima, 1990), 124.

25. *El Peruano*, May 7, 1842; Markham, "Travels" 1:43; *El Comercio*, September 27, 1851.

26. *El Comercio*, March 26, 1847; "Criminales contra Cayetano García y otros esclavos de la hacienda de La Molina por el homicidio del caporal Manuel Benito," AGN, CCrim, 1847, Leg. 592; "Seguido contra José Francia por homicidio perpetrado en la persona de Bruno Lopez" and "Criminal contra José Francia por homicidio, 1852," both in AGN, CCrim, 1854, Leg. 612; Aguirre, "Cimarronaje," 167–68. For other cases of

assaults and murders in bakeries see *El Peruano*, June 1, September 24, 1842.

27. *El Comercio*, January 4, 1854; *El Correo de Lima*, December 10, 1851.

28. Aguirre, "Cimarronaje," 146–48.

29. Flores Galindo, *Aristocracia*, 119–20; Carlos Lazo García and Javier Tord Nicolini, *Del negro señorial al negro bandolero: cimarronaje y palenques en Lima, siglo XVIII* (Lima, 1977), 51, 59, 63. In the early nineteenth century during his visit to Lima, Proctor noted the vegetation on the hills around Lima when the mists or *garrua* enshrouded the city: "During the *garrua* season, the high rugged hills, which rise at the back of Lima, are clothed with vegetation, and have a beautiful effect; they are covered with cattle climbing their craggy sides in all directions." See Proctor, *Narrative*, 296–97.

30. In 1831, *La Miscelánea* was urging the state to sell these unclaimed slaves who, it charged, were corrupting the rest of the slaves and assisting fugitives. See *La Miscelánea*, August 9, 1831; and Flores Galindo, *Aristocracia*, 117. For a study of fugitive slaves in the Lima area see Aguirre, "Cimarronaje," 145–56.

31. "Expediente sobre inventario de las haciendas nombradas San José y la Ventilla del valle de Nazca actuado al tiempo que las recibió el presbítero D. Manuel Barreto de D. Juan Bautista Mesa," AGN, 1828, P.L. 8-22; Valencia Avara, *Bernardo O'Higgins*, 432–35.

32. Between January 2, 1854, and January 8, 1855, *El Comercio* printed thirty-nine advertisements announcing fugitive slaves, five more seeking "lost" slaves who may have been fugitives, twenty-one selling slaves, seventeen requiring slaves, and five exchanging slaves. Some of these advertisements referred to more than a single slave. According to Aguirre, the majority of runaways in Lima between 1840 and 1846 was young and male. See Aguirre, "Cimarronaje," 148–49, 178–79, tables 2 and 3.

33. There is no explanation for the sex ratio of the fugitives. The incident led to charges that the estate exploited its slaves, which were subsequently denied. See *El Comercio*, November 19, 25, 1844.

34. For the San Nicolás and Santa Beatriz incidents see *El Comercio*, June 14, 1847, August 21, 1852. For other newspaper reports announcing the arrest of runaway slaves see *El Comercio*, July 5, August 2, 26, September 2, 23, 25, October 22, November 23, December 13, 1839. Some of these may not have been true runaways, since they included slaves without *boletos*.

35. *El Comercio*, September 2, 1839, October 30, 1840; *El Telégrafo de Lima*, November 3, 1828. A report in *El Comercio* for December 31, 1853, lists five slaves from the Huachipa estate who had been gone for periods from eight days to one year.

36. *El Peruano*, February 3, 1841.

37. Ibid., February 17, 23, 1850; Basadre, *Historia* 3:291; BN, Volantes, Hojas Sueltas, etc., 1850, 3. For cases of vendors being fined for selling prohibited goods to slaves see *El Comercio*, May 12, August 14, 1843.

38. *Mercurio Peruano*, January 17, 1829. For an examination of coastal banditry see Flores Galindo, *Aristocracia*, 139–48.

39. Aguirre, "Cimarronaje," 156–74. Brazil's highwaymen were also a racially diverse group. See Thomas Flory, "Fugitive Slaves and Free Society: The Case of Brazil," *Journal of Negro History* 64 (1979): 116–30.

40. *El Comercio*, May 22, 1839, January 18, 1840, September 10, 1846, April 17, 1847. For other examples of slave highwaymen see *El Comercio*, July 30, 1839, February 20, 1843, September 28, October 12, 1852.

41. "Criminales contra José Julian, Merejo, Salome y Justo N. por haber asaltado en la Pampa de Tacuay al indígena Bautista Guamanlaso y robadolo," AGN, CCrim, 1840, Leg. 577; "Seguidos contra Manuel Campos, reo presente y contra Mariano y Hermenegildo N., reos ausentes por salteadores de caminos," AGN, CCrim, 1842, Leg. 582; *El Comercio*, October 4, 1844; *El Peruano*, May 28, 1842. Echenique sold San Pedro in 1846 for over 100,000 pesos, as he had agreed to become minister of war. See Echenique, *Memorias* 1:104, 143–44.

42. *El Comercio*, November 16, 1843, March 14, 20, 1846, March 13, 1847; *Mercurio Peruano*, January 2, 1829; *Miscelánea*, June 1, 1833.

43. "Seguido sobre el robo hecho en las chacras del valle de Ate," AGN, CCrim, 1854, Leg. 613. On other occasions Lostaunau showed himself to be more concerned about defending the slaves under his jurisdiction before the courts. See Aguirre, "Cimarronaje," 162 n. 55.

44. "Contra José Roman y Lucas Vargas por salteadores, 17 de noviembre, 1853," AGN, CCrim, 1854, Leg. 613; "Seguido contra Joaquín Pardo (a) Cinco Varas y otros, por salteadores," AGN, CCrim, 1854, Leg. 613; "Seguido contra Eugenio Arguedas, Manuel Casimiro, y Manuel Ipinze por salteadores de caminos," AGN, CCrim, 1854, Leg. 614; "Seguido contra Mauricio Zabala y otros por salteadores," AGN, CCrim, 1854, Leg. 614.

45. *El Comercio*, April 29, 1847, January 22, October 19, 29, 1852, January 11, 1854; *El Correo de Lima*, January 22, 1852; Aguirre, "Cimarronaje," 172–93; Markham, "Travels" 1:36, 41. For a slightly different version of his confrontation with the highwaymen see Markham, *Cuzco and Lima*, 16.

46. *El Comercio*, August 31, 1852; Vicuña, *Ocho meses*, 171.

47. For a discussion of some of the problems with the term "bandit" in the historical record see Joseph, "On the Trail," 21–25.

48. E. J. Hobsbawm, *Primitive Rebels: Studies in Archaic Forms of Social Movement in the 19th and 20th Centuries* (New York, 1959), 16–24.

49. For a discussion of Hobsbawm and his critics, and for a bibliography on bandits, see Joseph, "On the Trail."

50. *El Conciliador*, November 30, December 7, 11, 1833; *Mercurio Peruano*, January 19, 1829; *Miscelánea*, December 2, 11, 1833.

51. More of the *montoneros* seem to have been anticonservative forces, perhaps because of their lower-class composition. See Walker, "Montoneros."

52. Basadre, *Historia* 2:120–21, 328–29; Scarlett, *South America and the Pacific* 2:87, 104–8; Smith, *Peru As It Is* 2:185–88; *Gaceta del Gobierno* (Lima), March 27, 28, 1835; Wilson to John Bidwell, Separate, March 25, 1835, F.O. 61/30; Wilson to Saunders or Murray, Private and Confidential, October 31, 1835, F.O. 61/34; Wilson to Palmerston, 95, November 9,

1835, F.O. 61/34; Wilson to Commodore Francis Mason, December 15, 1835, F.O. 61/34; Wilson to Palmerston, 5, January 11, 1836, F.O. 61/37. See *El Comercio*, August 23, 1839, for a report of the arrest of two slaves who were accomplices of those who had robbed the French consul.

53. *El Comercio*, February 5, March 12, 14, 15, 16, May 6, 1842; Aguirre, "Cimarronaje," 160–61, 166 n. 64.

54. *Gaceta del Gobierno* (Lima), June 10, 1835; *El Peruano*, October 26, 1838.

55. *El Comercio*, December 22, 1841; Alberto Flores Galindo S., "El militarismo y la dominación británica (1825–1845)," in *Nueva historia general del Perú: un compendio*, by Carlos Araníbar et al. (Lima, 1979), 115–16. Flores Galindo argues that the *montoneros* were a form of social protest but were spontaneous and ineffective.

56. Genovese, *Roll, Jordan, Roll*, 598.

57. Héctor Centurión Vallejo, *Esclavitud y manumisión de negros en Trujillo* (Trujillo, 1954), 9–10; Flores Galindo, *Aristocracia*, 95–96, 116–17; Kapsoli, *Sublevaciones de esclavos*, chap. 3.

58. "Cuentas que rindió al supremo gobierno Dn. Miguel Bernales, administrador de la hacienda San Javier de la Nazca, y corresponde a los años de 1826–1828," AGN, Temporalidades, 1819–1828, Leg. 70, Exp. 110; Basadre, *Historia* 1:333.

59. *Mercurio Peruano*, April 6, July 18, 1832.

60. Echenique, *Memorias* 1:112–13.

61. *El Comercio*, June 11, 1840.

62. For more on the modernization of the agricultural sector see Chapter 6 in this volume.

63. Concerning these events see *El Comercio*, February 4, 10, 13, 21, 24–28, March 1, 15, 17, June 25, October 30, 1851. The testimony of the arrested participants can be found in AD-LL, División Judicial, Corte Superior, CCrim, 1851, Leg. 877, Exp. 3771.

64. For the trouble at Chiquitoy see *El Comercio*, February 25, September 27, 1851; AD-LL, División Judicial, Corte Superior, CCrim, 1851, Leg. 877, Exp. 3767.

65. One account of the events claims that Olaya and Baca were converted to abolitionism by the black sacristan of the monastery of Santa Clara, Norberto Cedeño, whose views had been molded by the writer and jurist Fernando Casós, who in turn had been taught by the Trujillo law professor Alfonso Gonzáles Pinillos. Cedeño preached that it was right to take up arms to conquer injustice, and he assisted in rousing the slaves in the Chicama Valley, while Casós was responsible for editing the slaves' proclamation of freedom. Contemporary accounts, however, do not mention Casós's participation, and subsequent references seem to be based on his fictionalized autobiography, which is replete with factual errors, including erroneous dates, and is of questionable reliability. See Fernando Casós, *Los amigos de Elena: diez años antes* (Paris, 1874), 1:19–26, 320–22. Works that have relied on this source either directly or indirectly include Basadre, *Historia* 3:190–91; Héctor Centurión Vallejo, "Esclavitud y manumisión de negros en Trujillo," *Revista el Instituto Libertador Ramón Castilla* 5 (1959): 63–71; Cuche, *Poder blanco*, 30–31; and Rout, *African Experience*, 218–19.

66. Rebellions in the Caribbean and Brazil involved much larger numbers of slaves. See Genovese, *Roll, Jordan, Roll*, 588–91.

67. In 1846, Trujillo had 6,544 inhabitants, with 253 male and 364 female slaves. See *El Comercio*, March 24, 1846.

68. Eugene D. Genovese, *From Rebellion to Revolution: Afro-American Slave Revolts in the Making of the Modern World* (Baton Rouge, 1979), 11–12, 20–27.

69. Basadre, *Historia* 3:290–91, 295.

70. Genovese has argued that divisions among the elite were an important factor in the incidence of slave rebellions. See Genovese, *From Rebellion*, 20–27.

71. AD-LL, División Notarial, Escrituras, José V. Aguilar, 1850–51, Leg. 411; Nicolás Rebaza, *Anales del departamento de La Libertad* (Trujillo, 1898), 292–94.

72. Quoted in *El Comercio*, February 13, 1851.

73. See Chapter 7 in this volume.

74. *El Comercio*, March 7, 10, 1851, January 11, 12, 1854.

# 6

# Capitalism, Industry, and Immigrants

Central to the story of slavery in the nineteenth century were the socioeconomic developments occurring in response to the spread of Western industrial capitalism. Virtually all of Latin America was feeling its effects by the middle of the century. Factories were opening, transportation and communication networks were improving and expanding, landholders were switching from the production of food to cash crops, and machinery was being introduced in both urban and rural sectors. A new, urban middle class appeared, who propounded the more progressive ideas then current in Europe, supported the modernizing trends, and rejected the values of the old landed elite.[1]

The impact of these developments on slavery has been the subject of a long and inconclusive debate. On one side are those who see the spread of capitalism as central to slavery's destruction. They point to the fact that the new employers were committed to efficiency and the maximum return on their investment and wanted workers who could be "freely contracted, freely fired, freely sold to, freely moved—units to be joined and disjoined where and how economic imperatives might require." Employers such as these opposed slavery because it "slowed down capital formation and tied it up in immovable labor."[2] Even the strongest supporters of slavery, the rural landowners, became aware of this negative side of slavery to some extent. They discovered as they slowly began to mechanize their estates to take advantage of overseas markets and improvements in transportation that they could no longer afford the luxury of expensive slaves—especially aging slaves whose value was depreciating and who could not be replaced because of the suppression of the international slave trade. Manuel Moreno Fraginals has concluded that, in the case of Cuba at least, technology and slave labor were incompatible and the expansion of one inevitably led to the decline of the other.[3]

On the other side are those who argue that, while capitalism may have played a role in weakening slavery, it did not supply a deathblow. They point out that the real impact of capitalism was not felt until long after the establishment of factories and, in some cases, long after the abolition of slavery. According to D. C. M. Platt, Latin America was not firmly integrated into the transatlantic economy until the third quarter of the century.[4] Previously, little had existed to attract European investors, traders, and capitalists to this part of the world. Thus, while modernization was occurring, it was proceeding at a snail's pace, with the result that the institutions of the past survived and continued to influence developments. Among these colonial legacies was slavery, which managed to adjust to the new circumstances. Studies of Cuba and Brazil have shown that, contrary to Moreno Fraginals's view, technology and slavery managed to exist side by side, leading to the conclusions that capitalism and slavery accommodated one other without difficulty and that the old and the new coexisted without one necessarily bringing an end to the other.[5]

The Peruvian case provides further evidence to support this latter argument. The spread of industrial capitalism had made its presence felt by midcentury, largely due to the post-1840 guano boom. The resulting injection of capital helped stimulate modernization. Factories, railways, and mechanized operations became part of the Peruvian reality. Capital was available to finance new technology, employ more expensive workers, and remunerate slaveholders if the need arose. Promoting modernization was a small group of local entrepreneurs who were receptive to the new ideas and who recommended immigration as the obvious solution to Peru's chronic labor shortage. However, while these changes helped to weaken Peruvian slavery, modernization by and of itself did not destroy it. As a whole, Peruvians in the midnineteenth century still did not perceive slavery as an obstacle to progress. Moreover, the country was only gradually and incompletely absorbed into the capitalist mode of production, even after the beginning of the guano boom. Modernization occurred, but in a limited and incomplete way. Traditional structures remained strong and counteracted the effects of the new. Indeed, some of the changes associated with modernization, especially the growing need for workers, reinforced the desire to retain slavery. Thus, the midnineteenth century may have been a transitional period for Peru and the new developments may have helped to undermine slavery, but the changes were not sufficiently great to cause its collapse. Slavery and a nascent capitalist structure coexisted here as elsewhere, and prominent Peruvians were committed to both.

The gradual nature of Peru's transformation in the early nineteenth century was tied to the weak state of the economy. Geographically remote, politically unstable, and economically chaotic, the country had few attractions for the industrializing nations. At the time of independence it was in debt, its mines had been badly damaged or destroyed, its coastal estates were in ruins, any exports that it might offer could be obtained more cheaply elsewhere, its consumer class was small and offered a very limited market to European manufacturers and traders, and private capital was scarce since the country's major capitalists, the Spanish merchants, had fled. These problems continued over the next decades, leading one commentator to conclude that "during this period the country did not progress significantly on the road to civilization nor in the development of its sources of wealth."[6]

Lack of ready cash remained a serious problem. Robert Proctor noted in the early 1820s that "the richer inhabitants of Lima were at this time becoming dreadfully poor; the times were too unsettled to make it worth while to cultivate their farms and to repurchase slaves and cattle which in the space of the last three years had been cleared off at different times by the alternate occupation of contending armies. Most of the ready money also had been drained or had disappeared from the city," carried off to Europe, extracted by forced loans, or absorbed by the high cost of living in Lima. Proctor added that private credit had all but been destroyed, as debtors could avoid paying their debts merely by swearing an oath that they had no money. A decade later, capital and credit were still in short supply. That deficiency was blamed for the continuing weakness of the country's mining sector which, nonetheless, remained the major source of export earnings as it had during the colonial era.[7]

What was true of the private sector was equally true of the state. Even before the final expulsion of the Spanish, the country was in debt. In 1824 and 1825 the government contracted loans totaling £1,816,000 from British bondholders, but the precarious state of the economy and the lack of income forced the suspension of payments in October 1825. Successive governments recognized the debt and expressed their intention to meet their obligations when the financial situation improved. However, no improvement occurred, so that neither principal nor interest was paid and the debt grew to £4,380,530 by 1848. In addition Peru owed money to Colombia, Chile, Ecuador, Venezuela, and the United States, so that in the late 1820s the foreign debt was five times the government's annual revenue.[8] To meet its obligations the government tried raising money locally through voluntary and forced loans, usually imposed upon merchants (who were the only ones with capital), but this merely created further debts that could not be repaid. In 1830 the internal debt amounted to 4,477,717 pesos, and, like its external counterpart, it continued to grow, to an estimated 6,646,344 pesos in 1845, despite occasional servicing as governments sought to maintain friendly relations with domestic creditors.[9]

In spite of the flight of capital and the continuing debt problems, the government did have some money at its disposal, although figures are scarce, contradictory, and of questionable accuracy because no formal budget was drawn up until the mid-1840s. One source states that government revenues rose from 1,500,000 to 3,000,000 pesos between 1826 and 1840; another contends that they ranged from 4,500,000 to just over 6,000,000 pesos for the period from 1824 to 1849. In either case the government had access to funds from a variety of sources. An analysis of government revenues in 1840 shows that they came from customs duties (that made up about half the total); a head tax imposed on the Indian and mixed-blood populations, which produced about 1,200,000 pesos; taxes on mining profits; fees; rents; passports; patents; and other sources that contributed smaller amounts.[10] Temporary financial problems were met by new forced loans or the confiscation of salable resources. The government also had assets of its own, such as public land and slaves, which it could and did sell. In March 1827 it sold twelve slaves from San Javier de la Nazca for 3,150 pesos to a creditor who was owed 6,900 pesos.[11]

Revenue was available but hardly enough to meet the government's needs. Over the years budget deficits were "chronic." Expenses exceeded income by 1,664,550 pesos in 1831 and by 500,000 pesos in 1839. The first formal budget, drawn up for the years 1846–47, projected a shortfall of 1,771,561 pesos for each of the two years. As a result of these deficits there was not enough money, at least before the guano boom, to meet existing foreign or domestic debts or to consider new spending.[12]

The principal reason for the government's economic malaise was its various financial obligations, all of which seemed to drain the exchequer rather than generate new income. Primary among these were military expenses. The frequent wars and rebellions of the period absorbed vast amounts of money. In addition the government had officers' salaries, pensions of retired military personnel, and an extensive bureaucracy to pay. At times these payments may have been reduced or even neglected, but since they were vital to avoiding even more discontent and military unrest they constituted a high priority for government spending when money was available. Once these obligations were met, little, if anything, was left for other needs.[13]

The government had some options that might have improved its financial position. One possibility was to centralize the collection of revenues and thereby obtain access to the funds previously collected by the provinces, such as those used to pay local military and bureaucratic salaries. It could have tried to curtail the smuggling of silver and the influx of contraband goods which, according to estimates, deprived it of millions of pesos in lost customs duties.[14] Since these duties provided it with its major source of income it could have stimulated exports, which were still languishing as productive capacity had not increased significantly over late colonial levels. Before 1840 the major exports were bullion and specie, with wool, nitrates, cotton, bark, hides, copper, tin, and sugar of less importance. The returns on all of these amounted to only £1,612,318 in 1838 and £1,632,869 one year later.[15]

One obvious area for growth, as previous chapters of this volume have shown, was the agrarian sector, in particular the sugar industry. The value of sugar exports was only £10,430 in each of the years 1838 and 1839. Most of the sugar and its derivative products, such as cane alcohol, were

consumed domestically, which meant—if sugar was following the pattern of *aguardiente*, another agricultural product
consumed almost entirely within the country—that producers were barely covering their costs. In the 1820s high international prices tied to rising demand fostered an interest in
expanding Peru's sugar exports and led to investments in
modern technology. However, the price plummeted in 1829
as production rose. Three years later Peruvian producers
suffered a further setback when Chile, its major foreign
market—some claimed its only foreign market—imposed
heavy duties on Peruvian sugar. Political animosities between the two nations further complicated relations and led
to the termination of bilateral trade. Producers attempted to
open new markets, shipping a cargo of sugar to England in
1835, but the initiative failed. A slight recovery occurred
with the reestablishment of the Chilean market in 1839, but
this coincided with the beginning of a general decline in
sugar prices that continued for the rest of the century. As a
result, in the 1850s sugar exports were still modest, amounting to an annual average of only 1,672 metric tons for the
quinquennium 1850–1854.[16]

Thus, Peruvian sugar planters responded for the most
part to local, not overseas, markets. Their financial returns
were limited yet seem to have been adequate to meet their
needs, and they were essentially guaranteed by protective
tariffs. Consequently, few planters showed any interest in
expanding production, which might have improved the
country's economic position. They did not have to rationalize
their industry to compete in a world market, they could
remain with the tried and true methods that had proven
profitable in the past, and they could ignore the frequently
aired complaints about the deplorable state of Peruvian
agriculture.

In the 1840s attention focused on a new export that
seemed to provide the long-awaited nostrum that would propel
Peru into the modern era and solve all its financial woes.
Guano, the rich fertilizer formed from bird droppings, had
accumulated for centuries on the islands off Peru's coast and
was now in demand overseas due to efforts to expand agricultural production. This odoriferous but valuable commodity
attracted capitalists from various foreign countries to finance
its exploitation; it became the most important export from all
of Latin America to Great Britain in the mid-1850s; and it
produced sufficient revenue to pay off past loans, obtain new

ones, purchase all manner of European goods, and modernize the Peruvian economy.[17] According to W. M. Mathew, the major beneficiary of the guano boom was the government, which "nationalized" the industry in 1842 and by the end of the decade was taking the "lion's share" of guano sales.[18] Guano returns rose from 256,715 pesos out of total government revenues of 4,191,800 pesos in 1846–47, to 3,800,000 out of 7,113,500 pesos in 1852–53, and 4,300,000 out of 9,941,404 pesos in 1854–55.[19] As a result, the government settled its debt with Britain in 1849 and began to recognize its other foreign obligations, which made Peru attractive to investors once again. In 1853 it received a new British loan of £2,600,000.[20]

The situation, however, was not as promising as it seemed. The actual amount of money that the guano industry made available to the government was limited, largely because the industry was organized as a monopoly in which the government granted consignees the exclusive right to sell guano in return for monetary advances. These advances were loans on which the government had to pay interest, so that it was still in debt. On occasion it ran out of money and then either had to negotiate a bridging loan from the consignees or had to draw up a new contract providing additional money in exchange for an extension of the guano monopoly. It also was willing to break the monopoly and grant new guano concessions, a recourse adopted in 1847 when its "financial situation was desperate."[21] As a result, despite the enormous revenues from guano sales, the returns were modest, and a charge made in the 1860s that "the government's treasury was always without a dollar" seems to have been applicable to the earlier period as well.[22]

The lack of cash was tied to the government's continuing financial commitments. Paying off foreign debts was but one of these and a rare positive use of the guano funds. Otherwise the money was spent neither productively nor profitably, as much of it followed the old patterns of meeting military expenditures and paying bureaucratic salaries.[23] The principal reason behind the government's nationalization of the industry in 1842 was to finance an anticipated war with Bolivia.[24] The most controversial and perhaps most wasteful use of guano funds during this period revolved around President Castilla's "law of consolidation" of 1850, which recognized in their entirety all the claims made against the government since 1820. Before leaving office in 1851 his administration committed the nation to paying debts of some 5,000,000 pesos. His successor, José Rufino Echenique, proved to be even more generous, recognizing any and all claims that were supported simply by witnesses making a declaration before an official. His gesture increased the debt over fourfold to 23,211,400 pesos. Stories circulated that much of this debt was based on claims fabricated by speculators and that the chief beneficiaries were members of Echenique's administration. Adding substance to the rumors was the government's decision to convert 13,000,000 pesos of the debt into an external debt by floating a loan in Europe, thereby ensuring that future governments could not renounce it. Echenique's growing financial needs also caused him to demand larger and larger advances from the guano consignees in return for extensions of their contracts. His controversial economic policies and the rumors of ministerial corruption led to widespread criticism that fueled unrest and eventually triggered rebellion in 1854.[25]

The early years of the guano boom, thus, had rather limited effects on Peru. The financial situation had improved in comparison with the first decades after independence, as exports of guano now provided the government with access to capital, but the returns were uncertain, and most of the money was spent as unproductively as it had been in the past. Expectations of more profound developments may have been raised, and the existing socioeconomic realities may have come under closer scrutiny, but these were vague responses that translated into gradual and superficial changes rather than immediate and fundamental shifts in direction. The beginnings of the guano boom were accompanied by and partly responsible for a degree of modernization, but that modernization had little impact on the country's basic structures, which remained much as they had been in the preceding decades.

Like other countries in Latin America and elsewhere, Peru in the midnineteenth century sought to follow the industrializing trends that were then occurring in Europe and North America. International links tightened with the opening of steamship lines in 1840. In 1847 an electric telegraph was built between Lima and its port of Callao. Four years later a railway was completed connecting the two cities. Simultaneously industrialization was taking place, so that by 1851 Lima could boast factories producing cotton thread and cloth, paper, glassware, silk, gas, and beer.[26] In the countryside, too, modern methods were being adopted. A few sugar estates had been mechanized for years, in some cases almost since independence. The exiled Chilean war hero Bernardo O'Higgins introduced the most advanced techniques on his Montalván estate in the Cañete Valley. In 1826, Consul Ricketts noted that he was "making many improvements . . . by the introduction of our system of farming, of steam-engines for the manufacture of sugar, etc." In 1838 he began using machinery for the crushing of cane.[27] José Rufino Echenique was also interested in modern methods; he introduced steam-powered machinery on his San Pedro estate in 1837. Other estates around Lima began using steam power after 1841, and by 1852 Hualcará and La Quebrada in the Cañete Valley, Palpa in the Chancay Valley, and Larán, San José, and Caucato in the Chincha Valley all had steam-operated sugar mills or machinery. Cotton planters, too, were mechanizing, as cotton gins, mills for cleaning cotton, and steam-run plows began appearing on estates in the Ica region. Associated with this mechanization was a shift away from the traditional food and pastoral crops to cash crops such as sugar and cotton. This would become the norm in the 1850s, but some shifting was already evident in the preceding decade, leading to an expansion of land use and a search for money to purchase new holdings.[28]

These examples, however, seem to have been the exception rather than the rule. In general, industrialization and mechanization were slow and very limited. One reason for this, as a commentator in 1838 noted, was the unsettled state of the country: This had curbed investment in machinery and thereby hindered both industrial growth and trade. In addition, Peruvian manufactures, especially cloth, were hurt by the lower prices and better quality of imports. Protective tariffs had assisted the industrial expansion of the 1840s, but in 1852 the Echenique government reduced the rates, ended subsidies, and eliminated other protections, with the result that every factory except the paper mill closed.[29] In the agricultural sector the sugar industry, despite the efforts of the few forward-looking planters, was considered to be technologically archaic. The vast majority of the estates did not introduce steam engines until the 1860s, long after their general introduction in other countries. The industry was so backward that, according to Pablo Macera, a majordomo from the seventeenth century would have been quite at home on a Peruvian sugar estate in 1875.[30] Even in the guano industry, where money was plentiful and the consignees might have been expected to maximize their returns and resolve the problem of a lack of workers by using laborsaving devices, the extraction methods were "primitive in the extreme." Two steam-driven cutting and barrow-loading machines were in operation by 1853, but most of the work was done by hand. The labor force during the first decade of exploitation was composed of convicts, army deserters, slaves, some free wage labor, and increasing numbers of Chinese coolies. They loaded the guano onto trucks, which they pushed along tracks to the cliffs, and then poured the fertilizer down chutes into the holds of waiting ships. A significant amount of the guano was wasted, dumped into the ocean. However, both government and consignees were determined to minimize expenses, so the operations received little in the way of capital injections or technological improvements.[31]

Just as industrialization and modernization in Peru were limited, so, too, were the size and influence of the national entrepreneurial bourgeoisie. This group, which was to play a vital role in the later abolition of slavery in Brazil, constituted a minor force in Peru.[32] An identifiable industrial class emerged as a result of industrialization and urbanization, but the numbers of its members remained small, their interests often corresponded with those of the planters (for example, both groups in the early republic strongly supported tariff protection), and they virtually disappeared with the factory closings in 1852. Another urban group who might have propounded new ideas, the merchant class, was also small and largely foreign. The emigration of Peru's Spanish merchants at independence created a vacuum that might have been filled by local merchants, but instead foreigners came to predominate. In the late 1820s restrictive government policies, including the reestablishment of the monopolistic *consulado*, produced an expansion of the native merchant class so that "by 1839 about 80 major Peruvian merchants operated in Lima," mainly in the retail business. However, relaxation of these restrictions in the 1840s (together with initiatives taken by Peruvians to collaborate more fully with foreign firms and to benefit from the import trade, which was expanding because of the guano boom) brought increasing numbers of foreign merchants, who still dominated the wholesale sector, into the retail market. A reduced group of relatively prosperous native merchants merged with the foreign interests.[33]

A third indigenous entrepreneurial group might have been the native beneficiaries of the guano industry. The first guano consignee was a Peruvian, Francisco Quirós, but he was soon supplanted by foreigners because, like other Peruvians, he lacked the financial resources to meet the government's demands for large and immediate advances as well as the requisite commercial skills and overseas contacts. Wealthy Lima merchants were assigned guano rights again in 1850 by President Castilla, but they went bankrupt in a year. Subsequently, native involvement remained peripheral until the 1860s, when the Peruvian consignees emerged as a powerful and influential bloc. Until then their involvement was slight and their impact on developments was negligible.[34]

The small size of the bourgeoisie and their limited influence meant that issues that deeply involved them elsewhere, such as the debate over free wage labor versus slaves, received only a cursory airing in Peru. A few discussions appeared in the press, with anonymous proponents of wage labor arguing that it was cheaper than slave labor and was the only type of labor that offered security and wealth to the hacendado and a sense of well-being to the worker. In one of the few reports that made a detailed examination of the subject, the writer calculated that in a month of twenty-four workdays, a wage laborer receiving 4 reals per day would earn 12 pesos per month or 144 pesos annually, which was the total cost to the employer. In contrast, the basic annual cost of a slave was 152 pesos, which he calculated by adding 40 pesos in interest charges (reckoned at 10 percent on 400 pesos, the figure chosen as the average price of a slave); 1.5 reals daily, or 68 pesos, 3.5 reals annually for food; 17 pesos, 4 reals for clothing; 6 pesos, 0.5 reals for medical treatment and loss of work due to illness; and 20 pesos for fines, thefts, and damage. But the slave worked one quarter less than a free worker, and this, together with the basic annual cost plus an additional 8 pesos for miscellaneous expenses, totaled 44 pesos more per year for the slave.

Others calculated the difference to be much greater. One described it as "immense," a result of the slave's high initial price plus interest together with maintenance costs, which continued even during unproductive periods, such as the off-season for the sugar and grape industries and those times when slaves were ill or otherwise incapacitated. Slavery was also seen as uneconomic, since it retarded population growth because the slaves' fecundity was affected by poor subsistence. Even those who believed that slaves were cheaper because of the lack of alternative workers admitted that they were becoming more expensive because of the declining supply.[35]

The discussion of labor concentrated more on who would replace the slaves than on comparative merits, and here there was general agreement. Commentators tended to ignore the free blacks and other indigenous groups and, instead, cast their eyes beyond Peru's shores, seeking the panacea for the country's labor shortage in immigrants. Among the advocates of this position was the Lima newspaper *El Comercio.* An article in 1845 called for immigration to meet Peru's labor needs, as well as for studies of the likely impact of mechanization and statistical comparisons of the relative costs of free and slave labor. It blamed the country's political situation and religious intolerance for the past dearth of immigrants. Others held slavery responsible (claiming that immigrants equated certain tasks with slaves), and consequently supported abolition, believing that this would promote immigration and reduce the cost of free wage labor.[36]

Like other Latin American countries, Peru was interested mainly in European immigrants. Several immigration projects were introduced in the 1830s and 1840s to try to meet that interest, but the results left much to be desired. In 1846, José Gregorio Paz Soldán, the Peruvian foreign minister, lamented that "for twenty-three years we have futilely expected them, and even now the first has yet to appear."[37] Hopes rose in 1848 as revolution bloodied Europe and thousands of migrants fled overseas to escape the turmoil. Seeking to tap the flow, Peru's minister of government instructed departmental prefects to meet with local hacendados and discuss ways to attract European colonists. In Lima the prefect distributed a questionnaire that focused on the likely impact that European immigration would have on the slavery system. It inquired into the existing number of slaves, the extent of the decline of slavery in the past decade, the comparative productivity of slave and free workers, the problems other than the payment of wages that might arise from hiring free workers, the adequacy of 4 reals per day as a wage for European plantation workers, and the methods to be adopted to prevent troubles between slave and free workers. Responding through their Sociedad de Agricultura with answers that did not always correspond to the questions and indicated little real interest in attracting immigrants, the hacendados noted that they were not prepared to provide land to attract migrants unless it was absolutely necessary; slaves received 8 pesos per month; free workers worked only seven hours daily; and the maximum wage possible was 3 reals per day plus lodging. Elsewhere similar inquiries elicited similar responses. Piura's hacendados wanted more workers but recognized that their agricultural problems were also a result of a drought that had affected the region between 1838 and 1845. Hacendados in La Libertad were willing to support immigrants with land, equipment, seed, and what they thought was a fair wage. They wanted one thousand workers earning 3 reals per day, working three days per week on the planter's land. The rest of the time they would be free to work on their own.[38]

The growing interest finally produced an immigration law in November 1849. It was designed to counter "the prostration of agriculture" and offered Peruvian contractors a prize of 30 pesos per colonist, aged between ten and forty and imported in groups of fifty or more.[39] The hope was that Europeans would be the colonists contracted. The law was successful in stimulating immigration, but not in the numbers nor of the race generally desired.

The principal figures behind the law were Juan Rodríguez and the Ica planter Domingo Elías, and they wanted cheap, servile workers, specifically Chinese coolies. They believed that coolies could be easily attracted to Peru, because the living and working conditions there were as good as or better than those in China. They had already imported seventy-five coolies, and now they had a law that offered a prize to importers of colonists. They arranged to have the law applied retroactively, permitting them to recoup some of their expenses, and obtained the exclusive right to import coolies for four years into the departments of Lima and La Libertad.[40] Thus, while the law attracted some migrants from Germany and Ireland, leading to optimistic predictions that government-supported colonies of foreigners would be formed, the principal immigrants were Chinese coolies. They constituted such a large proportion of the immigrants that the law became known as the "Chinese law." However, even they did not add up to the numbers anticipated. In 1851 the government raised the prize to 40 pesos per head to try to increase the flow, but two years later the minister of government and foreign affairs could report that only 3,932 agricultural immigrants had been attracted: 2,516 Chinese, 1,096 Germans, and 320 Irish.

Like the majority of Peruvians, he viewed this preponderance of Chinese with serious misgivings. While some employers preferred them, considering them "better than slaves and without the problems" and cheaper and less troublesome than Europeans (who were perceived to have higher aspirations than the coolies), he regarded them as an unmixable group with objectionable cultural traits, such as a propensity to commit suicide, and immoral sexual practices, specifically masturbation and homosexuality. The British minister to Peru had an equally negative view of them. In an 1852 report he described them as physically superior to the natives but inferior to Europeans and blacks. They had been imported to solve Peru's agricultural problems, but only a small proportion of them worked in the agrarian sector—about 500 of the 1,613 coolies who had arrived in Callao between 1850 and 1852—and as agricultural workers they left much to be desired. They were susceptible to disease, had a reputation for being "obstinate and stupid," and were ignorant of Spanish. Unable to communicate verbally, they had resorted to striking to indicate their alienation.[41]

Thus the first wave of Chinese immigration was not a particular success, and the coolies were not a significant force for change. With regard to slavery, they probably helped to weaken the institution, but only to a limited extent. The expectation that substantial immigration would follow the opening of the coolie trade, thereby providing a new cheap labor force and reducing the importance of the slaves, may have undermined the strength of the commitment to slavery in some instances. However, as the British minister noted in his report, the major shortcoming of the coolies was their meager numbers. As a result, the search for alternative workers continued and slaves remained a vital sector of the labor force. In addition, many Peruvians found the coolies unsatisfactory, as their criticism clearly indicated. Consequently, they remained firm supporters of slavery.

The arrival of the coolies and other immigrants demonstrated that the general attitude toward labor in Peru was not changing in response to the developments of the period. Planters viewed the newcomers as an adjunct to the existing labor force, not a replacement. They still wanted a docile, servile labor force whom they could exploit without interference, as their treatment of the immigrants clearly revealed.

The coolies in particular suffered. Described as "midway between slaves and the European," they found that in their relations with the Peruvians they were closer to the former than the latter. One commentator, writing after two decades of Chinese immigration, claimed that Peru's slaves had been a favored group compared to the coolies.[42] It was an exaggeration, but it gives some indication of the hardships the coolies faced. Contracted by means of advances in China, they were herded into ships, where the degree of overcrowding recalled the worst of the slave ships and resulted in similarly appalling mortality rates. They were initially contracted for five years with the promise of a monthly wage of 4 pesos plus food and medicine. However, from their wage they had to pay for clothing and repay the advance at the rate of 1 peso per month. On the guano islands they received half the pay of free workers, most of which was deducted for their food, while performing duties that were described as "onerous." Coolies who failed to complete their assigned work or who resisted in any way could be punished by being flogged, suspended for hours in the sea, or left half-drowned on a buoy. Many coolies found suicide by leaping into the sea preferable to the conditions that they had to endure.[43] On the coastal plantations the situation was much the same, as the immigrants were confined to slave *galpones* that were locked at night; they worked from dawn to dusk, performing whatever tasks were demanded of them; and, like slaves, they were subject to the lash if they failed to comply. Also like slaves they were bought and sold by their employers, who advertised their availability in the local press.[44]

Proponents of the trade, citing the law that anyone who arrived in the country was free, argued that the coolies were not slaves, but almost as soon as the first Chinese arrived Peruvians began to show concern. Reports of the "numerous abuses" of the trade produced condemnation both internationally and at home and led to demands for its suppression. To counter the growing criticism, Elías and Rodríguez published a pamphlet in 1851 that claimed coolies were the cheapest and most logical solution to Peru's labor problems. They argued that coolies received only 4 pesos per month and could live on rice, while Europeans expected 20 centavos per day and demanded meat. They questioned the rationale of hiring free wage laborers who might be conscripted, or Indians and free blacks who were subject to a head tax that employers usually paid. They managed to convince congress for the time being, but reservations continued to grow, and in September 1854 the government halted migration to the Chincha Islands for five months. In 1856 the coolie trade was banned altogether. The ban, however, had only limited effect, for coolies continued to arrive and the full trade resumed in 1861.[45]

The Chinese were not the only immigrants to suffer at the hands of their Peruvian employers. Europeans, too, were exploited and mistreated. One case involved a German woman named Ursula Lang, a contracted estate worker. She had been shackled by a leg chain for three or four days by her employer, Tomás Villalva, who reported she had run away more than seven times. He claimed that the chain left no mark, and his lawyer explained it was simply a means to relieve Villalva's "anxiety" over his disappearing servant. Ursula charged that she had been starved for several days and hit by Villalva's wife. The court hearing the case concluded that no crime had been committed, but it was concerned about what had occurred (perhaps because of the international repercussions). It recommended that Villalva not chain his servants again, ordered him to pay Ursula an indemnity of 50 pesos, and terminated her contract.

Ursula's case was not unique. A Lima newspaper story in August 1853 entitled "European Slaves in Peru" described the abuse of other white immigrants, while newspaper advertisements announcing the flight of European employees suggest still further examples.[46] The employers may not have been completely to blame. An 1852 inquiry into the status of German immigrants found that many of them had suffered because German contractors had secured unfit or unsuited people who had been unable to cope with the nature of the work, the unaccustomed diet, the climate, and the different customs. Nonetheless, food and wages had been inadequate, resulting in disease, especially among field hands, and a death rate that was described as "appalling." The Germans, like the Chinese coolies, had responded by resisting the demands of their employers which, in turn, had led to conflict, imprisonment, and increased work loads.[47]

The treatment of the immigrant workers and the desire for a controlled, dominated labor force indicated how the ideas, attitudes, and institutions of the past continued to influence developments in early republican Peru. This conjuncture of the old and the new can be seen as well in the careers of many of the entrepreneurs who were prominent at midcentury. One of these was the Ica planter, politician, and businessman Domingo Elías. He was in the forefront of several of the period's economic developments and appeared to be among the most forward-looking Peruvians of the time. Clements Markham described him as "the most enterprising man in Peru" in the early 1850s. Yet, in some ways, particularly in his attitude toward labor, he was indistinguishable from his colonial forebears, showing that a commitment to modern enterprise did not entail a rejection of every tradition from the past.[48]

Elías was born in 1805 and at an early age became involved in various economic activities. He was primarily a planter, owning extensive estates in the Ica region including the former state-owned properties of San José and San Javier de la Nazca. Interested in improving the quantity and quality of his crops, he imported machinery and hired foreign experts to assist him in his operations. He is reputed to have been the first person in Peru to make wine following European methods and to produce cotton on a commercial scale. His experiments in the cultivation of cotton led to the development of a fiber known as Elías cotton. In addition he was a merchant, miner, and moneylender. He was involved in the guano industry, leasing the Chincha Islands in the late 1830s and exporting guano before the boom. His involvement in the guano industry suggests that his financial resources and foreign contacts were not unlimited, for he failed to obtain a guano contract when the boom began. Nevertheless, his wealth and his close political ties with President Castilla ensured some participation in the industry. In 1849 he obtained the guano-loading concession on the islands, which he held until 1853. Financial constraints were obviously not a serious obstacle to his ambitions. He borrowed extensively, both at home and abroad, demonstrating a willingness to take risks as well as a confidence in his own abilities.[49]

Elías was also prominent in the political arena, where he acquired a reputation for being "liberal and enlightened." He controlled the government for a brief period in 1844, prompting the British minister to comment that he "represents the principle of Government by the people as opposed to the military, and . . . he has been supported almost unanimously by the inhabitants of Lima, with a degree of enthusiasm which . . . has not for many years been exhibited in this city." Three years later he was reported to be head of "the Party of the People," and in 1851 he presented himself as a civilian candidate for the presidency. His campaign called for a civilian government, reduced military influence, budgetary restraint, monetary reform, immigration, industrialization, and the creation of technical institutions.[50] He became an outspoken opponent of Echenique—a probable factor in his losing the guano-loading concession—and he played a leading role in the 1854 rebellion that ended with Echenique's downfall.

While he was economically progressive and politically liberal, Elías remained staunchly conservative and traditional in other areas, particularly where labor was concerned. He was one of the country's largest slave owners and an outspoken defender of the system. Although he used sharecroppers, seasonal laborers, and other free workers in his operations and is reported to have been convinced "that the forces of the free man are worth three times those of the slave" and to have preferred free workers, he remained reliant on slaves, employing some of them on the guano islands. He sought slaves throughout the country and was the major purchaser of the slaves and *libertos* who were imported from New Granada in 1847. When the supplies of these dried up, he turned to Chinese coolies, indicating his continuing commitment to cheap, coercible, semiservile workers. He was the principal force behind the trade and a major employer of those imported.[51]

Elías and other similar-minded Peruvians who were interested in modern technology but remained firm defenders of slavery were not alone in their apparently contradictory behavior. Brazil's coffee planters displayed the same characteristics in the late nineteenth century, prompting Warren Dean's conclusion that they were "the most progressive and the most retrograde sector of Brazilian society."[52] The description could be applied equally to their Peruvian counterparts. Both groups seemed to believe that slavery or servile labor could coexist with the new technology. The changing times did not produce an automatic shift in attitudes, at least not where labor was concerned.

Peru thus remained much the same despite the spread of capitalism and the arrival of immigrants. New ideas and new methods may have been spreading, but they existed comfortably side by side with the old. This was clearly true of the guano boom and the accompanying abundance of capital. No significant changes were evident: Investment in the industry was paltry, and employers still sought cheap, exploitable workers. To argue that the guano boom "freed the black slaves" is to overstate the case.[53] There was no clear and direct link between the two. The boom may have created the revenues that were needed to compensate slave owners for freeing their slaves, but few if any Peruvians urged this use of guano returns on the government.

Nor did the arrival of immigrants as alternative workers reverse the commitment to slavery. Peruvian slaveholders, like their Brazilian counterparts, continued to consider slaves a more economical labor force as well as a more secure one. Where immigrants were concerned, employers hoped that sufficient numbers would arrive to drive down wages, making them as cheap as slaves and, as a result, more attractive as laborers. At that time slaves might lose their appeal. Even this was uncertain, however, for slavery had coexisted with other forms of labor in Peru since the arrival of the first black slave, and many prominent employers seemed to find the arrangement quite satisfactory. Although they were willing to experiment with a mix of different kinds of workers, they were not convinced that slavery should be abandoned, especially when commercial agriculture was expanding, estates were growing, and labor was in short supply. Even if slavery were to be abandoned, planters seemed to want equally servile and constrained workers as replacements, for they showed little interest in employing free blacks or indigenous workers as their principal labor force.

Nevertheless, despite the various continuities with the past, the socioeconomic developments of the period were undermining slavery to some extent. Changes were taking place, particularly from the 1840s, which caused some Peruvians to reevaluate their country's economic development and the nature of its social relations. The arrival of immigrant workers, especially coolies, revealed to at least a few employers that alternative cheap workers were available, thereby reducing the reliance on slaves and weakening the commitment to slavery. The guano revenues meant that by the 1850s money was available to introduce technological improvements, hire more expensive workers, and remunerate slave owners if necessary. The desire to obtain new equipment probably caused some employers to reconsider their investment in expensive slaves. Moreover, the modernizing trends experienced by Peru suggested some acceptance, grudging though it may have been, of the new ideas. This weakened the hold of the colonial past and broadened the willingness to consider associated changes, such as the employment of free wage labor.

In other words, changes were taking place in the socioeconomic sphere that threatened Peruvian slavery. By themselves they were not enough to overcome the strength of the slaveholders and ensure slavery's immediate and total destruction, but they exerted pressure in the direction of abolition by weakening the commitment of some Peruvians to the institution and indicating alternatives to slavery. Combined with other factors, they helped to establish the framework that in 1854–55 permitted the abolition of slavery and ensured its general acceptance by the Peruvian population.

## Notes

1. For an examination of these trends see E. Bradford Burns, *The Poverty of Progress: Latin America in the Nineteenth Century* (Berkeley, 1983).

2. Richard Graham, "Causes for the Abolition of Negro Slavery in Brazil: An Interpretive Essay," *HAHR* 46 (1966): 126, 128.

3. The classic presentation of this argument can be found in Williams, *Capitalism and Slavery*. See also Manuel Moreno Fraginals, "El esclavo y la mecanización de los ingenios," *Bohemia* 24 (June 13, 1969): 98; and Moreno Fraginals, *Sugarmill*, 106, 134.

4. D. C. M. Platt, *Latin America and British Trade, 1806–1914* (New York, 1972), 3 and part 1. Graham makes the same point about Brazil. See Graham, "Causes for the Abolition," 125.

5. For a thorough discussion of the argument concerning the incompatability of slavery and technology, in which it is rejected, see Scott, *Slave Emancipation*, 26–37 and chap. 4. For Brazil see Dean, *Rio Claro*.

6. Jesús Chavarría, "The Colonial Heritage of National Peru: An Overview," *Boletín de Estudios Latinoamericanos y del Caribe* 25 (1978): 42–46; W. M. Mathew, "The Imperialism of Free Trade: Peru, 1820–70," *Economic History Review* 21 (1968): 567–68; Mathew, *House of Gibbs*, 17; Dancuart, *Anales* 2:3–4.

7. Proctor, *Narrative*, 289–90; *Gaceta Mercantil*, July 5, 21, 1834.

8. Heraclio Bonilla, "Peru and Bolivia," in *Spanish America after Independence, c.1820–c.1870*, ed. Leslie Bethell (Cambridge, 1987), 254; Jonathan V. Levin, *The Export Economies: Their Pattern of Development in Historical Perspective* (Cambridge, 1960), 44–47; W. M. Mathew, "The First Anglo-Peruvian Debt and Its Settlement, 1822–49," *Journal of Latin American Studies* 2 (1970): 82–83; Charles A. McQueen, *Peruvian Public Finance* (Washington, 1926), 85; Emilio Romero, *Historia económica del Perú*, 2d ed. (Lima, 1968), 2:88; Ernesto Yepes del Castillo, *Perú,*

*1820–1920: un siglo de desarrollo capitalista* (Lima, 1972), 45; Memorandum, August 29, 1832, F.O. 61/21.

9. Bonilla, "Peru and Bolivia," 244, 247; Nils Jacobsen, "Taxation in Early Republican Peru, 1821–1851: Policy Making between Reform and Tradition," in *América Latina en la época de Simón Bolívar: la formación de las economías nacionales y los intereses económicos europeos, 1800–1850*, ed. Reinhard Liehr (Berlin, 1989), 333–34; Memorandum, August 29, 1832, F.O. 61/21.

10. Jacobsen, "Taxation," 313, 316–32; Levin, *Export Economies*, 29–31; Yepes, *Perú*, 43–44.

11. Levin, *Export Economies*, 51; Wilson to Palmerston, 18, April 3, 1834, F.O. 61/26; "D. Simón Ravago, reclamando un esclavo de su propiedad llamado José de los Santos, que existe en la hacienda de San Javier de la Nazca," AGN, 1828, P.L. 8-634.

12. Levin, *Export Economies*, 46; Mathew, *House of Gibbs*, 85; Yepes, *Perú*, 61 n. 5; Memorandum, August 29, 1832, F.O. 61/21.

13. Bonilla, "Peru and Bolivia," 243; Jacobsen, "Taxation," 335; Romero, *Historia económica* 2:70, 78; Wilson to Palmerston, 18, April 3, 1834, F.O. 61/26.

14. Jacobsen, "Taxation," 319; Romero, *Historia económica* 2:69, 75, 83.

15. Mathew, *House of Gibbs*, 19–20; Platt, *Latin America and British Trade*, 38; Yepes, *Perú*, 50–51.

16. Albert, *Essay on the Peruvian Sugar Industry*, 2a–13a; Gonzales, *Plantation Agriculture*, 20–22; Macera, "Las plantaciones azucareras," 28–49; Yepes, *Perú*, 51; *El Comercio*, September 16, 1848; *El Telégrafo de Lima*, October 31, 1832.

17. Concerning the guano industry see Levin, *Export Economies*, chap. 8; W. M. Mathew, "Antony Gibbs and Sons, the Guano Trade and the Peruvian Government, 1842–1861," in *Business Imperialism 1840–1930: An Inquiry Based on British Experience in Latin America*, ed. D. C. M. Platt (Oxford, 1977); W. M. Mathew, "Foreign Contractors and the Peruvian Government at the Outset of the Guano Trade," *HAHR* 52 (1972): 598–620; Mathew, *House of Gibbs*; Mathew, "Imperialism of Free Trade"; W. M. Mathew, "A Primitive Export Sector: Guano Production in Mid-Nineteenth-Century Peru," *Journal of Latin American Studies* 9 (1977): 35–57; and Yepes, *Perú*, chap. 2.

18. Mathew, "Antony Gibbs," 350. See also Mathew, "Primitive Export Sector," 56 n. 153; and Levin, *Export Economies*, 113.

19. Levin, *Export Economies*, 95, table 1. For the biennial budgets from 1846–47 to 1854–55 see McQueen, *Peruvian Public Finance*, 36.

20. Mathew, "First Anglo-Peruvian Debt," 81–98; McQueen, *Peruvian Public Finance*, 86; Romero, *Historia económica* 2:88.

21. Levin, *Export Economies*, 50–51, 60; Pike, *Modern History*, 97.

22. Quoted in Mathew, "Antony Gibbs," 353.

23. Mathew, "Primitive Export Sector," 56.

24. Mathew, "Foreign Contractors," 604; Mathew, "Antony Gibbs," 352–53.

25. Bonilla, "Peru and Bolivia," 259; Levin, *Export Economies*, 80–81; Pike, *Modern History*, 100–102; Yepes, *Perú*, 67–68.

26. Bonilla, "Peru and Bolivia," 241; Paul Gootenberg, "The Social Origins of Protectionism and Free Trade in Nineteenth-Century Lima,"

*Journal of Latin American Studies* 14 (1982): 343; Clements R. Markham, *A History of Peru* (Chicago, 1892), 342–43; J. Fred Rippy, "The Dawn of Manufacturing in Peru," *Pacific Historical Review* 15 (1946): 147; Romero, *Historia económica* 2:140, 142.

27. Ricketts to Canning, 26, December 27, 1826, F.O. 61/8; Basadre, *Historia* 2:214.

28. Basadre, *Historia* 2:300, 337–38; Engelsen, "Social Aspects," 208–10, table 30, chap. 4; Markham, *Cuzco and Lima*, 24–25, 33; Markham, "Travels" 1:48, 74, 79, 93, 110, 130; Vicuña, *Ocho meses*, 29.

29. Enclosure with Wilson to Palmerston, 64, September 29, 1838, F.O. 61/53; Gootenberg, "Social Origins," 355–56.

30. Macera, "Las plantaciones azucareras," 30, 31, 233. See also Basadre, *Historia* 2:300.

31. Mathew, "Primitive Export Sector," 42, 48–51; Markham, "Travels" 1:97.

32. Concerning Brazil see Graham, "Causes for the Abolition."

33. Gootenberg, "Social Origins," especially 333–38, 343–48, 352; Gootenberg, *Between Silver and Guano*, chap. 3. The reestablishment of the *consulado* in the 1820s provides further evidence of Peru's hesitant acceptance of the more progressive economic ideas of the time.

34. Levin, *Export Economies*, 78–79, 84–85; Mathew, "Foreign Contractors," 614; Mathew, *House of Gibbs*, 189–91; Pike, *Modern History*, 98; Yepes, *Perú*, 67–71.

35. *El Comercio*, August 8, 1845, July 26, 1848; *La Miscelánea*, August 16, 1830; *El Peruano*, May 4, 1850; Romero, *Historia económica* 2:47.

36. *El Comercio*, August 20, 1845; *El Peruano*, May 4, 1850.

37. Quoted in Watt Stewart, *Chinese Bondage in Peru: A History of the Chinese Coolie in Peru, 1849–1874* (Durham, 1951), 12. For other information on the failure of Peruvian immigration efforts see P. Emilio Dancuart, *Crónica parlamentaria del Perú: historia de los congresos, que han funcionado en la república desde 1822* (Lima, 1906–1910), 2:67; *El Peruano*, November 2, 1844.

38. *El Peruano*, August 23, 26, September 16, 1848; *El Comercio*, August 21, 29, 1848; Macera, "Las plantaciones azucareras," 154–55. By South American standards a wage of 3 reals was considered low. See Engelsen, "Social Aspects," 86.

39. *El Comercio*, September 7, 1849; *El Peruano*, November 21, 1849; Stewart, *Chinese Bondage*, 13.

40. Arona, *La inmigración*, 5; Levin, *Export Economies*, 87; Stewart, *Chinese Bondage*, 13–14, 17. The best survey of this early period of Chinese immigration is Stewart, especially chap. 1.

41. *Correo de Lima*, December 2, 1851; *El Comercio*, August 2, October 18, 1851; *El Intérprete del Pueblo*, July 14, 1852; *Registro Oficial*, August 20, 1853; enclosure with Barton to Malmesbury, 23, September 24, 1852, F.O. 61/134; Sulivan to Clarendon, 108, September 25, 1854, F.O. 61/148; Macera, "Las plantaciones azucareras," 224–26; Stewart, *Chinese Bondage*, 20–21.

42. *El Correo de Lima*, October 18, 1851. For the exploitation of the coolies see Stewart, *Chinese Bondage*, 18–23 and chap. 5.

43. Mathew, "Primitive Export Sector," 44–48; Stewart, *Chinese Bondage*, 95–98; Levin, *Export Economies*, 88–89; *El Peruano*, November

9, 1854. In 1853, Elías employed six hundred coolies, fifty slaves, and around two hundred Chileans and Peruvians on the guano islands.

44. See, for example, *El Correo de Lima*, December 24, 1851.

45. *El Heraldo de Lima*, June 16, July 6, 24, 1854; Gonzales, *Plantation Agriculture*, 88; Levin, *Export Economies*, 88–89; Stewart, *Chinese Bondage*, 21–23. The ban on migration to the Chincha Islands may have been politically motivated, a result of the hostility between Echenique and Elías.

46. *El Comercio*, August 14, 1853. An advertisement in this newspaper on August 21, 1852, announced the flight of three Portuguese, two Chinese, and ten slaves from the Santa Beatriz estate. Concerning the case of Ursula Lang see "Criminal contra D. Tomás Villalva," AGN, CCrim, 1852, Leg. 606.

47. H. G. Rodewald to Barton, December 30, 1852, F.O. 177/53.

48. Markham, "Travels" 1:103. For details of Elías's life see Engelsen, "Social Aspects," 208–14, 424–75.

49. Basadre, *Historia* 3:287; Echenique, *Memorias* 1:104; Engelsen, "Social Aspects," 144–45, 454–56; Levin, *Export Economies*, 49 n. 67; Macera, "Las plantaciones azucareras," 216; Markham, "Travels" 1:117; Mathew, "Primitive Export Sector," 37–38; Yepes, *Perú*, 315 n. 1.

50. Adams to Aberdeen, 31, July 18, 1844, F.O. 61/103; Crompton to Palmerston, 22, December 30, 1847, F.O. 61/116; Engelsen, "Social Aspects," 438. For Elías's liberalism see Pike, *Modern History*, 101–2.

51. Basadre, *Historia* 3:287; Engelsen, "Social Aspects," 429, 447; Mathew, "Primitive Export Sector," 37; Vicuña, *Ocho meses*, 70; Crompton to Adams, 9, June 29, 1852, F.O. 177/53.

52. Concerning the Brazilian planters see Dean, *Rio Claro*, 51–53.

53. Romero, *Historia económica* 2:96.

# 7

# Abolitionist Pressure

In January 1822 a Peruvian report on the condition of blacks in the newly independent country remarked on how "their forebears had been snatched from their native soil by ours," how "we committed the atrocious injustice of making slaves of those who had been born free," and how since coming to Peru they had "fertilized" the soil "with their sweat."[1] Over the next three decades comments similar to these that criticized both slavery and the slave trade appeared in other reports, articles, editorials, and speeches. They were proof that among Peru's elite there were at least a few who agreed with the goals enunciated by San Martín, who found slavery a barbarous and retrograde institution, and who were determined to see it destroyed. Some Peruvians who had been converted to abolitionism demonstrated their opposition by unconditionally freeing their slaves and *libertos*. Other opponents were found among government officials. They spoke out against the system, helped to organize lotteries that freed slaves, and introduced antislavery legislation. The number of abolitionists grew over the years, so that by the early 1850s many Peruvians had joined the cause.

To see this as the development of an organized, influential, and effective movement, however, would be to overstate what was a minor factor in the process of Peruvian abolition. Despite the evidence of growing antislavery sentiment, public pressure for abolition remained weak during the decades leading up to it. Unlike other countries such as England, France, and the United States, where abolitionists organized themselves and played an important role in altering the public image of slavery and converting the uncommitted to their cause, Peru produced no identifiable abolitionist group or organized movement. The country's abolitionists were a few voices crying in the wilderness, operating individually rather than as a group, with no apparent strategy or set of goals. None of them was particularly prominent; popular support was limited. The few who appeared provided an example for others to follow, convinced at least a few of their fellow citizens of the rightness and righteousness of their cause, and comprised another of the forces chipping away inexorably at the bastion of slavery, but their numbers were as modest as their influence. In many ways they paralleled the modernizing trends of which they were a part: They helped to undermine slavery, but in and of themselves they lacked the power to force its eradication.

The limited impact of abolitionism in Peru can be explained by some of the developments that have been discussed in preceding chapters in this volume. The strength of the slaveholders, the small size of the middle class, and the importance of the slaves were all relevant factors; so, too, was the weakness of liberalism among Peruvians. In a country long dominated by conservative values this, perhaps, was to be expected. Although liberals could be found in Peru, sharing the goals espoused by liberals elsewhere in Latin America (such as independence from Spain, republicanism, popular sovereignty, individual rights, elimination of group privileges, restrictions on the church, and free trade), they were neither especially numerous nor strong enough to challenge the conservatives who ran the country in the first decades after independence. With their strength centered in the south around Arequipa, they lacked national cohesion. Moreover, the depth of their attachment to liberal goals is suspect. Many seem to have adopted liberalism merely as a convenient tool to justify separation from Spain.[2] As a result, while Peru's liberals and conservatives differed over issues, their differences did not reach the ideological intensity that led to bloody strife in Mexico and elsewhere. They were prepared to accept and adopt elements of each other's programs: Liberals supported protectionist commercial policies in the 1830s, while a conservative president introduced a liberal tariff in the early 1850s; conservative governments in the 1840s oversaw the beginning of the modernizing trends and introduced some of the more progressive economic measures of the day; a conservative churchman proposed legislation to end the slave trade.[3]

Where slavery was concerned, Peru's liberals seemed willing to accept the views of the conservatives. Not many of them extended their concept of "the liberty of man" beyond the liberation of their nation to the freedom of everyone in it. Like liberals elsewhere in Latin America, they seemed more committed to the sanctity of property rights than to human rights.[4] Even among those who supported abolition, few displayed concern for the lives of the slaves. Some expressed abhorrence of slavery because of its impact on the enslaved, but more wanted it abolished because they feared slaves or blacks in general, held slave labor in low esteem, or were concerned about slavery's effect on the slaveholding class and Peru's international reputation. Even some of those who opposed slavery because of its effects on the slaves shared these views. Their call for European immigrants to replace the freed slaves was an obvious if unstated criticism of black labor as well as a racist response that revealed their desire to "whiten" the population and assimilate the blacks. Few opponents wanted immediate abolition; they considered it too disruptive. Instead, they supported gradualism. If "gradualism was the hallmark of the liberal mind" in countries such as England, the United States, and France, where liberals and liberalism had firm roots, in Peru with its weak liberal tradition resistance to rapid change was almost to be expected among those professing a commitment to liberal ideals.[5] Moreover, they had to contend with a powerful proslavery group. The result was limited support for abolition.

Nevertheless, although the number of abolitionists was small and no formal abolitionist movement appeared in Peru, opposition developed in a variety of forms. First and foremost were the antislavery comments that appeared in the newspapers in stories, editorials, and letters from concerned individuals and groups. They reflected the views of private citizens as well as those of the newspapers themselves. Some of the latter, including *El Genio del Rimac*, a short-lived Lima newspaper that was published during the 1830s, and *El Comercio*, the influential Lima daily that first appeared in 1839, adopted an openly abolitionist stance. Their harshest language was reserved for the slave trade, which was the target of almost universal condemnation. It was described as "odious," "execrable," "criminal," "dishonorable," and a "disgraceful blemish." Any law permitting it was a "deviation from the principles of humanity and philanthropy that the civilized nations have proclaimed." Critics of the trade applauded the activities of famous opponents, such as William Wilberforce and the King of Denmark, and expressed the hope that the international nature of the antislave-trade campaign would ensure its eradication. They realized that in the case of Peru a successful campaign required the complete abolition of slavery. Until it was abolished, slaves would continue to be smuggled into the country in an illegal trade, prolonging the institution's life, perhaps to the end of the century.[6]

Opponents also took aim at slavery itself, although not as frequently as at the slave trade. It drew the same epithets: "odious," "unjust," "evil," and "an abomination." The politician Nicolás de Piérola called it "the mortal cancer of society."[7] Female slaves attracted particular attention, as opponents charged that slavery produced "immodest" women who were condemned to satiate the "brutal sensuality" of the owners. A vineyard owner who kept ten to twelve slaves for this express purpose was cited as a case in point. Critics also denounced some of the other more exploitative aspects of the institution, especially excessive whipping. A group calling itself "enemies of the lash" urged the government to abolish this form of punishment, arguing that officials were subjecting slaves to more whipping than the law allowed and were ignoring proper procedures.[8] The treatment of *libertos* was another cause for complaint. One writer pointed out that they were being sold like slaves and called on the government and the courts to correct the evil. The fact that similar concerns were being expressed thirteen years later indicates that nothing had changed. Another writer observed that *libertos* working in the fields were supposed to be paid 1 peso weekly from the time they became twenty-five. Few, however, were receiving it, even though it was only half the pay of urban domestic servants. Moreover, they were having to cope with seeing their children, who were technically free, bought and sold as if they were slaves.[9]

Criticisms of slavery because of its impact on the slaves were not uncommon, but opponents seemed more concerned about its effect on themselves and on the country as a whole. One of their chief worries was the potential for violence. Pointing to the example of Haiti, they urged abolition to prevent the same upheaval from occurring in Peru. Reinforcing their fears were the newspaper reports of Peruvian slaves who had engaged in criminal acts, agitation, and rebellion, plus the general belief that slaves were incapable of virtue and possessed inherent vices that led to crime. They praised the country's existing antislavery legislation, especially the law of the free womb, specifically on the grounds that it had prevented social disorder.[10]

Critics also attacked slavery for having failed to produce effective workers. They charged that slaves lacked skills, were unproductive, put out poor quality work, and consequently were largely to blame for Peru's economic problems. As one Ica resident wrote in 1830, the slave had little commitment to his master or his work. He was given only a shovel with which to labor, as his "clumsy and slow hands" destroyed any other instrument. The general conclusion was that slavery had not transformed the slaves into useful or productive members of society and that, therefore, there was no economic reason to maintain it.[11]

A further concern was the institution's negative impact on slaveholders, who were described as a haughty, arrogant, callous, sensual, and ignorant group who were "accustomed to despising humanity." Their character flaws were blamed on their ownership of slaves. However, these same people were Peru's major landholders, and abolitionists accepted that agriculture had to be protected. They consequently agreed on the necessity for finding alternative workers, while arguing that the planters should be educated in the advantages of free wage labor.[12]

Finally, commentators expressed dissatisfaction about the impact that slavery had on the nation's reputation. An article in *El Comercio* in 1852 charged that Peru "appears before the civilized world more backward and less human than the Berber states" because of slavery, which it described as barbaric, and called the campaign for its rapid and total destruction a "holy cause." The newspaper was not above altering the facts to try to prove its point. Its claim that slavery existed in only five of Peru's sixty-four provinces, four in the department of Lima and one in La Libertad, was patently untrue, as was its conclusion that slavery was irrelevant to the country.[13] Nonetheless, the article indicated Peruvian sensitivity to the actions and attitudes of what were called the "civilized nations." As those nations condemned and abolished slavery, more and more Peruvians seemed to accept the idea that they should follow suit as quickly as possible.

Sentiments such as these were not restricted to the press and the private sector. Officials at various levels of government also opposed slavery and the slave trade and were equally open in expressing their beliefs. The officials who most consistently attacked slavery were the slaves' principal legal defenders, the *defensores de menores*. Conversant with their clients' legal rights and aware of the abuse and exploitation they had to suffer, most of the *defensores* were probably abolitionists. Their actions in assisting the slaves suggest as much, and occasionally they revealed their views during a trial. In 1839 a Trujillo *defensor* during a case involving an increase in the valuation of a slave dismissed the slave trade as having been "condemned by all the cultured nations," while Peruvian slavery was condemned by Peruvian law, which prohibited anyone from being born a slave in Peru. He argued that anyone who put obstacles in the way of a slave obtaining his or her freedom was challenging the spirit of this law.[14]

Another group of officials who seemed to have reservations about slavery were judges in the civil and criminal courts. Their attitude was evident in their willingness to ignore or interpret proslavery laws very narrowly while construing antislavery legislation broadly. As has been shown already in this volume, they implemented the constitutional restrictions concerning the importation of slaves and the enslavement of the newborn, and they freed slaves who had been mistreated as well as *libertos* whose care and education had not been properly supplied. Despite the lack of consistency in their rulings, they decided often enough in favor of the slaves that complaints were aired and charges made that judges were responding more to the concerns of the slaves than to those of the owners.

This may have been true, yet judges and members of the legal profession in general were hardly antislavery extremists, and their opposition was on an individual basis, not as a group. They expressed many of the worries that were appearing in the press, and like the press they had no desire to effect profound socioeconomic change. A court that refused to apply Gamarra's 1839 decree extending the period of patronal control condemned slavery, but on the grounds that it retarded agricultural productivity and hindered European immigration. It claimed that slavery was responsible for the small percentage of the land that was being cultivated, imperfectly and superficially, and that immigrants would not work alongside slaves. The court also expressed concern about the possibility of social unrest, noting the large number of naked and hungry blacks who were begging for money and attacking travelers.[15] Like the country's liberals, the court emphasized slow, deliberate change with a minimum of disruption. These views were encapsulated in an antislavery speech delivered by Dr. Juan J. Quintanilla on the occasion of his incorporation into the college of lawyers of Lima in 1851. He called for gradual, nonviolent abolition. Rapid abolition, he argued, would result in "social destruction," as the slaves, who had been brutalized, would seek revenge on their former owners and thereby hinder progress. Like other supporters of abolition, Quintanilla had absorbed many of the racist ideas of the day. He recommended that measures be taken before abolition to increase the slaves' intelligence and to educate them on how to use their new freedom.[16]

More influential than the judiciary were the executive and legislative branches of government. They had the power to pass antislavery legislation. Although in general they tended to support the slaveholders, nonetheless not every one of them shared the prevailing view. One president who was an outspoken opponent of slavery, and unique in this regard, was Andrés de Santa Cruz. According to his minister of foreign affairs, Santa Cruz considered the slave trade to have "degraded the human race, condemned man to the base price of the marketplace, and transformed reason into barbarism."[17] During his brief presidency he made numerous attempts to improve the lot of the slaves. Some legislators displayed a similar frame of mind. In October 1827, Ruiz Dávila, a deputy, introduced a proposal that would have permitted slaves to marry, to change owners on request, and to have their values determined when they wished. It was opposed by the deputy for La Libertad but passed to the chamber's constitutional and legislative commissions, where it seems to have died.[18] Between May and August 1831 the senate and the deputies discussed a number of possible slave laws, the most significant of which was the lower body's proposal to establish a maximum price for slaves and to give them, especially those who were ill or who had been excessively punished, more opportunities for obtaining their freedom. The proposal was in response to an argument that the internal slave trade was hurting agriculture and cutting into urban labor, as well as a desire to improve the lot of the slaves. It failed, however, to win executive support, for the government was still trying to undo the liberators' antislavery measures, such as Bolívar's order permitting slaves to change their owners, which was rescinded that year.[19]

In the 1840s the number of antislavery voices in congress multiplied and became more strident, as the slaveholders intensified their counterattack and tried to reopen the slave trade while Great Britain increased its pressure to end the international slave trade. Those who supported slavery still enjoyed a majority in congress, but the opposition was becoming more visible in both the executive council and the legislature. In May 1840 the council of state proposed a treaty that would have prohibited Peruvians from participating in the slave trade anywhere in the world, would have marked those who ignored the treaty as pirates, and would have established a joint commission with Great Britain to decide on the disposition of anyone arrested, their ships, and their slaves. It was widely supported, since the campaign to end the slave trade was seen as "morally right"—a factor, no doubt, in the rejection of Francisco Javier Calvo's proposal to reopen the slave trade in September.[20]

When the government reconsidered his proposal four years later at the behest of Senator Lucas Fonseca, the opposition had intensified, and even Calvo no longer supported it. In June the council of state unanimously rejected reintroducing this "detestable commerce" and equally opposed the second proposal to allow the importation of slaves from other American states. It was left unmoved by the argument that the status of the imported slaves would improve in Peru, explaining "the remedy proposed is worse than the illness it is trying to cure." Displaying an unexpected liberalism, the council ignored the recent constitutional changes on the issue. It argued that according to Peruvian law any slave who arrived in Peru was legally free, while African slaves could not be imported since trading humans who were born free was prohibited. It agreed to consult with congress to decide on the status of slaves who entered Peru as fugitives and those who arrived in service, although members seemed to view them as free; they referred to the decree of November 24, 1821, that declared free all slaves who arrived in Peru, an interpretation supported by the supreme court. The council of state also urged congress to promote immigration in order to obtain the workers required for the moribund agrarian sector.[21]

When the majority in the more conservative senate chose to ignore the lead taken by the executive and approved a new project permitting the importation of slaves from other American republics, it was attacked by some of its own members and by the public at large. One senator, Gervasio Alvarez, called the bill a reactionary step and slavery "as detestable as despotism." "Does not admitting slavery to the classic soil of freedom harm the development of the independence process, justice, humanity, and even the neighboring states that have renounced this disgraceful and horrible traffic?" he asked, eloquently embroidering the truth about his homeland. He questioned the legality of enslaving people whose ancestors had been free, as well as the difference between American and African blacks that permitted enslaving the former and not the latter. He wondered who would be allowed to import the slaves and what methods would be used to ensure that those imported were indeed slaves. He shared the view that wage labor was more economical than slavery and concluded that the senate was merely pandering to the interests of the hacendados.

Elsewhere the proposal "excited a considerable sensation, and very unanimous reprobation from the public press," according to the British minister. *El Comercio* had not expected this result, and in a series of editorials it challenged the reasons advanced by the senate to justify its actions. It described the slave trade as "unjust and barbarous" and beyond further comment. It rejected the contention that Peru was short of alternative workers, noting that while the senate had been approving its project, a deputy had been requesting a prohibition on the importation of foreign manufactured goods in order to create domestic jobs for the locally unemployed. It argued that slaves were not the only workers who could cultivate Peru's soil successfully, pointing out that since independence coastal sugar production had doubled with better methods and the application of machinery, not with more slaves, and that free indigenous workers in the departments of Chiclayo and Lambayeque produced the cheapest sugar in Peru.

The newspaper also questioned the senate's statistics showing that the value of agricultural lands had declined by five sixths in recent years because of a lack of workers. It listed a number of estates using free labor that were producing more than slave estates. It wondered about the source of the new slaves. Although Ecuador was frequently mentioned, the paper was skeptical, claiming that Ecuadorian slaves were much better treated than Peruvian ones and unlikely to migrate. It criticized the senate for failing to consider the question of the morality of slavery and referred to other slaveholding nations, such as the United States and Venezuela, that did not permit the importation of slaves. It concluded by urging the deputies not to follow the senate's example and approve this project that was "contrary to the religion of Jesus Christ and the institutions of the country."[22] The antislavery forces, however, were no match for those who wanted an injection of servile labor, and the project passed.

The setback produced no significant backlash, indicating further the weakness of those opposing slavery. In August 1845 the British minister wrote to Lord Aberdeen that there was still no abolitionist party in Peru, "nor does the subject seem to have occupied public attention in any political sense." Concern about the slave trade may have been rising, for one year later the new British minister wrote that two parties existed, of which one was against the trade while the other supported it, but he was uncertain which predominated.[23] The only other antislavery response at the time was a congressional attempt to help the *libertos*. In September 1845, Juan Arenaza, a deputy from Arequipa, introduced a project to abolish Gamarra's law of 1839, which had extended the period of patronal control. After a preamble, which described slavery as a kind of barbarism and noted that all the cultured nations of Europe and the nonslave states of America had abolished slavery as contrary to natural and divine law, that the Peruvian constitution prohibited slaves being born or imported into Peru, and that the congress of Huancayo had sentenced those born free to fifty years of slavery, it called for the abolition of the 1839 decree and the reinstitution of all previous laws concerning *libertos*.[24] However, it failed to pass.

The efforts of congressmen, government leaders, newspapermen, lawyers, judges, and private citizens may not have been successful in bringing about the immediate and unconditional end of slavery in Peru, but at least they had shown that there were Peruvians in addition to those in the country's black community who opposed slavery. While their numbers may not have been large, their attacks and legislative projects kept the issue of slavery and its associated problems alive in the public mind. And they had indicated that they had no intention of giving up the fight despite their limited success so far.

Other Peruvians who revealed at least some reservations about slavery during these years were those who were freeing their slaves. Not many can be considered abolitionists, for they usually delayed emancipation until they were beyond the need of worldly servants, but in the long run they may have been more important than the writers and critics in undermining slavery, for their actions actually reduced the numbers left in bondage. While in some instances emancipation may have been conditional upon the slave performing further service or designed to save the cost of maintaining an ill or aged slave, in others it was an unconditional reward for past service or the manifestation of a conversion to abolitionism. Rosa Rodríguez y Riquelme, the sister of Bernardo O'Higgins, freed as a reward for good service a slave she had inherited from her brother. Micaela Puertas left instructions for the freeing of her slave Silveria in recognition of her affection, goodwill, and service, which were like those of a daughter, "conduct quite rare at this time when it is very common for slaves to have no affection or love for their owners." She had nothing else to leave Silveria. Others provided their freed slaves with accommodation, utensils, and food, or, in one case, a shop as a source of income. Father Juan José Alvares left instructions in his will that his slaves Juana and Pedro Nolasco were to be freed unconditionally as a reward for their faithfulness, love, and conscientious service. Pedro was also to receive 100 pesos, while Juana was left 200 pesos, any utensils she needed, and the services of a slave for the rest of her life. If the latter served Juana well, he was to be freed on her death. Alvares also instructed that a *liberta* nine years of age be sold and the money given to the poor, but that she was to be freed when she reached twenty-five.[25]

The number of manumitted slaves could be substantial. Hipólito de Bracamonte (the marquis of Herrera y Valle Hermoso and count of Valdelomar de Bracamonte) freed all the slaves on his Chiclín and Sausal estates conditional upon their remaining until his death. He provided them with wages, food, clothing, and cigars and warned his foremen that any mistreatment of them would result in dismissal. Following his death, in April 1846, the slaves were unconditionally freed as promised, and all of them were reported to have attended his funeral.[26]

Even the government of President Gamarra got into the act of freeing slaves. It freed only a handful, suggesting that the aim was more for social control than for humanitarian reasons. Nevertheless, by its actions it had reduced the number of remaining slaves. Simultaneously, and perhaps more importantly, it created the impression that it was less committed to slavery's survival than were the slaveholders. The lucky slaves were chosen by a public lottery that was held in 1840 as part of the anniversary celebrations marking Gamarra's victory over Santa Cruz. On July 15 the president declared "that no demonstration of rejoicing is more reasonable, more appropriate for a civilized and democratic people, and more in agreement with the spirit of our unique laws than the manumission of some slaves." It was a sharp contrast to the proslavery legislation of the previous year and may have been designed to counter some of the residual animosity. The implementation of the decree indicated that there had been no real change in governmental philosophy. The authorities compiled a list of all the slaves of the province of Lima for the draw. The government agreed to reimburse the owners of the slaves chosen, but its generosity was rather limited. Only four names were drawn: those of three men and one woman. A spokesman explained that the number was dictated by the desperate state of the national treasury and promised more lotteries in the future, but eleven years would pass before the next occurred.[27]

These examples of abolitionist pressure in early republican Peru, even when added together, leave a sense of disinterest and ineffectiveness. The attacks on slavery had been infrequent and unorganized. Opposition had tended to be uncoordinated and on an individual basis. The commitment to the abolitionist cause had not approached the level that slavery's supporters had displayed. The weaknesses of the antislavery forces help to explain why by 1850 there was still no organized abolitionist movement in Peru, or even an identifiable abolitionist group.

Yet, despite problems, the picture was not entirely without its hopeful signs. Antislavery pressure had been exerted, and the slavery system had been undermined to some extent. During the 1850s more forceful challenges would be mounted, challenges that may have had their roots in the earlier developments. Alternatively, they may have been a response to the growing liberal trends that were evident in all of Latin America from the 1840s onward.[28] They may have been tied to the socioeconomic changes that were occurring in Peru at this time, or they may have been a result of external antislavery pressures. Regardless of where they originated, abolitionist voices were growing in volume, and even conservatives were joining the chorus. One result was some of the most dramatic antislavery acts since the liberators' legislation of the 1820s.

The government played an important role in these new attacks on slavery. In 1851, Bartolomé Herrera, the minister of government and foreign relations and a well-known conservative, asked the chamber of deputies to put together a law prohibiting the African slave trade. The relevant constitutional article, he explained, was no longer in force. He noted Britain's long crusade, "based on the laws of humanity and civilization," to declare the slave trade piracy, and the support that the United States, Russia, the German Confederation, and other nations had lent that crusade. The time had come for Peru to follow suit. While recognizing the right of property in slaves and thus the continuation of slavery, Herrera argued, "We cannot permit the abuse of enslaving men to continue. Peru cannot remain indifferent any longer in the midst of this censure with which the civilized world wishes to extirpate the monstrous crime of buying and selling men." The deputies' proposal was submitted to the chamber's legislative committee with the request that it be given preferential treatment. Simultaneously Herrera was trying to end the movement of slaves between Peru and Brazil. In September he signed the Herrera-Da Ponte Ribeyro Convention that closed this trade route.[29]

That same year the government held a second lottery for freeing slaves. Again the lottery was limited to the province of Lima, with its 329 urban and 670 rural slaves, but this time eight names were drawn. Six women and two men, three of them estate slaves and at least six of them over the age of fifty, received their freedom as a result of the draw. It prompted the observation that perhaps one day, "not very distant," every slave would be free.[30]

The following year President Echenique's government made a further dent in slavery's armor. It issued a Civil Code that systematized for the first time all the civil legislation that affected the people of Peru, with sections specifically directed at slaves, *libertos*, and *ingenuos*. In general the code compiled existing legislation, but where slaves and their offspring were concerned the most liberal laws and interpretations available appear to have been selected. By listing all of the slaves' rights, the code rejected one of the principal arguments of slaveholders: that slaves were "things." It recognized the civil rights of slaves, *libertos*, and *ingenuos*, considering the latter free. It declared that the only slaves were those who had not been free before Peru's independence; anyone born in or brought to Peru subsequently was a *liberto* or free. Owners had to supply their slaves with food, protection, and medical assistance. The lowest listed price of a slave could not be increased, and any violation of this clause would result in the slave's lowest price being cut in half. Slaves could not be sold distant from their place of residence unless they or a court approved. They could not be separated from a spouse or from children who were minors. They could change owners as they wished. They could obtain their freedom if their owner freed them or abandoned them for three years, through self-purchase or testamentary concession, or by saving the life of or marrying their owner. *Libertos* enjoyed the same civil rights as free persons, except for the service that they owed their masters, and they could demand their complete freedom if their master failed to feed, clothe, and educate them for a full year. Slaves still lacked complete equality, but as a result of the Civil Code their situation had improved markedly, and they now knew what they could demand and expect from their owners.[31]

Some hacendados asked the government to abrogate the articles giving complete civil rights to *ingenuos*, but otherwise the code was generally approved, perhaps because it maintained the gradualism that had marked the movement toward abolition since independence. As *El Intérprete del Pueblo*, a Lima newspaper, noted,

> Without altering essentially the previous laws, the codes have clarified and smoothed them in such a way that, without hurting the proprietor, they have prepared the road to freedom; they have taken into account that the slave is a man, and that his natural feelings cannot be violated with impunity; . . . the spirit of our codes is to recognize that the state of slavery is a transitory situation and that everything leads to the abolition of servitude; they preserve slavery only so as not to harm the owner, but they remove from the latter all prospect for speculating with the blood of his brother.[32]

More dramatic than the government's attacks was the action taken by a prominent official, planter, and slaveholder who came to the sudden realization that slavery was an evil, that it should end immediately, and that a public demonstration of his feelings would have widespread repercussions. Alfonso González Pinillos was a former professor of law and deputy for Trujillo and, in 1852, a member of the superior court. He was also a slaveholder, the owner of the Cajanleque and Nepén estates in the Chicama Valley, but in the early 1850s he experienced a sudden conversion to the abolitionist cause. He had bought and sold slaves and *libertos* in 1851, but on January 23, 1852, "moved by sentiments of humanity and justice," he freed all that he owned. The reason for his conversion is not clear. He may have thought that it was time to apply the concepts of equality that he had been teaching; he may have discovered that his slaves were more expensive than the free workers he employed. One definite factor had been the demands and concerns expressed by the Chicama Valley slaves during the rebellion of the previous year. Whatever his motivation he freed, according to his tombstone, 136 slaves. Of these, 32 came from Nepén, 71 from Cajanleque, and 9 were domestic slaves. Other slaveholders had freed their blacks before him but González Pinillos's act was different in that he attached no conditions to the manumission and he did it with great fanfare. It was the most widely publicized case of its sort during the republican era. He used the opportunity to condemn slavery and, by inference, his slave-owning colleagues. Freeing his slaves, he said, was "demanded by the light of civilization, by the eternal and sacred rights of man," as slavery was "an irritating anachronism, a criminal usurpation, a stupid remnant of cruel barbarism."

He was widely applauded for his act. Officials in Trujillo commended his "humane example." *El Comercio* wrote that it provided "immense pleasure," and the following year when the newspaper published *Uncle Tom's Cabin* it dedicated the work to him. *El Intérprete del Pueblo* commented that he had won "the respect and sympathy of his fellow citizens and the entire world. For this humanitarian and magnificent act, we are pleased to congratulate the noble magistrate from Trujillo who has provided the country with such a fine and fruitful example."

Not everyone felt this way. Friends in Trujillo condemned him, claiming he had demoralized the slaves. One critic charged that his former slaves had lost their source of food, clothing, medical treatment, and education, that is, "all the things a father provides his child." He added that the blacks were not really free because their lack of education opened them to continuing exploitation. He, however, had ignored or chosen to overlook the fact that González Pinillos had offered his former slaves work on his estates as wage laborers.[33]

The attacks on slavery were accompanied by new antislavery publications in the press. The most influential of these was a translation of Harriet Beecher Stowe's *Uncle Tom's Cabin* that was serialized in *El Comercio* between February 21 and May 14, 1853. It subsequently was published in book form, appeared in a dramatic version on the Lima stage in 1854, and has been cited as a factor in arousing popular opinion against slavery.[34] The aggressiveness of the antislavery voices also seemed to be intensifying. In September 1854, *El Heraldo de Lima* took not only the slaveholders but also the entire nation to task in a vituperative attack that charged:

> You have preserved slavery without knowing what to do with the slave except make him an enemy of his race, a *montonero*, a bandit. According to what has suited your interests, you have unchained his passions, flattering him on some occasions and tormenting him without measure on others. You have whipped him to cultivate your haciendas, you have intoxicated him and put a club in his hand to lead him to elections, you have armed him with a carbine and a sword to fight against this government or that party, and afterwards you have confined him in his slave hut with stocks and shackles at his bedside. By dint of repeating the word *equality* to the people, you have left the impression that in our country complete and absolute equality must exist, and that in its shadows even the inequalities created by nature disappear.[35]

The movement toward abolition seemed to be gaining momentum. Some Peruvians appeared convinced that slavery was about to end. One, a prospective slave buyer, published an advertisement in *El Correo de Lima* in 1851 (under the eye-catching title, "Communism Is Coming") that read: "In New Granada there are no slaves; in Ecuador now it is questionable whether there will be any; soon they will not want us to have them here in Peru; but before that occurs I require a slave who is a good seamstress."[36]

Despite the increased antislavery activity, however, there was still very little in the way of hard evidence to support conjectures such as this one that abolition was imminent. An organized movement still did not exist to press the crusade forward to its conclusion. Support for abolition remained limited, and even those who had emerged as leaders in the struggle showed themselves to be less than totally committed to the idea of complete and immediate emancipation. *El Comercio* maintained its policy of printing advertisements for the purchase and sale of slaves, even while it was criticizing slavery in its editorials and publishing *Uncle Tom's Cabin.* During the months that it serialized the novel, it published advertisements that offered slaves for sale, sought slaves for purchase, and listed runaways and the rewards for their capture. Many of these fugitives were in their teens or younger, so that they were *libertos,* not slaves. The government, too, had not accepted abolition. While its Civil Code may have circumscribed slavery, it continued to recognize the right of property in a person.

In other words, organized abolitionist pressures were still weak and uncertain. They had helped to undermine slavery but had not developed into a separate and identifiable force driving the country toward abolition. This pattern was not unique to Peru: In Cuba the abolitionist movement was similarly limited and slow to appear.[37] An obvious reason for this in the case of Peru was the continuing strong support for slavery and the slave trade. The majority of Peru's elite seem to have had few moral qualms about actively supporting slavery or remaining neutral on the issue. Economic pressures to get them to change their minds were notable for their absence. Further weakening the abolitionist cause were the facts that liberalism was a constrained force in the country and Peruvian liberals were inconsistent where slavery was concerned. Again this was not unique to Peru, for reputed liberals in other slaveholding countries displayed similar inconsistencies.[38] Taken together, all of these factors resulted in a gradual drift in the direction of abolition, without any clear route and with no certain or specific date for arrival.

The ineffectiveness of Peru's abolitionists explains in part why slavery survived, why the slaves and *libertos* continued to be exploited, and why blacks took matters into their own hands to alter the situation. Since the white community was unwilling or incapable of taking on the task set out by San Martín to end slavery once and for all, the black community had to assume the obligation. They were compelled to resist almost by default. Because of the weak abolitionist movement, it was the slaves who were in the forefront challenging the system. It was their resistance, not the opposition of the whites, that was vital to the withering away and eventual collapse of Peruvian slavery.

## Notes

1. *Correo Mercantil*, January 3, 1822.

2. For early republican liberalism and the liberal-conservative conflict see Cotler, *Clases, estado y nación*, 74–82; Daniel Gleason, "Anti-Democratic Thought in Early Republican Peru: Bartolomé Herrera and the Liberal-Conservative Ideological Struggle," *The Americas* 38 (1981): 205–17; Gootenberg, *Between Silver and Guano*, chap. 2; Fredrick B. Pike, "Heresy, Real and Alleged, in Peru: An Aspect of the Conservative-Liberal Struggle, 1830–1875," *HAHR* 47 (1967): 50–74; Romero, *Historia económica* 2:16; Charles Walker, "The Social Bases of Political Conflict in Peru, 1820–1845" (Paper presented at the 46th International Congress of Americanists, Amsterdam, July 1988), 5–6; and Yepes, *Perú*, 38–40.

3. For tariff policies see Gootenberg, *Between Silver and Guano*; Gootenberg, "Social Origins," 331, 335, 351; *El Peruano*, November 8, 1848.

4. For a brief discussion of similar attitudes among nineteenth-century liberals in Argentina see Andrews, *Afro-Argentines*, 47–48. Concerning the hesitancy of liberals throughout Latin America in the 1830s and 1840s about abolition see Safford, "Politics, Ideology and Society," 88.

5. Davis, *Problem of Slavery*, chap. 2 and 258–59.

6. Criticism of the slave trade became particularly acute at times when the government was considering reestablishing it in some form. See *El Meridiano*, November 3, 1833; *El Comercio*, September 11, 1841, August 20, 1845, July 26, 1848.

7. *El Genio del Rimac*, November 6, 1833; *El Comercio*, August 19, 1845; *El Peruano*, January 4, 1854. Piérola was the father of the later president of the same name.

8. *El Comercio*, March 20, 24, 26, 1847.

9. *El Genio del Rimac*, November 4, 1833, February 7, 1835; *El Comercio*, July 18, 1848, February 17, 1851.

10. *El Genio del Rimac*, November 4, 1833; *El Comercio*, August 8, 1845.

11. *La Miscelánea*, August 11, 1830; *El Genio del Rimac*, November 4, 1833; *El Comercio*, July 26, 1848.

12. *El Genio del Rimac*, November 4, 6, 1833; *El Comercio*, August 19, 1845.

13. *El Comercio*, December 27, 1852.

14. AAL, Apelaciones: Trujillo, 1830–1851, Leg. 44.

15. In one case, the courts freed the children of a slave whose late owner's husband had failed to comply with testamentary instructions that they be educated. See *El Peruano*, August 25, 1841. For other cases see *El Comercio*, February 10, 11, 14, 16, 23, 25, March 7, 1843, July 18, 1846.

16. *El Comercio*, April 2, 1851.

17. Enclosure with Wilson to Palmerston, ST5, December 12, 1838, F.O. 84/260.

18. *El Telégrafo de Lima*, October 23, 1827.

19. *El Conciliador*, August 3, 1831; Dancuart, *Crónica parlamentaria* 2:13, 14, 20, 23, 37.

20. *El Comercio*, June 2, 1840; *El Peruano*, September 15, 1841. See also Chapter 3 in this volume.

21. *El Comercio*, June 11, 26, 1845; Basadre, *Historia* 3:188.

22. Dancuart, *Crónica parlamentaria* 3:54; *El Peruano*, June 25, 1845; *El Comercio*, July 30, 31, August 1, 2, 4, 5, 7, 1845; Adams to Aberdeen, ST10, December 30, 1845, F.O. 84/595.

23. Enclosure with Adams to Aberdeen, ST5, August 4, 1845, F.O. 84/595; Barton to Palmerston, 3, October 10, 1846, F.O. 61/111.

24. *El Comercio*, September 10, 1845.

25. For examples of owners freeing their slaves see AGN, Notarial, Ignacio Ayllón Salazar, 1824, Prot. 41; AGN, Notarial, Eduardo Huerta, 1834–35, Prot. 267, 1839–40, Prot. 270; AGN, Notarial, Gerónimo de Villafuerte, 1848–1851, Prot. 1027; AD-A, Notarial, Juan N. Pastor, 1854–55, Prot. 775; AD-LL, División Notarial, Escrituras, José V. Aguilar, 1846–47, Leg. 409, 1850–51, Leg. 411, 1850–1852, Leg. 412; AD-LL, División Notarial, Escrituras, Juan de la Cruz Ortega, 1850–51, Leg. 454; AAL, CCiv, 1827–1831, Leg. 231; AAL, CCiv, 1837–1843, Leg. 233, LIX:19; AAL, CCiv, 1844–1847, Leg. 234; AAL, Causas de Negros, 1815–1855, Leg. 36, LXII:12.

26. Héctor Centurión Vallejo has written that this involved 115 slaves. However, when Bracamonte rented Chiclín in 1845, only 27 slaves were part of the transaction. See Centurión Vallejo, "Esclavitud y manumisión," 61–62; and AD-LL, División Notarial, Escrituras, José V. Aguilar, 1845, Leg. 408, 66.

27. *El Peruano*, July 22, 29, 1840; *El Comercio*, July 27, 29, 1840.

28. Safford, "Politics, Ideology and Society," 96.

29. Palmerston to Adams, ST1, March 10, 1851, F.O. 84/853; Palmerston to Adams, ST3, May 19, 1851, F.O. 84/853; Adams to Palmerston, ST4, October 4, 1851, F.O. 84/853; Adams to Palmerston, ST5, November 8, 1851, F.O. 84/853; Adams to Palmerston, ST2, February 8, 1852, F.O. 84/884; Perú, *Diario de los debates de la cámara de diputados: congreso de 1851* (Lima, n.d.), September 20, 1851; *Registro Oficial*, September 27, 1851; Dancuart, *Anales* 5:153; Basadre, *Historia* 3:320, 335; Roberto MacLean y Estenos, *Negros en el nuevo mundo* (Lima, 1948), 143.

30. *El Comercio*, July 29, 1851.

31. Miguel Antonio de la Lama, *Código civil del Perú con citas, notas, concordancias y un apendice* (Lima, 1893), 22–25; Perú, *Código de enjuiciamientos en materia civil del Perú* (Lima, 1852), 246–47; Basadre, *Historia* 4:112–13; Jorge Eugenio Castañeda, "El negro en el Perú," *Mercurio Peruano* 490 (1972): 92–93.

32. *El Intérprete del Pueblo*, July 28, 1852.

33. AD-LL, División Notarial, Escrituras, José V. Aguilar, 1850–1852, Leg. 412, 107, 131, 155, 156, 163; *El Comercio*, February 5, 11, 1852; *El Intérprete del Pueblo*, February 9, 1852; Basadre, *Historia* 3:191; Centurión Vallejo, *Esclavitud y manumisión*, 27–35; Rebaza, *Anales del departamento*, 290–91.

34. Basadre, *Historia* 4:56, 69; *El Comercio*, June 17, 18, 1853.

35. *El Heraldo de Lima*, September 6, 1854.

36. *El Correo de Lima*, November 17, 1851.

37. See Scott, *Slave Emancipation*, 284.

38. In England, Quakers had profited from slavery and the slave trade; in the United States there were similar contradictions in the first decades following independence. See Davis, *Problem of Slavery*, 152–59, 237.

# 8

# Foreign Involvement

In addition to the internal forces that were weakening Peruvian slavery during the first three decades after independence, pressures were being exerted by foreign nations. Of these Great Britain was the most influential. Its crusade to eradicate the international slave trade and, eventually, to abolish slavery in all its guises included Peru within its purview. Pressure also came from Brazil and New Granada, although any influence they might have had was circumscribed to a great extent by the fact that they, too, were slaveholding countries. Indeed, their involvement may have been intended simply to prevent their slaves from being exported to Peru. More influential were those European nations that manifested the growing international reprobation of the slave trade and slavery. They provided a model of what was considered to be "civilized" behavior, a model that members of the Peruvian elite sought to imitate. For some this included accepting the idea of abolition. Pressure from abroad also made clear to all of Peru's slaveholders that they could not expect to reopen the slave trade on a scale that would permit slavery's survival. They were going to have to prepare for abolition and consider using alternative means of labor.

Nonetheless, foreign pressure by and of itself did not end Peruvian slavery. The distances involved, the chronic political unrest in Peru, and the xenophobia of Peruvian governments all limited the power that foreign countries could wield. Moreover, foreign nations lacked any kind of leverage that might have compelled Peru to follow their wishes. Their involvement was another of the elements that were weakening Peruvian slavery, undermining domestic support, and assisting in the creation of an environment that made emancipation possible, but alone it was incapable of forcing the slaveholders and the government to agree to the abolition of slavery.

Outside pressure on Latin American slavery, in the form of British demands, began even before the colonies had secured their independence. Britain's support for the rebels had been conditional upon their prior condemnation of slavery and the slave trade. Its subsequent recognition of the new states required, among other things, that they abjure and abolish the slave trade.[1] Britain would eventually direct its crusading zeal at the institution of slavery as a whole, but during the 1820s slavery was still legal in parts of its empire, so its efforts at this time were aimed at ending the international slave trade. Because of San Martín's antislavery legislation and the 1823 constitution with its article abolishing the slave trade, Peru seemed to be in step with British concerns—even if the constitution never was implemented. Moreover, in 1826, at the Congress of Panama, Peruvian delegates introduced a proposal that called for cooperation in the abolition and extirpation of the African slave trade.[2]

Three years later, Peru signed a peace treaty with Colombia containing articles that committed the two countries to cooperate in the complete eradication of the African slave trade and that declared any Peruvian or Colombian involved in the trade a pirate.[3] With Peru expressing open opposition to the international slave trade, the British seemed prepared to accept that slavery would continue in that country. In 1826 the British consul explained to the Foreign Office that immediate abolition would be "impracticable" at that time, since "the manumission of the slaves, who are the only cultivators of the soil, would be followed by their desertion from the Estates on which they were employed; and . . . the Landholders would hence be exposed to have their lands left waste."[4] The Foreign Office adopted a policy that corresponded closely with the wishes of the Peruvian government and the planter class: Peruvians would be allowed to maintain their slavery system as they wished, as long as they condemned and refused to participate in the international slave trade.

British policy with regard to this trade became increasingly rigid following the appointment of Viscount Palmerston as foreign secretary in 1830. Palmerston was committed to the complete extirpation of the slave trade, and one area of his concern was Latin America.[5] To secure its abolition in the region he tried to compel the Latin American states to sign either formal slave-trade treaties or other treaties that included slave-trade clauses. A proposed treaty of amity, commerce, and navigation with Peru in 1832 contained the article that the two countries would cooperate in the "total abolition of the slave trade, and . . . prohibit all persons inhabiting within the Territories of Peru, or Subject to their Jurisdiction, in the most effectual manner, and by the most solemn Laws, from taking any share in such trade."[6] The proposal seemed to be little more than a formalization of existing relations. Peru's past opposition to the slave trade was well known, and the negotiations for the friendship treaty seemed to indicate that its attitude had not changed.

In 1835, however, the situation changed dramatically as a result of Salaverry's decision to permit the reopening of the slave trade. Although Britain had become committed to the total destruction of slavery following its abolition throughout the British Empire two years earlier, its primary concern continued to be the international slave trade.[7] The British consul general, Belford Hinton Wilson, therefore responded immediately and critically to the Peruvian initiative. He delivered a protest to the Peruvian foreign minister, in which he noted his own nation's "philanthropic exertions . . . to effect the total extinction of the Slave Trade: and, with this view, to induce Foreign Countries, by amicable representations, to unite with it in its endeavours to procure the mitigation and the gradual suppression of slavery, by prohibiting any future importation of Slaves into their respective Dominions." He lauded Peru's past actions in terminating the slave trade upon its declaration of independence and in "adopting effectual measures for the gradual and final suppression of Slavery within its Territories." These were "fully appreciated by His Majesty's Government, and by all others co-operating with it in the cause of civilization and humanity." He warned that he was required to communicate the Peruvian government's decree to London, but before doing so he wanted to know whether the proposed trade would involve all of North and South America or only the Spanish American republics. He concluded that he regretted sincerely "a measure which may possibly be construed as a retrogression from those principles of philanthropy uniformly acted on by Peru since her own declaration of independence."

The Peruvian foreign minister tried to allay British concerns. He explained that his government was taking the present action because of the deteriorating state of agriculture, which was a result of a shortage of workers. He stated that the decree only applied to the Spanish American republics, "in which the condition of the Slaves never has been, or is, so happy as in Peru," and claimed that it was a provisional measure that "should be considered more as a mitigation of the rigors of Slavery than as a stimulus to promote its traffic."

British worries may have been soothed to some extent by Wilson's prescient prediction that no trade would develop. He forwarded the decree and his correspondence to the Foreign Office, dismissing the claim that Peruvian slavery was more benign than elsewhere in Spanish America and commenting that the decree violated the constitution but probably not Peru's treaty with Colombia, which referred only to the African slave trade. He believed that no slaves were likely to come from Colombia, since it, too, suffered from a shortage of workers.[8] Any further action that he might take now became virtually impossible because of the political chaos that divided the Peruvian nation. When Wilson was instructed by the Foreign Office in May 1836 to cooperate with his Brazilian counterpart in pushing for treaties abolishing the slave trade and declaring involvement in it piracy, the two men decided to delay approaching the Peruvian government until the crisis was resolved.

In August of that year the situation appeared to change in Britain's favor with the victory of the liberal Andrés de Santa Cruz. Wilson presented his instructions to the new government and found a sympathetic audience, although a still-hesitant one. Santa Cruz indicated that he had no personal objection to a treaty abolishing the slave trade, but he was not prepared to support it now, "dreading that it might prejudice his Government with the Slave Owners . . . who are anxious for the promulgation of an enactment doing away with the Law for the Abolition of Slavery in Peru; for replacing those already emancipated by it in a state of Slavery; and for allowing in future the Importation of Slaves from Africa."[9] Nevertheless, Wilson achieved a minor success. In June 1837, Santa Cruz signed a treaty of amity, commerce, and navigation with Britain that included a slave-trade clause. According to Article 14, the two governments would cooperate "for the total abolition of the Slave Trade, and to prohibit all persons inhabiting within the Territories of the Peru-Bolivian Confederation . . . from taking any share in such trade."[10] It did not meet all British demands, but the British were hopeful that this would soon be rectified. In 1838, Santa Cruz expressed his willingness to negotiate a formal treaty "for the entire suppression of the Slave Trade." The Foreign Office responded by offering to use the Royal Navy and British courts for all the police and judicial work involved in catching and prosecuting slave traders. Although it made the offer as an altruistic gesture designed to spare the confederation any expense, it was probably trying to ensure complete British control over the situation. In November, Wilson presented a draft treaty to the confederation government.

Once again internal problems frustrated the British initiative. Santa Cruz was still interested in a treaty, but an invasion of Chilean forces backed by Peruvian opponents of the Bolivian caudillo threatened his regime. Desperate for support, he dared not risk alienating Peru's slaveholders by publicly opposing the slave trade. His strategy, however, failed. Defeated at the Battle of Yungay in January 1839, he was forced to flee, thereby ending any possibility of a slave-trade treaty. His defeat also placed in doubt the status of the 1837 treaty of amity, for the new government declared all of Santa Cruz's legislation null and void.[11]

The British government's experiences with Salaverry and Santa Cruz clearly showed that it exercised very little influence over Peru. The British wanted an amenable president, but they could not impose one. Moreover, they had discovered that even if they had one in office, he was more responsive to internal pressures than to external demands. Treaties regulating bilateral relations had virtually no meaning, since rulers felt free to ignore their predecessors' legislation. The British could do little to alter the situation. They were operating in a milieu in which strongly nationalistic feelings predominated and demands by any foreign power produced resentment and almost-automatic rejection. British political pressure was further hampered by the frequent changes of government in Lima and by the small number of warships on the Pacific station that could be used for more forceful actions.

The possibilities for economic pressure were equally limited. Before the 1840s and the guano boom, economic relations were weak, as Peru had few exports to sell and little buying power. The value of exports and imports grew over the years, but not at a rate to provide the British with any economic leverage.[12] That impotence had been evident since the late 1820s, when Peru had defaulted on the loans it had

negotiated at the time of independence and subsequently
failed to pay any of the interest or principal despite British
pressure.[13] Peruvian governments were thus aware that they
could ignore British demands with some impunity. They also
may have wondered why they should support the British
antislavery crusade, when the British themselves appeared
to be responding more to economic self-interest than to humanitarian concerns and were willing to ignore their lofty
principles when the property of British subjects was involved.
In 1835, while Wilson was objecting to the reopening of the
slave trade, he was simultaneously asking the Salaverry
government to exempt British subjects and their slaves from
a decree ordering compulsory military service for all able
men. And, until Palmerston issued a directive in 1841 banning the practice, British functionaries in countries where
slavery existed, such as Peru, could be slave owners.[14] The
situation raised some obvious questions: Were the British
really opposed to slavery, or were they merely trying to
demonstrate their power at the expense of weaker nations?
Why should Peru comply with British antislavery demands
when the British attitude toward slavery seemed inconsistent, even hypocritical?

Wilson recognized the difficulties. Moreover, in Agustín
Gamarra he now had to deal with a president who was a
conservative and a nationalist and who was unlikely to look
favorably on the requests of a country that had strongly
supported his predecessor. Wilson also was aware of the
slaveholders' growing influence under Gamarra. He noted
that past abolitionist legislation and treaties conformed more
"to the prevailing principles of the age and . . . the personal
enlightenment and humanity of the rulers and parties by
whom these were executed, than with the feelings of the
slaveholders in Peru who exercise over its Government a
powerful political influence."[15] That influence was indicated
by the government's proslavery legislation, to which the British responded with new complaints. Wilson protested the
1839 constitution for failing to include the usual article stating that nobody could enter Peru without immediately becoming free. The change was an essential prerequisite to the
renewed importation of slaves, and the Peruvian foreign
minister made no attempt to hide the fact that this was the
intent. He told Wilson that the government favored importing slaves from Brazil or other countries outside Africa and
would repeal any legislation that prevented this.

Wilson also objected to Gamarra's decree extending the period of patronal control over *libertos*. He reported that he, like others who were "possessed of a particle of humanity," had been "scandalised" by the decree, showing that he was as concerned about slavery as he was about the slave trade. "This law robs of their birthright men declared by law to be born free, and dooms them to a state of continuous slavery until the period of their lives at which in the debilitating and unhealthy climate of the coast of Peru, manual labor can no longer be available to a task-master; and when life itself in these unfortunate men is generally but disease and wretchedness." He lamented that congress, by accepting the new constitution and promulgating the law concerning *libertos*, "has been induced to set at defiance a vital principle of universal morality and of Peruvian national policy; namely the complete extirpation of the traffic in slaves and of slavery itself, in Peru, out of deference alone to the personal interests of three large slaveholders, political partizans of the actual government. The curse of slavery is therefore another of the many evils inflicted upon Peru by the overthrow therein, by the arms of Chile, of the honest and enlightened Government of . . . Santa Cruz."

The growing influence of the slaveholders also may have been responsible for Wilson's failure to obtain a slave-trade treaty in 1840. He had been authorized to negotiate such a treaty with the Gamarra government, and in May 1840 the council of state, in response to the continuing British pressure, considered the question. It noted that the trade was now largely in the hands of Spanish Americans or ships flying Spanish American flags. Unexpectedly, it then proposed a treaty that followed the 1838 British draft treaty: prohibiting Peruvians from participating in the trade anywhere in the world, declaring participants pirates, and establishing a mixed tribunal. It foresaw no problems, since the proposal complied with existing laws and treaties, was morally right, and, according to the council, followed the principles upheld by Peru since independence. Furthermore, other states, including Chile, Venezuela, and the province of Buenos Aires, had concluded similar treaties. The council recommended that the proposal be passed to congress.

The Peruvian response suggests that either British pressure was finally working or domestic opposition to the slave trade was having some effect on the Gamarra government. Alternatively it may have been nothing more than a charade for British consumption, as the proposal quickly died. Having made its recommendation, the council announced that no negotiations could proceed at this time because according to the constitution it could not negotiate a treaty without congressional authorization, and the present congress was authorized only to confirm the election of Gamarra as president. Wilson did not conceal his annoyance, and although he made no accusations he was all too aware that the president of the council, Manuel Menéndez, was a slaveholder. Frustrated once again, he turned his attention to Bolivia, where he succeeded in securing a treaty. This, however, only caused the Foreign Office to urge greater effort in drawing Peru into the fold.[16]

Wilson next had to cope with a new challenge. In 1841, Francisco Javier Calvo made his proposal for importing African slaves into Peru. The council of state considered the proposal at the same time it reconsidered a slave-trade treaty with Britain. Both were shelved for the time being. Wilson was suspicious of Calvo's motives, speculating that his real aim was to gain entry into the far more lucrative Cuban market under the cover of Peruvian authorization. He feared that the proposal might have a chance of success, because Menéndez was in charge of the executive and was keen to see the trade reestablished. He urged the Peruvian government to reject it and reported that the consuls general of New Granada and Ecuador intended to make clear to the Peruvian government that the 1829 treaty between Peru and Colombia prohibited the African slave trade. The Foreign Office under its new foreign secretary, Lord Aberdeen, was also annoyed and instructed Wilson to remonstrate "strongly against the proposed measure." Aberdeen argued that Peru was already committed to the abolition of the slave trade as a result of its 1837 treaty with Britain and that it could not "absolve itself from those obligations." He seemed to believe that moral suasion and an appeal to national pride might have some effect, for he instructed Wilson to "express the earnest hope of Her Majesty's Government that the Peruvian Government will not thus stand almost single among the civilized Powers of Christendom in declining to conclude a Treaty for the effectual and final extinction of a traffic proscribed by all."[17]

The 1837 treaty remained Britain's major weapon in its attempts to compel Peru to forswear reopening the slave trade during the three years of political chaos that followed

Gamarra's death in November 1841. The Foreign Office was still suspicious of Peruvian intentions, suspicions that were proved well-founded when President Vivanco in August 1843 decreed on the basis of Gamarra's 1839 constitution that the status of foreign slaves did not change on entering Peru. The British considered this to be an effort to "encourage and to protect the revival" of the slave trade, and Lord Aberdeen ordered the new British consul, William Pitt Adams, to "address a strong remonstrance" on the basis of the 1837 treaty and "those liberal and enlightened principles" of the 1835 constitution. The danger seemed to pass with the defeat of Vivanco by the more liberal Castilla in July 1844, the nullification of Vivanco's legislation, and the appearance of a government that was reported to be "strongly opposed to the Slave Trade."[18]

Britain, however, still had little influence over the direction of Peruvian affairs. Those who viewed Castilla as the ideological successor to Santa Cruz seemed to be ignoring the fact that he had demanded obedience to the 1839 constitution during his rebellion. Moreover, relations between Britain and Peru had seriously deteriorated since the fall of Santa Cruz. Gamarra's removal of Santa Cruz, his proslavery initiatives, and his preferential treatment of domestic and Chilean debts over the long-standing British one had alienated the British, who made little effort to hide their views of the new president. Relations failed to improve upon his death, as the ensuing political unrest resulted in a number of attacks on British subjects and demands for compensation. In 1842 a belligerent Lord Canning authorized British officials to call in the navy "to make reprisals upon Peruvian vessels to the full amount of the compensation required."[19] Events during Castilla's rebellion against Vivanco soured relations even further. In 1844 a mob led by Peruvian officials invaded the British vice consulate in the southern port of Islay and attacked the consul. In retaliation the British embargoed four ships belonging to Castilla that were moored at Islay, demanded the removal of the official considered responsible for the fracas, and threatened further actions if their demands were not met. After three months, and the reduction of Castilla's ships to abandoned, stripped, and plundered hulks, the Peruvians complied.

While this was occurring, a Peruvian official in Arica denied watering rights to a Royal Navy ship on the grounds that a state of hostilities existed between the two nations.

The British minister, who happened to be present, instructed the ship to bombard the port. According to his report, the bombardment lasted an hour and knocked down a few huts and mud walls. The Peruvian prefect conceded that the British were justified in their actions, and Adams, in a rather eccentric gesture, agreed to pay for the damage caused by the bombardment.[20]

The final act of this drama was played out in May 1845, when the British demanded that General José Félix Iguaín, who had been involved in the earlier troubles, be removed from office. A British warship in Callao threatened hostilities if the demand was not met. Clements Markham witnessed the events as a young midshipman on board the British flagship, noting in his journal how close they came to firing: "We snaked our stays down, got the cabin guns up, and got everything ready for action, on seeing which Castilla complied with our demands and . . . amity was thus again restored." A protocol signed by Adams and the Peruvian foreign minister at the end of May finally resolved the differences.[21]

Adams realized that securing a slave-trade treaty was impossible under these circumstances. He reported in December 1845 that he was waiting until relations improved before he pushed for a treaty. He claimed that there was no particular Peruvian hostility toward the British; there was just no Peruvian desire to establish treaties with any European power at this time, perhaps reflecting the general animosity to foreigners that marked the Castilla presidency.[22]

The events clearly show that in the 1840s Britain was prepared to use its gunboats in the Pacific when respect for the Union Jack was at stake, and that by doing so it could force Peru into making minor concessions. In the case of the slave trade, however, the British seemed hesitant to use force, and the Peruvians were still prepared to resist any outside pressure. Early in 1845, following reports that slaves and *libertos* were being imported illegally from New Granada into northern Peru, Adams wrote to the Peruvian government, which agreed to instruct its officials to pay attention to all blacks brought by sea and to prevent imports from New Granada. British vessels were not authorized to stop the shipments, possibly because of the hearsay nature of the reports, possibly because of the limited number of these ships in the area. Even following confirmation of the trade by British subjects in Paita and by the Royal Navy, Adams did not instruct British ships to intervene but limited himself to complaining to the Peruvian foreign ministry.[23]

The complaints had little impact on the slave-trade supporters in the government. They were now in the ascendancy and pushing through the proposal to reopen the trade. Despite continuing objections the Castilla government agreed to resume the slave trade on January 14, 1846. Adams had earlier asked for information about Peruvian intentions, and with those intentions now apparent the minister of foreign affairs, José Gregorio Paz Soldán, issued his memorandum of January 19 that sought to justify the reopening of the trade. He rejected the claim that Britain's treaty with the Peru-Bolivia Confederation was still binding and insisted that Peru's slaves were better off than those in neighboring countries and even factory workers in England. Adams commented in a letter to Aberdeen: "I am prepared to bear my personal testimony to the general good treatment of the slave population in Peru. . . . I am convinced that the condition of slaves imported from Brazil would be improved by their transference to Peru, but whether they would be benefited by being brought from the gold districts of New Granada is a more doubtful question."[24] His evaluation may have been correct, but it seemed to ignore the entire thrust of British policy, which was to abolish the slave trade regardless of the treatment of slaves in individual countries.

New protests followed the sailing of the Peruvian ship *Tres Amigos* in August 1846 with its cargo of slaves and *libertos*. In New Granada the British minister pointed out that the trade contravened treaties between the two countries. In Peru the acting minister, John Barton, argued that it violated the treaty of amity and insisted that Paz Soldán "take every necessary precaution to prevent the introduction of the aforesaid slaves into the Peruvian Territory." When the foreign minister replied that the treaty was null and void and refused any discussion of the subject, Barton suggested to the captain of a British warship in Callao that he prevent the landing of the slaves, citing Aberdeen's past insistence that the treaty was to be considered in effect. The captain thought that further discussion with Paz Soldán might be more appropriate, but the latter maintained that there was no treaty and that any attempt to stop the ship would be seen as a hostile act "of employing force to humble the Peruvian flag."

Barton was unwilling to resort to gunboat diplomacy without the backing of his superiors, so he wrote to the Foreign Office for directions. His unwillingness may have stemmed from his uncertain position, as the Peruvian government did not recognize him as a diplomatic agent. He was also aware of the confused political situation, which made any kind of pressure problematic. He reported: "In Peru there are two parties, and it is very difficult to find out which preponderates in interest, the one who would willingly see a Slave Trade Treaty entered into between this country and that of Great Britain, whilst the other, whose interests lye in estates, principally cultivated by blacks, will use every means in their power to prevent its being carried into effect, and amongst the latter is the Minister himself [Paz Soldán] and his relations." Barton added that Paz Soldán was rumored to have a share in the cargo of the *Tres Amigos*.[25]

With its hands tied in Peru, Britain directed its attention toward New Granada, where it seemed to have more scope for action. New Granada was the source of the slaves and a country with which it had an unequivocal slave-trade treaty. Demanding the complete suppression of the trade, Palmerston expressed particular concern about the *libertos* being exported, noting that they would be held in bondage in Peru until the age of fifty, rather than eighteen as would be the case in New Granada. He instructed the British minister to try to convince New Granada to stop this trade at least. All British demands were satisfied in April 1847 when New Granada issued its law prohibiting the export of slaves, a decision that in the final analysis owed little to outside pressure.[26]

Although New Granada's law ended the flow of slaves to Peru and more or less assured that Peruvians would not be able to obtain slaves from the Western Hemisphere, Britain still wanted Peru to formalize its opposition to the slave trade. With the closing of its last source of slaves and the growing antislavery sentiment in the country, Peru now showed itself amenable. The treaty took the form not of a formal slave-trade treaty but of a new treaty of friendship, commerce, and navigation. The British proposed that the slave-trade article that was included in the 1837 treaty be included in the new one. The Peruvians wanted "slave trade" to read "African slave trade," but Palmerston refused, commenting, "Slave Trade is Slave Trade whether the slaves bought and sold be Africans or Americans; and such Traffic ought equally in either case to be put an end to." On April 10, 1850, the treaty was signed in London. The Peruvian congress, which had to confirm it, procrastinated, leading to delays and further pressure, but in November 1851 it finally complied. The relevant clause was Article 15 which stated: "The Republic of Peru engages to co-operate with Her Britannic Majesty for the total abolition of the Slave Trade, and to prohibit all persons inhabiting the territories of the Republic, or subject to its jurisdiction, in the most effectual manner, and by penal laws, from taking any share in such a trade."[27]

Britain continued to press for a formal treaty abolishing the slave trade and declaring it piracy. Early in 1851, Palmerston instructed the British minister to communicate to the Peruvian government details of its treaties with Russia, Portugal, Germany, Argentina, New Granada, and Brazil abolishing the slave trade and to urge Peru to follow suit. That pressure was one reason why the old conservative cleric Bartolomé Herrera, the minister of government and foreign relations in the new Echenique government, recommended to the chamber of deputies in September that it pass a law declaring the slave trade piracy. It also may have had some bearing on the treaty he signed with Brazil one month later prohibiting the movement of slaves between the two countries. Despite this executive interest and further diplomatic letters from Adams, however, the congressional committee considering the slave-trade law failed to report, forcing a delay until the next congressional session.

While still trying to negotiate a slave-trade treaty, the British now also became involved in trying to secure the freedom of slaves in Peru, specifically those who had been imported from New Granada. In 1850, New Granada approved a law, effective January 1, 1851, that emancipated all of its slaves, including those living outside the country, such as the slaves who had been exported to Peru in the 1840s. Early in 1852, New Granada's chargé d'affaires in Peru, Mariano Arosemena, in concert with Adams, sought to secure the freedom of these slaves. He proposed that Peru's government purchase their freedom and deduct the sum from its debt to his country. The government refused, unwilling to involve itself in the private sector in this fashion or to intervene in the debt question, since the amount was still under negotiation. Arosemena also sought the return of the slaves' children. They constituted two groups: those who had left

New Granada with their parents and were entirely free; and those who were *libertos* and, according to New Granada law, subject to service until they reached the age of eighteen. A new disagreement seemed in the making, as Adams urged Arosemena to use diplomatic and legal pressure to ensure that the *libertos* were freed at eighteen, while Herrera argued they were subject to Peruvian law, which meant that they could not receive their freedom until the age of fifty. A survey taken of the *libertos*, however, revealed that there was no real problem: They were already being freed at the earlier age.

The Peruvian government also was unwilling to legislate the freedom of these children despite charges that many of them were being treated like slaves by their parents' owners. It claimed that it had investigated the charges and, except for one instance, found no supporting evidence. Even that one case was less than clear-cut, for it involved the 116 *libertos* who had arrived on the *María de los Angeles* and were in the possession of Domingo Elías. He was accused of treating them like slaves, even of selling them as if he owned them. Adams noted that these *libertos* had not been sold to Elías but were in his possession only by dint of their having accompanied their parents. In early June a supreme decree ordered their release. When Elías refused to comply, a second decree had to be issued to secure their freedom. The government's apparent concern may have owed more to politics than to humanitarian considerations or foreign pressure: Elías's opposition to Echenique was well known, and the president was not about to miss an opportunity to strike back at his most vociferous critic. Publication of the charges at the very least embarrassed the Ica planter, and his apparent refusal to obey the law provided an unexpected bonus: Elías also suffered financially from the affair. Following the loss of the *libertos* he sued the estate of Felipe Revoredo, from whom he had bought the slaves in 1847, to recover some of his expenses.[28]

With the question of the *libertos* more or less resolved, the Peruvian government returned to the problem of the New Granada slaves. In July 1852 it appointed Santiago Tavara minister plenipotentiary to New Granada to settle this and other issues involving the two countries. Tavara was instructed to inform the Bogotá government that it was financially responsible for returning the slaves and *libertos* to New Granada, but that Peru would provide up to 150,000 pesos to purchase the slaves. New Granada sent an official to locate and arrange the purchase of the expatriate slaves. He included not only those imported during the 1840s but also slaves who had arrived earlier, even during the period of the Independence Wars, as New Granada sought to ensure that all of its nationals were free.

One of those freed was a man by the name of Juan Bautista Escobar, who showed himself to be an extraordinary individual, a man whose enslavement in two countries over several years had failed to destroy his basic human decency. In Peru he had distinguished himself by his honesty, which was attested to by several merchants who had employed him to carry considerable sums of money. He spent the wages he earned unselfishly, even raising a German child whose mother was dead and whose father was incapacitated. On learning of New Granada's intention to include expatriate slaves in its abolition scheme, he had gone to the legation in Lima and told the minister to free those who were confined or worked in bakeries and mills first, because he and others had "good masters and should be the last to be freed." Finally, on October 13, 1854, dressed in his best clothes, he received his freedom in the legation. His owner, having been paid Escobar's price, said to his former slave: "This money isn't for me; it's for you. I want to reward your integrity. . . . I am not now your master but always shall be your protector and your friend."[29]

The ceremony might be seen as the culmination of the campaign to free the slaves from New Granada, as Escobar was one of the last to receive his freedom. Moreover, it seemed to demonstrate the generosity and common aim of all the parties involved, suggesting the development of a more liberal attitude in Peru and a willingness to deal with slaves as human beings rather than as property. However, this was hardly the case. Escobar's freedom marked nothing more than the liberation of another slave, the final act in a campaign that had taken over two years to complete. If a more liberal attitude existed among Peruvians, one might ask why Escobar's owner had not freed him earlier, especially since the slave's value was apparently no longer of any importance. Rather than marking a break with the past, the incident demonstrated once again how the country remained tied to its colonial heritage. It underlined the continuing labor shortage and the determination of employers to hold on to their workers even if this meant retaining them as slaves. It also reiterated the obvious fact that many Peruvians were still committed to slavery despite the pressure of foreign nations and the example of neighboring countries.

The freeing of the slaves from New Granada was one of the few accomplishments of those foreign nations led by Great Britain that had long urged Peru to alter its stand on the slave trade and slavery. That pressure had eventually helped to end the slave trade, thereby seriously weakening Peruvian slavery by preventing further imports, and it had provided support for abolitionist sentiment within the country. It could not secure the complete abolition of slavery, however, simply because, as the history of Peru's foreign relations in the first decades following independence shows, the influence of foreign countries, even Great Britain, was slight. Peru resisted British demands with impunity. Britain was restricted by the chaotic political situation in Peru, the tenuous economic relations between the two countries, and the uncertainties of gunboat diplomacy. Peru's presidents, regardless of their personal views, revealed themselves to be far more responsive to internal pressures than to external ones, an understandable attitude in these years of political instability. Political longevity was determined not by satisfying British demands but by maintaining alliances with and respecting the wishes of the country's elite, many of whom were slaveholders.

By the early 1850s this situation was beginning to change. Peru was now more responsive to British pressure, as a result of the financial links established with the guano boom and the desire for economic expansion. It could no longer obtain slaves, and it had money to compensate slaveholders, as its purchase of the New Granada slaves demonstrated. It was probably influenced by its neighbors as they abolished slavery: Bolivia and New Granada in 1851, Ecuador in 1852, the Argentine Confederation in 1853, and Venezuela in 1854. It could still resist pressure to sign a slave-trade treaty and showed no signs that it was about to abolish slavery, but it had been willing to sign a treaty of friendship. The international slave trade was now formally dead, and the opposition to slavery was growing. The final battle that would destroy it still had to take place, but the day of reckoning was approaching, slowly but surely.

# Notes

1. Enclosure with Canning to Rowcroft, 2, December 15, 1823, F.O. 61/1; King, "Latin-American Republics," 389–91.

2. Basadre, *Historia* 1:117–19.

3. Ibid. 2:300–301; *La Prensa Peruana*, October 17, 1829.

4. Ricketts to Canning, 24, December 19, 1826, F.O. 61/8.

5. King, "Latin-American Republics," 393–400.

6. Enclosure with Palmerston to Wilson, 10, September 24, 1832, F.O. 61/21.

7. The British response raises questions about David Brion Davis's contention that "officially, the British drew a distinction between the criminal export of slaves and systems of 'domestic' slavery with which they had no right to interfere." See Davis, *Slavery and Human Progress*, 302. The Peruvian case indicates that, by the mid-1830s, Great Britain seemed prepared to interfere with slavery systems while continuing to focus its main attention on the slave trade.

8. Wilson to Wellington, and enclosures, ST1, July 9, 1835, F.O. 84/182.

9. Enclosure with Wilson to Palmerston, 51, August 9, 1838, F.O. 61/50; Basadre, *Historia* 2:302.

10. King, "Latin-American Republics," 401–2; enclosure with Masterton to Bidwell, 13, May 13, 1839, F.O. 61/63; Wilson to Palmerston, ST1, May 31, 1836, F.O. 84/206; Wilson to Palmerston, ST2, October 22, 1836, F.O. 84/206.

11. Wilson to Palmerston, ST5, December 12, 1838, F.O. 84/260; Wilson to Palmerston, 18, September 4, 1839, F.O. 61/62; enclosure with Wilson to Palmerston, 14, April 30, 1840, F.O. 61/71.

12. The average annual value of exports and imports between Peru and Great Britain for the four quinquennia between 1826 and 1845 measured £355,953, £441,052, £767,297, and £986,236. The last figure reflects the effect of the guano boom. See "No. 656. Account of the Value of Imports and Exports between the United Kingdom and Cuba, Chili, Peru and Columbia Respectively, in Each Year, from 1824 to 1845," in Great Britain, *Parliamentary Papers* 60 (1847): 2–3.

13. Peru failed to meet any interest or principal payments before 1849. See Mathew, "Imperialism of Free Trade," 568, 575.

14. Wilson to Palmerston, 73, September 8, 1835, F.O. 61/33; Wilson to Palmerston, ST2, August 30, 1841, F.O. 84/375.

15. Luis Martín, *The Kingdom of the Sun: A Short History of Peru* (New York, 1974), 204; Palmerston to Wilson, ST2, August 28, 1839, F.O. 84/294; Wilson to Palmerston, ST1, March 24, 1839, F.O. 84/294; Wilson to Palmerston, ST2, November 30, 1839, F.O. 84/294.

16. *El Comercio*, June 2, 1840; *El Peruano*, June 6, 1840; Wilson to Palmerston, ST1, January 11, 1840, ST6, February 20, 1840, ST12, June 6, 1840, ST15, July 18, 1840, all found in F.O. 84/331.

17. *El Peruano*, September 8, 15, 1841, June 18, 1842; Wilson to Palmerston, ST2, August 30, 1841, F.O. 84/375; Aberdeen to Wilson, December 31, 1841, F.O. 84/375.

18. Sealy to Aberdeen, ST4, June 14, 1842, F.O. 84/418; Miller to Aberdeen, ST3, March 16, 1843, F.O. 84/483; Aberdeen to Adams, ST1,

May 25, 1844, F.O. 84/537; Adams to Aberdeen, ST4, December 4, 1844, F.O. 84/537; Pike, *Modern History*, 88.

19. Mathew, "First Anglo-Peruvian Debt," 95; Canning to Admiralty, March 29, 1842, F.O. 61/96.

20. Adams to Aberdeen, 38, 39, September 30, 1844, F.O. 61/104; Adams to Aberdeen, 34, June 14, 1845, F.O. 61/108; Adams memorandum, November 5, 1846, F.O. 61/111; Crompton to Aberdeen, 10, January 12, 1846, F.O. 61/113; Iturregui to Palmerston, May 15, 1847, F.O. 61/117.

21. The threat may have been a bluff, but the fourteen-year-old Markham was convinced war was imminent. He wrote to his mother on May 18 that there was "every chance of a war," adding plaintively, "I hope I shan't be killed," and concluding, "I'll write to you when all the row is over, if I'm alive." See C. R. Markham, "Private journal, September 7, 1844, to August 10, 1845," 70, C. R. Markham, "Correspondence," Royal Geographical Society, London, Clements R. Markham Special Collection (hereafter cited as RGS-CRM), 2 and 36. See also Basadre, *Historia* 3:82–85.

22. Adams to Aberdeen, ST8, December 30, 1845, F.O. 84/595; Crompton to Palmerston, 11, February 28, 1851, F.O. 61/131; Gootenberg, "North-South," 284–85, 290–91, 294.

23. Enclosure with O'Leary to Aberdeen, ST1, May 30, 1845, F.O. 84/595; enclosure with Adams to Aberdeen, ST4, August 4, 1845, F.O. 84/595.

24. *El Peruano*, January 31, 1846; Adams to Aberdeen, ST, February 4, 1846, F.O. 84/645; Basadre, *Historia* 3:188–90.

25. Barton to Palmerston, 3, October 10, 1846, F.O. 61/111; O'Leary to Palmerston, ST3, October 6, 1846, F.O. 84/645; O'Leary to Palmerston, ST6, December 4, 1846, F.O. 84/645; Barton to Palmerston, ST4, September 11, 1846, F.O. 84/645; Barton to Palmerston, ST5, October 6, 1846, F.O. 84/645; Barton to Paz Soldán, September 9, 1846, F.O. 177/34.

26. Palmerston to O'Leary, ST4, October 22, 1846, F.O. 84/645; Palmerston to O'Leary, ST6, December 7, 1846, F.O. 84/645; O'Leary to Palmerston, ST4, March 9, 1847, F.O. 84/689.

27. "Treaty of Friendship, Commerce, and Navigation," F.O. 61/124; *El Comercio*, November 15, 1851.

28. Santiago Tavara, *Misión a Bogotá en 1852, a consecuencia de la expedición de Flores al Ecuador, &c.* (Lima, 1853), xi; Adams to Palmerston, 8, January 8, 1852, F.O. 61/133; O'Leary to Palmerston, ST6, May 24, 1851, F.O. 84/853; Adams to Palmerston, ST1, January 8, 1852, F.O. 84/884; Adams to Palmerston, ST3, February 8, 1852, F.O. 84/884; Adams to Malmesbury, ST4, June 9, 1852, F.O. 84/884; *Registro Oficial*, June 24, 1852; "Promovido por el señor D. Domingo Elías con la testamenta de Don Felipe Revoredo para que le descuentera una cantidad de pesos," AGN, CCiv, 1852, Leg. 168.

29. Tavara, *Misión*, xii, 20; *El Comercio*, October 13, 1854; "Seguidos por D. José Miguel Najera, defensor de la esclava María Cordoves e hijos, con su amo Don José Vicente Delgado sobre su libertad, 1852," AGN, CCiv, 1852–53, Leg. 169. For slaves purchased by the minister of New Granada see AGN, Notarial, Lucas de la Lama, 1854–55, Prot. 333, September 5, October 13, 1854.

# 9

# Abolition

By the early 1850s, Peruvian slavery was visibly weakening. Its end, which had long been a vague hope, was now becoming an increasing possibility. Although many Peruvians remained committed to the institution, they did so without the intensity that had been evident twenty or even ten years earlier. The declining number of slaves, the international antislavery crusade, the availability of alternative workers, the growing acceptance of free wage labor, and the demands of both whites and blacks for abolition had all assisted in undermining the support for slavery. Even the slaveholders themselves had weakened the system, by ignoring the laws that protected their interests and hiring runaways to work on their estates. Yet, despite the various antislavery pressures, the date of abolition was still uncertain. The government was not prepared to legislate slavery out of existence, for slaves were still too important and the slaveholders too powerful. To surmount this final obstacle, to secure abolition before the last slave had either died or been privately emancipated, some new crisis was required, a crisis that would bring the issue of slavery once more to the forefront of political consciousness and produce the conditions for abolition. That crisis came in the form of a new civil war that engulfed the nation in 1854.

The Peruvian conflict did not approach the destructiveness of the cataclysm that divided the United States in the 1860s. Slavery was not central to it, nor did it have the sweeping impact of the American Civil War. According to David Brion Davis, "Hispanic emancipation brought no sense of an apocalypse, of collective rebirth, or of the self-purgation of deep national guilt."[1] It is a description that accurately captures the events preceding the last days of Peruvian slavery. Perhaps the only similarity between the Peruvian and American conflicts was that they helped secure the destruction of their respective countries' slavery systems. In the case of Peru the end of slavery has also been seen as part of a liberal shift in the country's political direction, an offshoot of the spread of European ideas throughout South America, especially those ideas associated with the 1848 revolution in France. The change indicated the rising influence of the urban middle class as well as a new concern for the oppressed sectors of the population.[2]

The spread of liberalism and the rise of a new middle class may have supplied additional pressure for ending slavery in Peru, but the real impetus for the abolition decree had far more pragmatic and less philosophical origins. The decree was nothing more than a self-serving, opportunistic gesture by a military leader seeking popular support during a civil war. It came without preparation or warning, it was not tied directly to the preceding abolitionist pressures, its implementation was designed to ensure first and foremost that the slaveholders suffered as little as possible, and it did nothing to assist the slaves' transition to freedom. Although it ended slavery, Peru's abolition decree changed virtually nothing else.

While they were conscious that slavery was dying, Peruvians seemed unaware as the days and weeks of 1854 ran their course that its demise was imminent. Still dependent on slave labor, Peru's slaveholders continued to buy slaves, in some cases offering freedom in return for a few years of service to try to induce a change of owners. They neither engaged in a frenzy of selling in anticipation of a decree that would deprive them of their property and might deny them compensation nor stopped freeing slaves and selling those of little value in expectation of a forthcoming abolition law that would award them generous compensation. Slave advertisements still appeared in the press. *El Heraldo de Lima* published its last in early October, but other papers such as *El Comercio* continued advertising. Slaves and *libertos*, too, were unaware of the impending change in their status. They were still buying their own freedom and that of their relatives with their hard-earned funds. In October one couple paid 600 pesos to free themselves and 90 pesos to free their six-month-old son; on December 14, Juana Vasquez paid 300 pesos to free her daughter.[3]

In view of the weaknesses of the abolitionist forces and the ideological persuasion of the president, the actions of both slaves and slaveholders are not particularly surprising. A conservative and former slaveholder, President Echenique seemed an unlikely person to alter the status quo. Even though his Civil Code, his abolitionist activities, and his initiatives to formalize the end of the slave trade seemed to indicate that he was more responsive to abolitionist demands than his reputedly more liberal predecessor had been, these were token gestures that may have added to the groundswell of support for abolition but did not presage slavery's immediate demise. The slavery question, in fact, did not seem to occupy much of his attention during his presidency. Of far greater concern were threats from neighboring republics and internal crises related to his domestic policies. By 1854, Echenique's control was seriously threatened. Charges of corruption related to his law of consolidation had multiplied and unleashed the hostility and ambitions that gestated just below the surface of Peruvian politics.

Particularly alienated was Domingo Elías, who in August 1853 had published a number of letters condemning the government. Arrested and exiled, he now resorted to more violent opposition. In October and again in December he mounted armed expeditions against the government. Although he suffered defeat in both cases, others followed his lead, so that Echenique found himself in an increasingly insecure position. In January 1854, Arequipa rose in rebellion. That same month former president Castilla, ignoring his previous pledge to forgo military conspiracy, joined the rebels after condemning what he called the tyranny, theft, and immorality of the administration.[4] By mid-February he was the recognized leader of the opposition and had won the support of other centers that rose against the government. In April, as the rebellion increasingly took the form of a popular movement against the military, he was declared "The Liberator." On July 5, to widen his support further, especially in the heavily populated sierra, he abolished the detested Indian head tax. Echenique responded with decrees that ended the use of forced recruitment and freed the provinces of Huarochirí and Yauyos from paying the head tax and other taxes for the second half of the year.[5] His efforts, however, failed to halt the rebellion, and the areas remaining under his control were gradually being whittled away.[6]

To this point slavery had not been an important issue in these events. The few contemporary references to slaves revolved around their activities as *montoneros*, for once more the countryside was infested with irregulars. Robbery, as usual, was their principal motivation, with political allegiances providing justification for their acts, but a few bands displayed an awareness of social issues. In February, progovernment *montoneros* raided Elías's San Javier estate, freed his slaves, released his German and Chinese settlers from their contracts, and then expelled everyone before looting and destroying the estate. Other prominent families suffered similar depredations as local officials either would not or could not protect them. In May forty assailants attacked the white administrator of La Molina. Over the next month what may have been the same band (many of the participants were later identified as coming from the Villa, La Molina, and San Pedro estates) robbed travelers, attacked estates, and freed slaves in the Lima area. When they killed a subprefect, the government dispatched two hundred soldiers to suppress them, a difficult task since the *montoneros* could easily "disappear" into the estates. Nonetheless, by late July the troops reported success. They seem to have taken justice into their own hands, for several of those captured were killed "while trying to escape." Civilians assisted the troops, arming themselves and hunting down the bands. But despite the actions of troops and civilians, late in the year black *montoneros* terrorized the coast from Lima to as far north as Lambayeque, attacking and occasionally killing hacendados, assaulting administrators, and luring away slaves.[7]

With his control restricted largely to the coast and challenged by growing rebel forces and local unrest, Echenique needed to widen his support and reverse the flow of events. To that end he issued a decree on November 18 that was designed primarily to bolster the size of his army. However, by couching the decree in a wider socioeconomic context, Echenique provided the element that would hasten the complete and final destruction of Peruvian slavery. The decree stated that in order to crush the rebellion threatening the country the government needed to organize an army reserve that also could be used to satisfy other social concerns. Thus, deserters were to be allowed to return without punishment, every soldier and noncommissioned officer was to be rewarded with 10 pesos, each new recruit was to be relieved from paying taxes for life, and "every domestic or hacienda slave who enlists in the army will receive his freedom . . . and the reward will be extended to his legitimate wife." The slave had to serve for two years but would receive his emancipation documents immediately, with the state indemnifying the owners.[8]

According to the official newspaper *El Peruano*, the principal reason for the decree was "the urgent need to bring an end to the revolution"; nonetheless, the attack upon slavery, an institution that was "rejected by justice and the dominant ideas of the century," was of great importance. The government believed that the legislation would provide the framework for a new army, while at the same time opening "new horizons" to national industry and assisting the agricultural sector. With regard to the latter, free wage labor would bring about improvements on those estates, little changed since the time of the conquest, whose owners had ignored new methods and treated their slaves as nothing more than "beasts of burden." A switch to wage labor also might attract *serranos* and immigrants to the coast. For the government, therefore, the decree marked "a new era in the Republic." It would stimulate production and the accumulation of wealth, and by "scrupulously" respecting property rights it would not alienate the hacendado class.[9]

Echenique's own recollections were that his decision was "not so much because I believed that slavery was prejudicial to them [the blacks], for I had proof to the contrary, but for being inappropriate to human dignity." He had not previously made a proposal to congress because he believed that he first had to obtain replacements for the agricultural workers and funds to import them. He claimed that he was sincerely interested in abolition and that he was gradually achieving it, as demonstrated by his lottery and his freeing of the slaves from New Granada. The civil war gave him a new abolitionist opportunity, one that also allowed him to increase the size of his army.[10]

The decree received praise in some quarters. *El Heraldo de Lima* concluded that Peru was now "no more than a step from complete abolition." It accused the hacendados of having exploited their slaves and claimed that the government had long been considering abolition but had not found the right method or moment. It contended that the decree would result in further efforts to attract Asians to assist the agricultural sector. It also made the odd but prescient statement that, should Castilla's rebellion succeed, those who had been freed would remain so.[11]

Other commentators were less favorably impressed. Some viewed the decree as nothing more than a self-serving gesture. Echenique's forces had recently been withdrawn to Lima from Jauja in the sierra and could not be reinforced with new recruits from the north in time to face Castilla.[12] Some alternative source had to be found, and Echenique seemed to have settled on Lima's slaves. The British minister noted that "as the compensation to be granted to the slave owners is more apparent than real, the landed proprietors, who are all slave owners, are on this account much enraged against the Government." Consequently, many slaveholders threw their support behind Castilla.[13]

As to the decree's impact on the slaves, the sources are contradictory. Echenique recalled: "I knew very well there would not be many, because I knew their repugnance to army life, but some 350 showed up, and I gave them their freedom."[14] An antigovernment newspaper in Arequipa, on the other hand, claimed that not one slave responded and that Echenique had to resort to forced recruitment to create a battalion of three hundred blacks. It also reported the case of the Larán estate, whose owner asked his slaves whether they wanted to be freed by serving Echenique. They unanimously rejected the offer, saying that they wanted to defend the lower classes, at which the owner gave them arms to support Castilla. Perhaps the most accurate picture came from an antislavery writer in Trujillo. He wrote that the decree had "not been of benefit to many." Nevertheless, it had had some effect, for he had seen several slaves approaching the prefecture, "some half naked, others having been imprisoned for two to six years, and all dead from hunger, to ask for their inscription into the ranks of the army" to alleviate their suffering. He commented that the "tyrannical masters" had only themselves, their indolence, and their avariciousness to blame for the loss of their "martyr slaves."[15] Some certainly took advantage of Echenique's offer, for the notarial records list slaves who were freed in accordance with the decree. More might have responded if they had known about it, but owners deliberately kept news of the decree from their slaves to limit the response.[16]

Echenique's decree thus directly freed a small number of slaves. Indirectly its impact was even greater, for it extracted a response on the slavery issue from Castilla. The former president had justified his participation in the rebellion on the grounds that he was protecting the rights of the oppressed and the exploited—hence his decree ending the Indian head tax. Echenique's decree openly challenged that position and therefore required a quick riposte. From a military point of view, it also necessitated a response if Echenique was to be denied a new injection of manpower. Castilla consequently had to turn his attention to the slaves.

His response was simple and straightforward: He issued a decree of his own. On December 3, from his headquarters in Huancayo, Castilla (referring to himself as provisional president) declared: "Men and women until now held in Peru as slaves and *libertos*, whose condition arises from having been transported as such or from having been born of a slave womb, who by whatever means are subject to perpetual or temporary servitude, are all without distinction of age from today and always entirely free." Four reasons were given for the decree: justice required it; one of the principal objectives of the revolution had been to guarantee the rights of oppressed and exploited Indians and black slaves; waiting until after the rebels' military success would arouse owners' worries about indemnification and unjustifiably ransom the slaves' participation in the civil war; and, since "ex-president" Echenique had demanded that slaves enlist for two years and had disturbed property rights with "his vague offer of indemnity, . . the name of Peru would be besmirched if the provisional government did not declare immediately its national principles and condemn this new horrible traffic in human flesh." According to the decree, the government would care for aged slaves; "only those slaves or *libertos* who take up arms and sustain the tyranny of ex-president D. José Rufino Echenique, who makes war on the freedom of the people, will be unworthy of freedom"; the owners of slaves and masters of *libertos* were guaranteed a "just price" through special bearer bonds payable in five years with annual interest of 6 percent; the bonds could be used to pay a portion of taxes and other fiscal responsibilities; and the government would stimulate European immigration to reanimate coastal agriculture.[17]

The decree seemed to indicate that Castilla had undergone some sort of ideological transformation, that he had finally come to realize that moral issues were a part of the liberalism that he claimed to profess. In a speech made to the national convention on July 14, 1855, he recalled:

a sacred debt weighed on the conscience of the provisional government; it had freed the Indians from the abject tyranny of tribute, but slavery remained, degrading society and destroying the personality of humanity. The fortunes of war are uncertain, and the government was devoted to the moral revolution, to complete its work, and to complete the program that the heroes of independence had left undone. It must end at once the shameful anomaly of slavery, and at Huancayo, where the ignominious institution had been extended for one generation, the provisional government proclaimed freedom for all who tread the surface of the republic, indemnifying the owners from the national treasury for the value of those who the law demanded be free.[18]

Some claim that The Liberator, a title that now acquired new significance, was responding to the pressures of his liberal advisers, men such as José and Pedro Gálvez Egúsquiza and Manuel Toribio Ureta. The British minister described them as being "well imbued with socialist doctrines." José Gálvez Egúsquiza was minister of government in Castilla's provisional government, his brother and Ureta had been deputies, Pedro was Castilla's secretary during the insurrection, and Pedro and Ureta became ministers in Castilla's government after his victory. It was they who provided the revolution with its ideological direction and, according to many, pushed Castilla toward abolition. José had pressed for abolition in the past, while Pedro had been involved in drawing up Echenique's Civil Code.[19]

However, it was not liberal or humanitarian concerns that propelled Castilla in the direction of abolition. Like the appeals of San Martín and Bolívar thirty years earlier, Castilla's appeal to the slaves was essentially opportunistic and self-serving. It was to satisfy military and political concerns, as both his detractors and his admirers recognized. Manuel Atanasio Fuentes described the decree as an opportunistic act designed to popularize the rebellion and win support. To Santiago Tavara, it was a military action, a "barracks decree," while to Ricardo Palma it was "an arm of war, at the same time the expression of humanitarian sentiments." *El Heraldo de Lima*, commenting five months after Castilla's return to power and subject to the pressures of the new regime, saw it as nothing more than a war measure introduced to prevent Echenique from winning recruits. Pointing to Castilla's lack of action during his first presidency and the decree's inconsistency with the rebel program, the newspaper astutely observed: "The social question was converted into a measure of the circumstances and ceded its place to the necessities of the campaign."[20] That Castilla in rebelling had rejected the very principles for which he had fought in the 1840s raises doubts about his commitment to any principle, while his refusal to free slaves who supported Echenique raises questions about the depth of his commitment to abolition.

Nonetheless, the decree gave the impression that Castilla had freed the slaves, and it provided the military advantage that he had sought. Announced by Castilla's commanders as they advanced, it drew slaves into his army, between two thousand and three thousand according to one report. Slaves also supplied military intelligence. In December, as the two armies faced one another outside Lima, a black woman who sold food in Echenique's camp reported his troop movements to Castilla.[21] One measure of the decree's success was Echenique's desperate search for something similar to win supporters to his own cause.[22]

While the slaves' response was almost predictable, the same cannot be said of that of the slaveholders. In view of what was at stake in terms of income and control over labor, they showed a surprising lack of concern. Perhaps their response can be explained by the general animosity toward Echenique, who had alienated important sectors of the population with his political incompetence, his Civil Code, and now his abolition decree and its vague plans for compensation. Castilla, on the other hand, seemed to have the slaveholders' interests at heart despite his decree. His record showed that while president he had reestablished the slave trade, and he numbered among his supporters such prominent slaveholders as Domingo Elías. They may have viewed his decree as nothing more than barracks rhetoric that would be rescinded or modified once he had ousted Echenique. And even if the decree remained in force, many of them may have been more concerned about compensation—which Castilla had promised—since they now could obtain alternative servile workers through the coolie trade.

Regardless of how the various groups responded to it, Castilla's decree in the first weeks after its issuance was little more than a moot point. To become the law of the land it required a military victory. The indicators of the likely outcome of the rebellion had been apparent for months, but the decisive battle was not fought until January 5, 1855, at La Palma,

near Lima. Castilla was victorious; Echenique resigned and
went into exile, and Castilla resumed the presidency. His
provisional decrees now had the full force of law, and Peru
seemed to have an all-encompassing abolition decree.

Would the decree be implemented? Some people seemed
to believe that nothing had changed—an early indication
of the limited impact abolition was going to have. On
January 8, *El Comercio* advertised the sale of a female slave.
Justo Lostaunau freed one of his slaves for good service on
January 11; Francisca Sánchez de la Concha freed one of
hers on January 26. In February some Arequipa masters
were reported to be still selling their *libertos'* children; in
March the owner of a Lima bakery was charged with having
a private prison, committing an offense against the person of
a free man, and contempt after a fire in the bakery led to the
discovery of a cell where two blacks and four Chinese were
found chained.[23] These examples indicate that, although a
decree abolishing slavery was now the law of the land, many
people were either confused as to what the decree meant or
were prepared to ignore it.

In some cases the uncertainty may have been justified,
for the situation was far from clear. How the decree was to be
implemented had not been explained, Castilla had to worry
about maintaining support among the former slaveholders,
and slaves had begun taking matters into their own hands.
The British consul, J. N. Sulivan, demonstrating little sympathy toward the slaves despite his being Lord Palmerston's
nephew, wrote to the British foreign secretary on January 21:

> The slaves of various landed proprietors have risen against their
> masters and have committed all kinds of excesses, they refuse to
> work and in most instances have transformed themselves into high-
> waymen, the estates are left to ruin, and though the proprietors are
> to receive compensation it will remain to be seen whether the prom-
> ised compensation will be real. To render the measure valuable the
> slaves should not have been liberated but under certain conditions
> being insisted upon; though free they should have been forced to
> serve as apprentices, and kept in order, for this mass of lawless
> negros left to themselves may be very dangerous; already constant
> murders are being committed, and the cry of death to the white men
> has been raised.[24]

Peruvians were equally critical and equally insensitive to
the blacks. One who thought that the decree was going to be
amended after the military victory charged that it was im-

moral and contrary to existing laws, and that it prejudiced those affected, attacked property, and hurt agriculture. He claimed that slaves were not prepared for overnight abolition: They were uneducated and depraved, they had a propensity to steal, their relationships with their families and activities as *montoneros* indicated their cruelty, and only the "vigilance and morality of the masters" who had taught them religion and moral practices had controlled their inherent immorality.[25]

Criticisms such as these were a major part of the defense that was now launched to ensure that the decree, if not revoked entirely, would be gutted and the status quo would be left untouched. The harm done to agriculture and the slaves' lack of preparation for freedom were commonly cited, as was the negative impact on the planters, who attracted widespread sympathy. Even opponents of slavery appeared to accept these views. One, who considered slavery inequitable and consequently undemocratic, and who saw abolition as an "obligation imposed by the century's civilization, by philosophy, and by religion," nevertheless argued that the decree was harmful to agriculture and would demoralize the former slaves, "whose vicious tendencies have been developed by the effects of their very unhappy and humble condition."

Many critics saw disaster in the making, predicting that abolition would drive the price of essentials out of the reach of the poor, thus fostering epidemics, increasing the death rate, limiting population growth, and provoking political unrest. Their solution was additional laws: to protect agriculture; to prevent crime, disorders, and prostitution; and to force the blacks back to work. Some called for a period of apprenticeship during which the former slaves would be taught about liberty. One suggested that all former slaves be returned to their owners as wage laborers earning 5 pesos per month plus their clothing, food, medical treatment, and funeral costs. Another added that, if any apprentice fled, he should be whipped on the first occasion and condemned to perpetual hard labor on the guano islands on the second. The immediate hope of many planters was that officials would compel the former slaves to remain on the estates as wage laborers, collecting the harvest and thereby preventing financial ruin. Their hopes indicated once again that what many wanted was not necessarily slaves but rather a guaranteed labor force, hopes that now seemed doomed by

Castilla's decree. The government had sent troops to the estates to announce the decree, permit the slaves to leave, and prevent unrest. Nonetheless, disorders were occurring, perhaps not to the extent claimed by critics of the decree but sufficient to create a tense situation.[26]

Castilla responded on January 23 with a new decree, which reiterated that the slaves were free but pointed out that this meant they were subject to the same obligations and laws as everyone else. In addition, they would have to work for a living, would be considered delinquent if they failed to obey the authorities, would have to work now for three months as wage laborers collecting the harvest on their old estates or on other farms to meet the labor shortage, would be sent to work on the guano islands if they were still unemployed three months after the harvest, could not take animals from the estates nor remain against the owner's wishes, and would have to stay with their former masters if they were orphans under the age of twenty-one. Officials were to begin an inscription of former slaves and *libertos* for the purpose of indemnifying owners.[27]

This decree fixed the rights and obligations of the former slaves by satisfying many of the demands of the owners. In effect it created a kind of apprenticeship system by supplying a guaranteed work force and placing restrictions on the former slaves. It dictated that they had to work and designated where they were expected to work: on the estates and guano islands. Castilla later said that his aim had been to "prop up the morality of the ex-slaves, to induce them to work."[28] In fact, his actions had underlined the constancy of his views regarding blacks, despite his abolition decree, and raised further doubts about his supposed liberalism and commitment to the oppressed. He had indicated that in his mind abolition did not mean complete freedom, nor did it mean equality. Freedom was to be restricted, as the former slaves had to obey rules and regulations that applied only to them. But would they comply?

By January 23 many former slaves already had fled their estates. Others were to follow. They refused to work and threw away the papers that they were supposed to carry showing that they were free and had been registered. The frustrated authorities began folding the papers before distributing them in a half-hearted attempt to hide their contents and prevent them from being thrown away, but the incongruity of carrying documents verifying one's freedom after an abolition decree had not been lost on the former slaves, who must have been aware that the real purpose was to assist in identifying them and indemnifying their former owners.[29] Thus, their rejection of the papers and refusal to be counted were quite understandable. Moreover, the restrictive nature of the recent decree may have aroused fears of further limitations on their freedom, and therefore they may have believed that they had to separate themselves from their former status and their old owners as completely as possible.

The slaveholders were still not satisfied, despite Castilla's decree of January 23. At the end of February a meeting of the most influential hacendados in the department of Lima produced a demand for compensation and for legislation that would furnish them with replacement workers. Recent developments had altered at least their public statements if not their private beliefs, for they now declared that they recognized the sacrosanctity of the right to freedom. However, they still believed that property rights were paramount, arguing that without them society did not exist. They claimed that since January all their slaves had fled their estates but remained in the area, returning at night to steal. They wanted troops stationed in the countryside to stop this thievery.

On March 3 yet another meeting of prominent slaveholders, including Pedro Paz Soldán (José Gregorio Paz Soldán's brother), Mariano Osma, Isidro Aramburu, Francisco Quirós, José María del Valle, and Manuela Pando, issued a protest that criticized the abolition decree for its "iniquity" and the government for its failure to provide prior indemnification and replacement laborers. They asserted (and in the process contradicted their earlier statement that all the slaves had fled) that the former slaves were demanding "fabulous" wages and only working half days, while planters were so poor that they needed to be indemnified immediately and generously. They also wanted compensation for the machinery that they had bought which now lay idle. These points were reiterated when a number of the planters subsequently met with Castilla. They pleaded absolute ruin because of the shortage of workers, charged that blacks who had remained on the estates were confronting their former masters and refusing to work, and demanded a law that would compel them to work.[30]

On March 9 a further decree informed the former slaveholders how they were to be indemnified. In charge was an administrative body, the Tribunal Mayor de Cuentas.

Slaveholders would have to appear before it with their records listing the slaves and *libertos* that they had owned or controlled on December 3, 1854. Lima owners had twelve days in which to appear; those outside Lima had one month. The tribunal was to adjudicate the claims, and local officials were to distribute letters of freedom. The state would pay 300 pesos for each slave or *liberto* regardless of sex and age, including fugitives who had fled before December 3 if their whereabouts was known. It set aside 1,000,000 pesos to compensate owners of rural slaves, would satisfy immediately the owners of one or two slaves, and would pay the rest one quarter of their compensation in specie and three quarters in bearer bonds that returned .5 percent monthly interest from January 5, 1855. A special fund of 70,000 pesos was assigned to amortize these bonds.[31]

Once more Castilla seemed to be pandering to the owners. He later remarked that his desire was to protect agriculture and the lower classes, but his new decree benefited only the slaveholders, as the remuneration of 300 pesos overvalued many slaves and created a huge debt that the state would have to pay.[32] Castilla may have acted unwillingly, bending to the will of his cabinet. The British minister noted on March 11 that

> the landed Proprietors who have been seriously injured by the ill considered Decree for the manumission of the slaves, have addressed a strong, and threatening remonstrance to the Provisional Government demanding compensation. I have learnt that General Castilla refused to accede to their demands but that Señor Elias, the Minister of Finance, has engaged that a sum of One Million of Dollars shall be distributed among the landed proprietors; by so doing he not only shows that he acts independently, but conciliates a powerful Body, highly useful for the success of his plans of ambition.[33]

To distribute the funds the government on April 30 created a Junta de Manumisión. Hardly a disinterested body, it was composed of ten prominent proprietors, including Francisco Quirós, who was president and considered a liberal; Isidro Aramburu, vice president; José María Sancho Dávila, treasurer; and Pedro Paz Soldán, Ignacio Osma, José Antonio Lavalle, José María de Sotomayor, Francisco Sagastaveytia, Antonio Salinas, and José Manuel Salas. All were former slave owners, and many had signed the March protest note.[34] They reported to Minister of Finance Elías, to whom, they would decide eventually, was owed compensation for 493 slaves. Nevertheless, despite its slaveholder ties, the committee demonstrated a notable degree of independence and objectivity in its operations and strictly complied with its mandate. In May, Quirós inquired whether the committee should pay less for slaves whose papers indicated that their value was less than 300 pesos, what it should do with aged slaves, what steps it should take in cases in which a promise of freedom had been reneged upon, and whether it should pay for the slaves owned by religious orders. The government replied that the committee should pay 300 pesos regardless of the market value, the state would look after invalids and the aged, payment should be altered for those whose papers indicated that they should be free, and the number of slaves owned by the orders should be verified but no compensation paid at this time. In late May the committee reckoned on the basis of the various claims in its possession that there had been between twenty-one thousand and twenty-two thousand slaves at the time of abolition. The necessity for the calculation was a telling comment on the abysmal state of official records regarding slaves at this time, while the figure indicated the complete inadequacy of the initial million pesos. Nevertheless, in mid-June the committee began paying the owners of one and two slaves.[35]

The start was promising, but the committee quickly ran into obstacles that were to plague it throughout its short existence. Even before it began paying compensation Sancho Dávila resigned, and no one could be found to replace him. Lack of funds became another major problem. The committee tried a number of ways to meet the challenge: paying only partially in specie, issuing letters against the guano consignees that were payable in one to three months, paying the interest on the bonds with other bonds, and continuing to withhold payment to the church. The cash shortage continued, however, fueling rumors that creditors were never going to be paid. The committee also had to contend with a constant flow of new claims. The government tried to stem this by declaring June 11 (plus the arrival dates of the subsequent two steamships in Callao—to satisfy slaveholders outside the capital) as the final date for submitting claims. But claims continued to arrive, and two years later the chamber of deputies was still trying to decide on a final cutoff date.

With a limited budget and mounting claims, the committee was an easy target for complaints and criticism, mainly from unpaid creditors. One wrote that for more than two thirds of his life the work of four slaves had supported him; and now he had nothing. Another, who previously had received 63 pesos monthly from the earnings of six slaves worth 1,950 pesos, claimed that now he had only vouchers, one of which he had sold for 200 pesos and another for 100 pesos. He wanted his full compensation so that he could buy a *callejón* of rooms to rent. Owners of one or two slaves complained that they were not being compensated first, as the March decree stipulated. Those with vouchers or interest bonds could sell their paper on the speculative market that appeared as a result of the uncertainty surrounding compensation, but they received only 40 percent or less of the face value. The problems produced recommendations for easing the slaveholders' plight. Manuela Pando suggested that the former slaves be compelled to remain with their masters until the latter had received full compensation, a suggestion that even *El Comercio* was seriously considering by July 1856, when many bonds still had not been redeemed. The newspaper commented that, since the owners had not been paid, the blacks were still slaves.[36]

Only one voice was raised against these efforts to help the slaveholders. In November 1855 a deputy from Arequipa named Valdivia launched a vituperative attack following a proposal that the executive provide 300,000 pesos more for paying the owners. "The masters," he said, "have been no more than exploiters of humanity; they trafficked in their fellow creatures, buying and selling them like animals, . . . they were tigers who, rather than being compensated, should be obliged to indemnify their slaves for the unjustified time the latter have served, for they have been free since General San Martín published his decree."[37] His, however, was a single, uninfluential voice, and the long process of compensating the former slaveholders continued.

By the end of 1855 the constant pressure on the committee had taken its toll. In early December it was reduced to two members and could no longer function. It was dissolved, a new committee was established, and the Tribunal Mayor de Cuentas began to play a more prominent role in the proceedings. On December 10 one of the remaining incumbents, Isidro Aramburu, submitted his resignation, complaining of the unremitting demands and pestering of the interested parties and the interference of the new minister of finance, José Fabio Melgar. He was willing to continue offering advice to the committee, but not to be a member.[38]

Despite the problems, the original committee and its successor performed admirably in enumerating the surviving slaves and *libertos* and in inaugurating the process of indemnification. They made slow progress, but checking the validity of the claims and coping with a shortage of documents almost ensured a snail's pace. As of June 21, 1855, only 752 former owners had been paid for 1,431 slaves. The committee published lists of those whose claims had been approved and whose money and bonds were available for collection.[39] By October it had pushed its initial estimate upward and now reckoned that the final total of slaves would not be more than 24,000. This still proved low: *El Peruano* reported in August 1856 that the number of slaves manumitted was 26,419, of whom 1,454 belonged to religious orders. In 1860 the Ministry of Finance announced that 25,505 slaves worth 7,651,500 pesos had been freed.[40] The committee had had to determine ownership among competing claims, assign documents long after many slaves had left their owners, and prevent fraud. Attempts at cheating were to be expected in a situation in which individuals were dependent on this one source of revenue and validation could take the form simply of swearing an oath as to the state of one's holdings on December 3, 1854. One newspaper counted seventy-two instances of fraud that involved such matters as attempting to obtain compensation for dead slaves, presenting false documents of ownership, and claiming freedmen as slaves. Someone went so far as to issue counterfeit manumission bonds, which appeared in London, Paris, and Brussels and necessitated the replacement of the legitimate ones.[41]

Claimants turned to the courts in order to establish rightful ownership of their slaves and to congress to try to secure compensation. They asked the deputies to intercede with the committee, repeating explanations and complaints that had been heard since the committee was first established: that distance had prevented them from learning about the manumission decree and presenting their claims, that their rights were not being respected, that those holding consolidation bonds were receiving preferential treatment, that those holding slave vouchers were receiving preferential treatment, and that Echenique supporters had been paid while Castilla supporters had not. The majority simply asked that they be paid, and as quickly as possible.[42]

Castilla promised payment, but the creditors remained uncertain about when that might take place. Their hopes rose and fell with the passage of new legislation. They received a scare in October 1856, when rumors of further cuts followed the government's termination of earlier policies that applied one fifth of the national income to payment of the bonds and permitted bonds to be used to pay up to one fifth of all federal taxes and contributions. In March 1857 a law renewing the amortization on the bonds for three years raised their market value to 80 and 85 percent, while the bonds for deferred interest were now quoted at 96 and 97 percent. By June of that year a number of former slaveholders still had not received compensation, although in some cases they had only themselves to blame, having failed to collect their money despite newspaper announcements of those whose money was available.[43]

By 1860 the government had committed 7,651,500 pesos for compensating owners. Of this, 2,617,600 pesos had been paid in specie and the rest in bonds. It now owed only 414,975 pesos or 331,980 soles (the new currency), virtually all to the religious orders. Gradually, it paid off the debt. The 1866 budget listed 10,860 soles still owing for manumission; the same amount appeared in the budget twelve years later.[44]

Abolition had been accomplished. The denouement of the thirty-year struggle had come suddenly and with little preparation, it had produced widespread criticism and new problems in its wake, but it had met its aims of freeing the slaves and paying the owners, and it had done so in a relatively short time. It had made Castilla and Ureta heroes among the black community. The former would always be The Liberator, deserving of the unquestioned loyalty of ex-slaves. In 1856, when Echenique and Manuel Ignacio Vivanco, with the support of unpaid creditors, rebelled against the government, the former slaves enlisted in Castilla's army, unconvinced by the claim that a Vivanco victory would guarantee their freedom as he intended to compensate all outstanding creditors immediately.[45] They viewed Ureta as a possible presidential candidate. In June 1855, on his birthday, they presented him with a gold card bearing an inscription that thanked him for his efforts on their behalf.[46]

On its first anniversary abolition was described alongside the ending of Indian tribute as one of the "most profound marks of the revolution. . . . Today [the former slaves] can raise their heads peacefully and calmly breathe the precious air of freedom. The word 'slave' has been removed forever from our legal codes and Peru, composed in its totality of free men, marches in step with the civilized people in pursuit of progress and social improvement."[47] But had the country really changed? Slavery had ended, the blacks were free, but what did this mean? Had attitudes shifted? Had racial prejudice accompanied slavery into oblivion? Could the former slaves really expect to compete with whites on an even footing? Could an event that had been as unexpected and as politically motivated as Castilla's abolition decree lead to fundamental changes? Subsequent developments revealed that it did not. Despite the freeing of the slaves, the defeat of conservative counterrevolutions, and the introduction of a new liberal constitution in 1856, Peru remained a country much dominated by its past. Rebellion and a few new laws had not altered that reality. Indeed, in the broad sweep of Peruvian history Castilla's abolition decree was almost inconsequential. The basic underpinnings of Peruvian society remained virtually intact, as the former slaves quickly learned.

## Notes

1. Davis, *Slavery and Human Progress*, 290.
2. Labarthe, "Castilla y la abolición," 20; Quiroz Norris, "La consolidación," 248–51. For further evidence of the popularity of liberalism at this time see Engelsen, "Social Aspects," 322–24; and Gootenberg, *Between Silver and Guano*, 80–91, 93–99, 111–32.
3. *El Comercio*, May 5, September 16, 1854; AGN, Notarial, Lucas de la Lama, 1854–55, Prot. 333; AGN, Notarial, Manuel de Uriza, 1854–55, Prot. 972; AD-LL, División Notarial, Escrituras, José V. Aguilar, 1854–55, Leg. 414.
4. *El Peruano*, February 25, 1854.
5. *El Heraldo de Lima*, July 7, 14, 1854.
6. For details of the 1854 rebellion see Basadre, *Historia* 4:72–76 and chap. 47; Quiroz Norris, "La consolidación," 259–81.
7. "Seguido sobre el robo hecho en las chacras del valle de Ate," AGN, CCrim, 1854, Leg. 613; *El Comercio*, November 8, December 5, 16, 1854; *El Correo de Lima*, February 15, 1854; *El Heraldo de Lima*, June 14, 27, July 25, December 5, 1854, January 2, 4, 1855; Aguirre, "Cimarronaje," 170–71.
8. Tavara, *Abolición*, 24; *El Comercio*, November 21, 1854.
9. *El Peruano*, November 23, 1854.
10. Echenique, *Memorias* 1:169.
11. *El Heraldo de Lima*, November 25, December 6, 1854.
12. *El Comercio*, January 20, 1855.
13. Sulivan to Clarendon, 127, November 25, 1854, F.O. 84/947; *El Comercio*, January 20, 1855.
14. Echenique, *Memorias* 1:169.

15. *El Heraldo de Lima*, December 7, 1854; *El Republicano Extraordinario*, December 7, 1854.

16. AGN, Notarial, Lucas de la Lama, 1854–55, Prot. 333. This lists eleven males and one female freed by the decree on November 22 and 23. See also *El Comercio*, January 20, 1855; and Manuel Atanasio Fuentes, *Biografía del exmo. e ilustrísimo señor Don Ramón Castilla, Libertador del Perú, escrita por el más fiel de sus adoradores* (Valparaíso, 1856), 101. Fuentes was being sarcastic in his choice of a title: He was a conservative slaveholder and critic of Castilla.

17. Dancuart, *Anales* 6:66–67.

18. Pedro Ugarteche and Evaristo San Cristoval, eds., *Mensajes de los presidentes del Perú, 1821–1867* (Lima, 1943), 1:309.

19. Basadre, *Historia* 4:112, 123, 153–54; Centurión Vallejo, "Esclavitud y manumisión," 78; *Diccionario enciclopédico del Perú*, prepared under the direction of Alberto Tauro (Lima, 1966), 2:10–12; Miguel A. Martínez, *La vida heroica del gran mariscal Don Ramón Castilla* (Lima, 1952), 109; Paredes, "Castilla y la abolición de la esclavitud," 12; Sulivan to Clarendon, 21, February 10, 1855, F.O. 61/153.

20. Fuentes, *Biografía*, 103; Palma, *Tradiciones* 18:190; Tavara, *Abolición*, 25; *El Heraldo de Lima*, June 1, 1855. See also Romero, "Papel de los descendientes," 87.

21. Echenique later complained of his inability to obtain satisfactory intelligence about Castilla's troop movements. See Basadre, *Historia* 4:114.

22. Ibid.; Tavara, *Abolición*, 26.

23. AGN, Notarial, Lucas de la Lama, 1854–55, Prot. 333; AGN, Notarial, Manuel De Uriza, 1854–55, Prot. 972; *El Comercio*, January 8, February 24, May 26, 1855. In Trujillo the executor of a will freed a slave and *liberto* on February 12, 1855, explaining that the owner wrote her will before Castilla's victory. He renounced any claim for compensation. See AD-LL, División Notarial, Escrituras, José V. Aguilar, 1854–55, Leg. 414, 135, 136.

24. Sulivan to Clarendon, 12, January 21, 1855, F.O. 61/145.

25. *El Comercio*, January 19, 1855.

26. Ibid., January 22, 23, February 1, 3, 11, July 14, 1855; *El Heraldo de Lima*, June 2, 4, 5, 6, October 25, 1855; *El Murciélago*, March 15, 1855; Labarthe, "Castilla y la abolición," 21.

27. *El Peruano*, February 6, 1855.

28. Basadre, *Historia* 4:343; Ugarteche and San Cristoval, *Mensajes* 1:314.

29. *El Heraldo de Lima*, June 5, 1855.

30. Ibid., June 6, 1855; *El Comercio*, February 15, March 8, April 13, 1855.

31. *El Peruano*, March 10, 1855; *El Comercio*, March 11, 1855; Basadre, *Historia* 4:344.

32. For one example of a slave whose market value was less than 300 pesos see "D. Lorenzo Figueroa a nombre de Da. Joaquina Uribe, reclamando el pago del valor de una esclava," ACD, 1855, 1856, 1857, Leg. 15, Expedientes de particulares pasados a la Comisión de Memoriales, 1857, 26. This discusses the case of a slave named Petronila who had been sold at the age of fifteen in 1826 for 150 pesos, with the condition

that she could not be sold for more. She subsequently was sold sixteen times, once to Isidro Aramburu who resold her four days later. She was last sold in 1849 for 100 pesos, to Joaquina Uribe who now was "reduced to the unhappy condition of losing that [property], which is not just."

33. Ugarteche and San Cristoval, *Mensajes* 1:315; Sulivan to Clarendon, 31, March 11, 1855, F.O. 61/154.

34. Quirós was later compensated for 23 slaves, Aramburu for 41, Paz-Soldán for 163, Lavalle for 322, and Sotomayor for 46. See *El Comercio*, April 24, 1856; and *Diccionario* 2:24.

35. *El Heraldo de Lima*, May 11, 1855; *El Peruano*, May 10, June 5, 15, 1855; *El Comercio*, June 5, 1855.

36. For the activities of the Junta de Manumisión and assorted criticisms see "Junta de Manumisión," Lima, July 1855, BN D2342; *El Comercio*, April 23, May 18, July 2, 11, October 24, November 14, December 6, 1855, April 24, May 20, July 22, August 2, 1856, June 15, July 1, 1857; *El Heraldo de Lima*, June 5, 22, July 21, September 13, October 16, 23, November 19, December 27, 1855; and Dancuart, *Anales* 6:67.

37. *El Heraldo de Lima*, November 15, 1855.

38. For some of the problems of the committee, including the dispute between Aramburu and Melgar, see "Junta de Manumisión," Lima, July 1855, BN D2342; and *El Comercio*, December 4, 6, 7, 27, 1855, January 17, February 11, 19, 22, March 8, 1856.

39. For some of these lists see *El Comercio*, January 11, 17, 18, 19, 21, April 24, 25, May 19, 20, 31, 1856, March 4, May 5, 1857.

40. The reason for the difference is not clear, unless church-owned slaves and others were subtracted. The statistics in *El Peruano* leave some doubts as to their accuracy: Its calculation of the value of the slaves is wrong by 21,300 pesos in one case and 300 pesos in another. The difference may indicate that at least some slaves were valued at less than 300 pesos. See *El Peruano*, August 21, 1856; and Dancuart, *Anales* 6:67. For a list of the principal slaveholders indemnified by the manumission decree see Quiroz Norris, "La consolidación," table 2. The Convento de Buenamuerte was the largest owner, with 517 slaves; other orders also owned significant numbers.

41. See, for example, "Doña Petronila de Santiago Concha, sobre el pago de su esclava Juliana," AGN, CCiv, 1854–55, Leg. 173, November 28, 1855; "Don Juan Pedro Lostaunau con Don Vicente Alfaro sobre retención del precio de la esclavatura de la chacra de Pró," AGN, CCiv, 1854–55, Leg. 174, April 19, 1855; "Tercera escluyente de Doña Jacoba Salazar de Rivera en la causa que sigue Don Julian Layseca contra Don Ignacio Rivera, su esposo," AGN, CCiv, 1854–5, Leg. 174, October 19, 1855; "D. Manuel Ballesteros—un esclavo," ACD, 1856/1857, Convención Nacional, Leg. 21-25, 99; *El Comercio*, June 15, 1855, October 8, 16, 1856, June 15, October 21, November 10, December 24, 1857; *El Heraldo de Lima*, December 22, 1855; and *El Peruano*, August 27, 1856.

42. "Se desaprueba un decreto del Gobierno, relativo a vales de consolidación y de manumisión," ACD, 1855, 1856, 1857, Leg. 6, Convención Nacional, Asuntos Generales Resueltos, 52; "Del Sr. Bandini pidiendo se exitase al Ejecutivo para que ordenase a la Junta de Manumisión la continuación del examen de los expedientes de esclavos," AGN, 1855, 1856, 1857, Leg. 9, Proyectos y proposiciones a la orden del día, 1855, 16; "De los SS Muga y Escudero para que se pague de preferencia

el principal e intereses aduedados por la manumisión de esclavos," ACD, 1855, 1856, 1857, Leg. 9, Proyectos y proposiciones a la orden del día, 1855, 17; "De los SS Eguisquiza y Matute para que se abone el valor de los esclavos pertenecientes a individuos que no pudieron hacer uso oportunamente de sus acciones," ACD, 1855, 1856, 1857, Proyectos y proposiciones a la orden del día, 1857, 9; "De Don Pablo Patrón, a nombre de los tenedores de vales de manumisión para que se derogue el decreto de 4 de Octubre de 1856," ACD, 1855, 1856, 1857, Leg. 16, Expedientes particulares pasados a las Comisiones que se indica, 8; "D. Juan Teodoro Calderón por D. José Mateo Ramírez—un esclavo," ACD, 1856/1857, Convención Nacional, Leg. 21-25, Junta de Manumisión, 206; "Palmieri y Patroni por D. Simón Cuneo," ACD, 1856/1857, Convención Nacional, Leg. 21-25, Junta de Manumisión, 210; "D. José María Vidal—un esclavo," ACD, 1856/1857, Convención Nacional, Leg. 21-25, Junta de Manumisión, 211.

43. Lists were published at least three times. See *El Comercio*, April 24, May 20, July 12, August 2, 1856, June 2, 13, 1857.

44. Basadre, *Historia* 4:344–45; Dancuart, *Anales* 6:67, 7:107, 8:8, 10:96.

45. Pike, *Modern History*, 107–8; *El Comercio*, December 11, 1856, January 5, 27, 1857.

46. *El Comercio*, March 10, June 9, 1855.

47. *El Peruano*, January 5, 1856.

# 10

# The Aftermath of Abolition

In 1857, in a reference to the recent abolition of slavery, Peru's minister of foreign affairs observed:

> By legislation passed during the first days of our independence, the importation of Africans, that repugnant trade which was still occurring, was prohibited along the whole coast of Peru. Through subsequent dispositions, slavery, which still survived in the country, should have disappeared with the hazy passage of time. However, the entire nation with its essentially humanitarian character was watching. It saw this as an aberration and desired rapid abolition. To satisfy that national demand and as a consequence of the moral revolution of 1854, the decree of December 3 of that same year was issued that abolished slavery once and for all throughout the territory of the Republic.[1]

With its references to widespread support for humanitarian goals and long-standing opposition to slavery, this account was typical of the half-truths and hyperbole that began to mystify the true story of the struggle for abolition almost as soon as Castilla implemented his decree. In a similar fashion, commentator after commentator obscured and distorted the effects of abolition, arguing that the end of slavery had been an unmitigated disaster for Peru and Peruvians as it had undermined the country's economic development and harmed social relations. They provided corroborating evidence in many cases so that their comments cannot simply be dismissed as the embittered ravings of former slaveholders. However, a close examination of events after abolition reveals that they often used their evidence selectively and ignored the broader picture.

Cutting through the mythology and the distortions, the self-interest and the short-term evaluations, also leads to the conclusion that the end of slavery had very little impact on Peru. Abolition did not spell disaster, but neither did it mark a watershed in the country's history. Castilla's decree did not significantly affect the direction or the nature of Peruvian developments; the liberal focus of the 1854 revolution did not indicate that the dominant sectors of society had become proponents of liberalism; attitudes toward blacks and toward workers in general did not change. Denied black slaves, employers turned to alternative sources of the servile workers they desired. They secured the reopening of the coolie trade early in the 1860s, and during that same decade they imported several hundred Polynesian workers, exploiting both groups as they had slaves in the past.[2] Some former slave owners may have pleaded hardship because of the loss of their workers, but the government's compensation helped cushion the blow, and the transition to free wage labor seemed to improve the financial position of many of them. In common with the British Caribbean, the plantation system remained intact, as did the political influence that went with it.[3]

As for the former slaves, they obtained their freedom but little else. They still had to cope with the prejudice and discrimination of the ruling class and the rest of the white population. Moreover, no longer were they the crucial labor sector that they had been in the past. Replaced by coolies, European immigrants, and indigenous workers from the sierra, they possessed no leverage in the labor market and had to accept whatever jobs were made available to them. They even seemed to be disappearing as a separate demographic group. Their proportion of the population had been declining for decades because of the termination of the slave trade, high mortality rates, and low reproductivity. That decline now accelerated as a result of racial mixing, the immigration of other groups, and a conscious decision among blacks to redefine themselves racially. Even their cultural influence began to wane, as the dominant group adopted and championed what had been elements of black culture, while coastal culture in general was being reshaped by the waves of *serranos* who were migrating to the coast in ever-increasing numbers.

The view that the end of slavery had a profoundly negative effect on Peru remained commonly held for many years after abolition. The arguments that critics made in the first months after the implementation of Castilla's decree were repeated time and again: abolition had paralyzed agricultural production, inflated the price of foodstuffs, and left slaveholders destitute; former slaves lacking paternalistic control were refusing to work or had abandoned their masters; and many slaves had became vagabonds and thieves, leading to a new crime wave. Seventy years later these views were still accepted. In 1926, Pedro Dávalos y Lissón argued in his influential four-volume work *La primera centuria* that the Castilla revolution had cost four thousand lives and 13 million pesos and then caused further hardships as a result of the abolition decree. He wrote that it had produced "calamities of immense gravity" in the agricultural sector and in social relations and had been "harmful to the interests of the treasury and to those who lived from the work of the slaves." Many poor urban families whose income had been derived from the wages earned by their slaves had been left in misery, while former slaves—men, women, and children—had delivered themselves to "the vices of alcohol, lust, sloth, and brigandage." Their refusal to work except when they were hungry had reduced agricultural productivity and driven up the price of essentials. Their criminal activities had resulted in the appointment of a special judicial tribunal that found so many former slaves guilty of capital offenses that the gallows had been kept in constant use.[4]

Of the problems arising from abolition, the most frequently mentioned was the decline of agriculture. Some critics went so far as to claim that it was "destroyed," and with it the landholding class.[5] They pointed to examples such as that of the Bocanegra estate, whose owner in 1855 refused to pay his taxes—the unremarkable sum of 120 pesos—because of the state of "ruin" of his estate, which he blamed on abolition. In the province of Cañete former slaves were reported to have delivered themselves to "laziness and licentiousness," leaving the fields empty and uncultivated and causing the price of agricultural produce to rise. Despite making large expenditures in an attempt to survive, many Cañete farmers eventually abandoned the land. Elsewhere owners followed a similar course, undermining agricultural production in the process and providing additional evidence of a sector in crisis. They almost invariably blamed their difficulties on a shortage of labor, claiming that the ex-slaves and their families had fled the estates. Five years after abolition Cañete owners stated that former slaves would still not work on the estates, but lived in nearby villages and "came for a few days to work, and then disappear, as the humour takes them." The finance minister in 1855 accepted this view, ascribing agriculture's difficulties to a shortage of labor. So, too, did later commentators such as Emilio Dancuart, who noted that emancipation, which had hurt mining, had had "ruinous consequences for agriculture." The proprietors had not foreseen it, "and they found themselves unexpectedly without the workers necessary to gather the harvest or to operate their industries, suffering consequently a serious and irreparable loss."[6]

The situation, however, was not the complete disaster that these writers suggest or claim. For one thing, agriculture had not been a dynamic sector previously. Thus, any decline following abolition was probably marginal, although further research may prove otherwise. In some respects the situation had improved. *El Comercio* reported in 1857 that haciendas were producing more now than they did when they had employed slaves. It cited the example of the Mataratones estate, which had been divided in 1855; each half was now producing more than the entire estate had before abolition. In the Cañete Valley, a recovery was evident within the decade due to the arrival of new coolie labor, the introduction of machinery, and the increased demand arising from the American Civil War.[7]

Moreover, contrary to what many commentators wrote, the land had not been abandoned by either its owners or its workers. Large numbers of blacks remained on the estates after abolition, as even former slaveholders admitted when they complained of the high wages that they now had to pay. Some contemporary accounts contend that the majority of the former slaves continued to work as they had done before, in the same places and under the same circumstances, only now they received a wage. Most domestics as well as those lacking a profession also remained in their former owners' houses, often working under the same conditions. This may not have been a totally voluntary choice, but rather a decision forced on them by hunger and want and an inability to find a job elsewhere. Whatever the reason, the fact remains that many ex-slaves stayed with their owners, so the picture of abandoned lands and masters is not an altogether accurate one.[8]

Furthermore, while some landholders may have suffered and been forced to sell their property, others, like the owner

of Mataratones, were benefiting. Many planters who owned
large numbers of slaves profited from the indemnification,
people such as Domingo Elías who as finance minister was
rumored to have participated in an association that bought
undervalued slave vouchers. Elías remained a wealthy man
whose fortune was not substantially affected by abolition.[9]
Some merchants bought slave vouchers and used the profits
from their speculation to purchase or recapitalize estates,
revealing their confidence in this sector. Their financial deal-
ings, in the words of Pablo Macera, converted a fixed capital
(the slaves) into circulating capital (the indemnity), "permitting a shifting of investments." Those who rented property
found themselves in an improved situation because they no
longer had to pay for rented slaves and thus had a smaller
capital outlay. Some of the capital that was now available
was used to modernize the agrarian sector. Creditors of planters assisted in this process by pressuring the latter to up-
grade their operations. As the agrarian sector improved, so,
too, did the nascent industrial sector, which also received
some of the freed capital.[10]

However, the role of the slave indemnification in Peru's
post-1855 economic growth and modernization and in the
creation of a new coastal plutocracy should not be
overstressed.[11] Compensation for the slaves was only one
source of the funds that were available for investment in the
1850s. Millions more, up to 15 million pesos, were in circulation as a result of the earlier consolidation law, while even
more funds were provided by the continuing expansion of the
guano industry.[12] Thus, while the financial impact of abolition
was not negligible, it was relatively small in comparison with
the other major financial developments of the time.

Associated with the postabolition agricultural difficulties
was a widely predicted inflation in food prices. Critics of
abolition at the time contended that prices would rise, and
later commentators proved them right. Santiago Tavara made
a survey of prices shortly after abolition and found that the
cost of living had risen. A later and more complete examination of 1850s prices came to the same conclusion, noting a
pronounced increase between 1855 and 1856, especially after
February 1855. But while there is agreement on the fact of a
price increase, opinions differ as to the reasons for it. The
critics blamed it on abolition, while Tavara believed that the
maintenance of armies and the destruction during the civil
war had been responsible. He noted that, since most slaves

had been involved in the production of sugar and grapes rather than foodstuffs, emancipation would have had little impact on the price of essentials. A more recent study contends that the timing of the rise supports the view that abolition helped push up prices, but other factors such as international pressures on the Peruvian currency also played a role. The increased circulation of money from the slave vouchers, the consolidation bonds, and the guano revenues; the specialization in commercial crops and rising transportation costs; and the end of Indian tribute payments, which cut back on agricultural surpluses—all of these had inflationary effects on food prices.[13]

Prices rose. Who suffered as a result? Little has been written on the subject, but reason suggests that the lower classes and those on a set income would have been the most affected. This may in part account for the reported hardships suffered by former urban slave owners who without their slaves providing an income could not afford the increasingly expensive food. Some of the lower classes may not have been especially affected, since the labor shortage was driving up wages, doubling them in some cases. Few workers, however, benefited from this windfall. For the rest, jobs were uncertain, wages were not guaranteed, and the rising prices must have been the source of much grief.[14]

While the poor suffered, other sectors of the population had little cause for complaint. Paramount among these were the producers of foodstuffs, whose position improved enormously from the higher prices as well as from the reduced expenses that followed abolition. To what extent they actually profited is unknown, for this aspect of Peru's economic history remains unstudied, but the assumption is that their returns were sufficient to counter any losses arising from emancipation.

In addition to the various economic problems, abolition was blamed for causing social unrest. Critics charged that it released "uncivilized" blacks from the controlling hand of the master and left them to disrupt the social fabric of the nation. They could cite instances of former slaves rising up, attacking coastal estates, and even killing their owners. In July 1856 a former slave was reported to have raped, hanged, decapitated, and further mutilated the body of Doña Joaquina Arana, an estate owner in the Pacasmayo Valley. The alleged assailant was arrested, but before he could be brought to trial, local townspeople raided the jail, abducted the prisoner, and lynched him.[15] More common were the brigandage and theft that seemed to multiply following abolition. Newspaper reports give the impression that robbers and highwaymen plagued the country in 1855, and their raids seem to have gone beyond merely stealing and disrupting communications. One report on a group of well-mounted black *montoneros* operating near Surco referred to them as "black communists."[16]

Once again, the situation may not have been as bad as the critics charged, and the relationship of the crime wave to abolition is not at all clear. Although crimes were occurring, no one has proved that the perpetrators were ex-slaves, nor has anyone tried to make a comparison with earlier periods when banditry was rife to see if the postabolition situation was significantly worse. Only Santiago Tavara made what might be called a scientific study of the problem, and he restricted himself to the 1854–55 period. His examination of police reports for January to June of both years revealed no increase in the crime rate for the later period; in fact, there was a slight decrease. Addressing congress in October 1857, he remarked: "When the blacks were emancipated, it was said that they would be lazy, that they would steal to survive, that from theft they would progress to highway robbery, murder, and arson. False! Most blacks work. There are idle and vicious ones, but just as there are idle and vicious whites." He added that recent highly publicized crimes could not be blamed on Peru's black population.[17]

As further proof of increased criminal activity after abolition, critics referred to the appointment of a special Tribunal de Acordada and its sentencing of numerous former slaves to the gallows. The tribunal had existed some years earlier, had been suppressed in 1839, and then was reinstituted on June 20, 1855, by supreme decree. In its first year of renewed operations it heard 172 cases involving 287 persons. Of the accused, 144 were absolved, 92 were sentenced to prison, and 10 were condemned to death. During this period, however, no one was executed, and the government commuted at least one capital sentence to ten years of hard labor. How many of those who were convicted had been slaves is not recorded. The picture, therefore, of a long line of black criminals proceeding inexorably to the gallows is a fanciful one, and the relationship between the tribunal and abolition is open to doubt.[18]

What is surprising is that the former slaves did not engage in more acts of violence, for, while they had received their freedom, they had obtained virtually nothing else. Like Brazil's slaves thirty-three years later, Peruvian blacks soon realized that "emancipation from slavery marked the beginning of the struggle for freedom, not the end."[19] Official energies following abolition had been directed toward assisting the slave owners, not the slaves. The interests of the latter were almost completely ignored, as little was done to ease their passage to freedom and to welcome them as equals into Peruvian society. One of the few gestures in their direction was an attempt early in 1856 to establish a college for former slaves. It aroused public hostility, however, failed to attract government support, and was a dead issue by July.[20] Some former slaves may have believed that their situation had improved. For example, wet nurses were demanding such high wages that only the rich could afford them, while black plantation workers found that planters preferred them to Indian labor, employed them as foremen over the *serranos*, and even sought to import African settlers to replace the departed slaves.[21] But even these privileged few had to cope with living in a hostile society marked by prejudice and racial discrimination.

The widespread racism was evident in the criticisms of the emancipation process as well as in more overtly antiblack statements. In 1855 an article in a Cuzco newspaper accused blacks of being "the worst race of the human species for their intellectual unsuitability" and "a terrible plague for Peru." It recommended that they be sent to form a colony in the Amazon, isolated from others to prevent the spread of crime "that always has been the heritage of this caste." Even sympathetic individuals, such as Santiago Tavara, believed that blacks were intellectually brutalized and morally insensitive, a natural consequence of slavery. Later writers shared these views, helping to ensure that racism and prejudice toward blacks survived into the twentieth century.[22]

Faced by open hostility, the former slaves also had to contend with no longer being a vital sector of the laboring population and, consequently, having no leverage in the labor market. The reintroduction of the coolie trade in 1861, the arrival of European immigrants, and renewed efforts to employ the indigenous population created an alternative labor supply.[23] As a result most blacks found themselves with little choice in jobs, restricted to the less attractive ones, and expected to engage only in their traditional occupations. In contrast to postabolition Haiti, few of Peru's former slaves had access to land so that they could become independent farmers and separate themselves from their former owners.[24] Forced to remain on the estates, some found that their old owners ignored the abolition law and treated them as if nothing had changed. Working conditions did not improve. In the Chancay Valley, blacks were reported to be "held in virtual slavery" or at least bound in some manner to the estates. As sharecroppers or tenant farmers, they lived on the fringes of the estates and for many years had to provide unpaid labor at harvest time.[25]

The passage of time did little to alter the situation. A study of Afro-Peruvians at the beginning of the twentieth century shows that those in Lima were still largely restricted to a small handful of traditional artisanal, skilled, and unskilled jobs in the urban sector, or to plantation labor and domestic service. In part this continuity was a result of "a system of personal relations" in which blacks chose to follow the occupation of a relative or friend. More relevant, however, were the limited job opportunities open to them and the continuing obstacles to social mobility created by the dominant groups.[26]

Confined to the bottom of the social ladder, discriminated against because of their color, and exploited like other members of Peru's laboring class, many blacks struck back at their exploiters, following familiar patterns of resistance. Occasionally they turned to violence and attacked their former owners, as in the case of Joaquina Arana. More often, as they had done in the past, they adopted less militant methods, resorting to what the white community perceived as insulting or obnoxious behavior. In the months immediately after abolition, *El Murciélago*, an antigovernment newspaper published by Manuel Atanasio Fuentes, described a number of incidents involving blacks that may or may not have occurred. The stories stressed the insolence of the blacks but revealed simultaneously the racism in the white community. The reports described blacks who obstructed a sidewalk and forced a white woman "of more than half a century" to walk in the street; a group of blacks who insulted a white man and threatened to break his jaw; an "insolent black" on a burro who knocked over a small boy and then loudly cursed him when the child began to cry; a black who approached a young white woman in the street, tapped her on the shoulder, and announced: "Blanquita, soon we'll get married, now that we're all equal"; and six "free citizens" who assaulted a little black girl, who was attending a number of white women on their way to church, and threw the rug she was carrying into a ditch.[27]

Attracting particular attention, once again, were Lima's water carriers. They were still drawn almost entirely from the black population, they still carried out additional duties such as catching and killing stray dogs, and they were still notorious for their insolence. In one reported case a number of them rubbed the bloody carcass of a dog against the dresses of some "elegant" young ladies on their way to the theater. When the latter remonstrated, the water carriers replied, "These are the fruits of liberty."[28] Alcohol may have been the lubricant for some of these incidents, as the newspapers reported clashes between inebriated blacks and police in which the former were heard to shout: "Death to the police, long live Castilla, death to the whites."[29]

The animosity simmered for twenty-five years and finally boiled over into open rebellion during the War of the Pacific (1879–1883). Following the Chilean invasion of the coast of Peru and the consequent breakdown in central authority, blacks in the Chincha and Cañete valleys attacked whites and, more frequently, Chinese. Although the coolies were another exploited sector of the population, they were still perceived to be assisting in the oppression of the blacks, partly by taking away jobs, partly through their role in small commerce. They were also less capable of defending themselves and were an easy target, since many of them had sided with the Chilean invaders. In the case of the Cañete uprising, several hundred Chinese were killed before Chilean troops restored order.[30]

This marked the last collective attempt by Peru's blacks to alter through violence the situation in which they found themselves. Subsequently, opportunities were far more limited, largely because of the declining size of the black population, both absolutely and as a percentage of the total population. This pattern had been evident since the abolition of the slave trade and the termination of black immigration. The fertility rate of the black population may have risen with emancipation and the concurrent improvement in living conditions, but the other major racial groups were increasing more rapidly in size, and natural reproduction within the black community did not keep pace. As a result, by 1876 blacks and Asians together comprised only 4 percent of the Peruvian population. In Lima, in 1857, around 11 percent of the population of 90,000 was black; the figure declined to just under 5 percent of a population of 140,884 in 1908, and to 2 percent of 562,885 in 1940. Only in Ica, where in 1940 they constituted just over 4 percent of the population, were they still a distinct group. Elsewhere blacks did not total over 1 percent of the local population.[31]

The decline may not have been as large as the statistics suggest, for mistakes in the censuses almost certainly occurred. Where blacks were concerned, errors were especially likely. One reason for this was that they, like other nonwhite groups, were altering their self-classification, "whitening" themselves as they tried to improve their opportunities for advancement in a racially rigid environment. Accepting the dominant group's views, many of them displayed a negative self-image, rejected their African heritage, and refused to recognize themselves as "black." They also married with other racial groups in a further act of denial, producing offspring whose racial identification was difficult to determine.[32] The result was fewer and fewer Peruvians who defined themselves or were recognized as black.

As their numbers declined, the blacks' influence followed suit. This was evident in the labor sector; it was also true in the cultural sphere. In the past blacks had made a significant contribution to the country's cultural developments, to its music, dance, religious festivals, food, and even language. Elements that had been introduced by African slaves had been kept alive and spread by their descendants over the following centuries, and in some cases they were adopted either wholly or in part by other sectors of society. Neither the end of the slave trade nor the abolition of slavery completely reversed this process, and celebrations that maintained the black communities' traditions continued to be held in their barrios for years after abolition. Nevertheless, changes became evident as the black population declined. Some of their principal celebrations began to be taken over by others. Perhaps the most obvious example of this was the Lima religious cult associated with the image of Nuestro Señor de los Milagros. It had originated among the slaves, but by the early twentieth century the annual celebrations were increasingly under the direction of members of the white community. At the same time the blacks' pervasive influence along the coast was being challenged by Indian migrants. Just as black workers were being replaced by newcomers, their culture was being "swamped by consecutive waves of *serrano* migration." The Afro-Peruvian cultural heritage remained alive, but, like the black population, it was losing its influence and being overshadowed by the new developments.[33]

With the abolition of slavery many changes occurred in Peruvian society. Much remained the same, however, as abolition did not mark a social revolution or a cathartic break with the past. Vestiges of colonial attitudes and traditions could still be found. The elite continued to dominate the country, leaving their imprint not only on the early republic but also on developments for years thereafter. Their interests prevailed, and they remained committed to maintaining the old ways. Only grudgingly were they prepared to accept change; when they did, it was gradual, for they had no intention of permitting more fundamental transformations that might threaten their political, social, and economic dominance. Their resistance, plus the weak and uncertain nature of the abolitionist process, had ensured that the slaves secured nothing more than their freedom in 1855. Nonwhites and the laboring classes in general were still exploited and downtrodden sectors of the Peruvian population, a fact clearly shown by the subsequent experiences of Chinese coolies, Polynesian immigrants, sierra migrants, and Amazonian rubber workers. One colonial institution had fallen, but many more remained, supporting the elitist, exploitative, undemocratic system that dominated this nation and in which the blacks now had to find their way.

These negative and depressing aspects, however, should not be permitted to hide the fact that slavery had ended and the black population was finally free. Peru and Peruvians should be commended for this accomplishment. The struggle to end slavery had revealed the courage, spirit, and determination of numerous individuals, both slave and free, and marked a noble chapter in the country's history. Peru may not have been the first country to abolish slavery, but neither was it the last. The pressures to maintain the institution had been enormous, yet they had been overcome. There were still many problems; other elements of the colonial past survived, and social inequities, discrimination, and racial prejudice were still part of the Peruvian reality. Nonetheless, the example of the abolitionist process showed that change could occur. Much still needed to be done, but the end of slavery gave proof that those striving to improve the situation were not engaged in a futile effort. Peruvians could alter their lives. It might require outside influences, it might take many years, but it could be accomplished.

# Notes

1. Enclosure with Barton to Clarendon, ST1, November 13, 1857, F.O. 84/1025.
2. Engelsen, "Social Aspects," 118–19; H. E. Maude, *Slavers in Paradise: The Peruvian Labour Trade in Polynesia, 1862–1864* (Canberra, 1981), especially chap. 17; Stewart, *Chinese Bondage*, 25–30.
3. Concerning the British Caribbean see Eric Foner, *Nothing but Freedom: Emancipation and Its Legacy* (Baton Rouge, 1983), 14.
4. Pedro Dávalos y Lissón, *La primera centuria: causas geográficas, políticas y económicas que han detenido el progreso moral y material del Perú en el primer siglo de su vida independiente* (Lima, 1926), 4:105–6.
5. Manuel Atanasio Fuentes claimed that the abolition decree had "been prejudicial to those who were masters, . . . the larger part of [whom] . . . are now insolvent." See Fuentes, *Biografía*, 105.
6. Dancuart, *Anales* 5:8, 6:4; E. Larrabure y Unánue, *Cañete: apuntes geográficos, históricos, estadísticos y arqueológicos* (Lima, 1874), 49; Clements R. Markham, "Private journal kept during the voyages and journeys from Southampton to Arequipa from December 17th, 1859, to March 21st, 1860," RGS-CRM 64:45; *El Heraldo de Lima*, June 4, October 29, 1855; *El Comercio*, August 16, 1855, June 2, 1856; AAL, Causas de Negros, 1815–1855, Leg. 36, LXII:17. See also Cotler, *Clases, estado y nación*, 97; Cuche, *Poder blanco*, 34–36; and Paredes, "Castilla y la abolición," 13.
7. See also the quotation in Denys Cuche, *Pérou nègre: les descendants d'esclaves africains du Pérou des grands domaines esclavagistes aux plantations modernes* (Paris, 1981), 44, that indicates that there was an agricultural recovery by 1861.
8. *El Comercio*, September 1, 1855, January 11, 1856, May 8, 1857; Cuche, *Pérou nègre*, 37–39; Cuche, *Poder blanco*, 36–38, 41; E. A. Hammel, *Power in Ica: The Structural History of a Peruvian Community* (Boston, 1969), 69; Larrabure y Unánue, *Cañete*, 49; Macera, "Las plantaciones azucareras," 173; Rout, *African Experience*, 220; Ulloa Sotomayor, *La organización social*, 18.
9. *El Murciélago*, April 21, 1855. The rumors may have been politically motivated, but there were grounds for suspicions. One of the members of the Junta de Manumisión, Francisco Sagastaveytia, was a former associate who had been involved in the purchase of New Granada slaves and the coolie trade. Elías subsequently suffered financial reverses, but these were not directly related to abolition. Concerning his later career see Quiroz Norris, "La consolidación," 197–202; and Engelsen, "Social Aspects," 144–45, 455, 461.

10. Macera, "Las plantaciones azucareras," 126–29. See also Gonzales, *Plantation Agriculture*, 22; and Quiroz Norris, "La consolidación," 28–29.

11. For a brief discussion of the emergence of a new coastal plutocracy after 1860 see Basadre, *Historia* 4:368–69.

12. Mathew, *House of Gibbs*, 194–96.

13. Tavara, *Abolición*, 45–46; Quiroz Norris, "La consolidación," 286–88, 290–91, 295–99; Bonilla, "Peru and Bolivia," 252; Cuche, *Pérou nègre*, 40; Engelsen, "Social Aspects," 272–75.

14. Quiroz Norris, "La consolidación," 300–301, 304–5.

15. *El Heraldo de Lima*, June 5, October 23, 1855; *El Comercio*, July 29, 1856.

16. *El Comercio*, September 10, October 12, 15, 1855; *El Heraldo de Lima*, October 15, 1855.

17. *El Comercio*, October 30, 1857; Tavara, *Abolición*, 36–43.

18. Concerning the activities of the Tribunal de Acordada see *El Comercio*, February 11, April 1, 26, May 3, June 4, July 9, 17, August 6, November 22, 1856; and *El Peruano*, July 26, 1856.

19. Toplin, *Abolition of Slavery*, ix.

20. *El Comercio*, February 1, July 26, 1856.

21. *El Comercio*, February 17, 24, 1860; Cuche, *Pérou nègre*, 42–43; Hammel, *Power in Ica*, 71; Macera, "Las plantaciones azucareras," 267.

22. The Cuzco article appeared in *El Heraldo de Lima*, September 3, 1855. For Tavara's comment see Tavara, *Abolición*, 25. See also Cuche, *Pérou nègre*, 56–59; Rout, *African Experience*, 222–24; and Susan C. Stokes, "Etnicidad y clase social: los afro-peruanos de Lima, 1900–1930," in *Lima obrera, 1900–1930*, vol. 2, by Laura Miller et al. (Lima: 1987), 203, 208, 215–18, 242–43.

23. The number of Europeans, who included Basques, Germans, and Italians, was small but may have raised hopes of further immigration. See Basadre, *Historia* 4:365–67, 374–76; and Hammel, *Power in Ica*, 57.

24. On some of the British Caribbean islands, former slaves also had access to land. See Foner, *Nothing but Freedom*, chap. 1.

25. Cuche, *Pérou nègre*, 62–64; Cuche, *Poder blanco*, 41; Louis C. Faron, "A History of Agricultural Production and Local Organization in the Chancay Valley, Peru," in *Contemporary Change in Traditional Societies*, vol. 3, ed. Julian H. Steward (Urbana, 1970), 232, 238; Paredes, "Castilla y la abolición," 13; Jean Piel, "The Place of the Peasantry in the National Life of Peru in the Nineteenth Century," *Past and Present* 46 (1970): 125.

26. Stokes, "Etnicidad," 193, 194, 198, 201, 206–7. This is not to say that Peru's social barriers were impassable. Chinese coolies, for example, managed to transform themselves from semiservile labor into petit bourgeois and, in time, came to dominate much of Peru's petty commercial sector.

27. *El Murciélago*, March 18, 22, 1855. The accuracy of these reports is open to question. They were written in a rather sarcastic and caustic vein, with the writer concluding, "*Viva la Libertad!*" For more on Fuentes see Basadre, *Historia* 4:130–31.

28. *El Comercio*, July 9, 1856. For a picture of black water carriers with the carcass of a dog see Angrand, *Imagen*, 189–90.

29. *El Comercio*, January 9, September 2, 1857.

30. Arona, *La inmigración*, 99–104; Cuche, *Pérou nègre*, 81–87; Carmela Sotomayor Roggero and Ramón Aranda de los Rios, *Sublevación de campesinos negros en Chincha, 1879* (Lima, 1979), 32–46; Stewart, *Chinese Bondage*, 121–24, 218–21.

31. Manuel A. Fuentes, *Estadística general de Lima* (Lima, 1858), 42, 619; Enrique León García, *Las razas en Lima: estudio demográfico* (Lima, 1909), 14, 81; Jeffrey L. Klaiber, *Religion and Revolution in Peru, 1824–1976* (Notre Dame, 1977), 46; MacLean y Estenos, *Negros en el nuevo mundo*, 145–54; Romero, "El mestizaje negroide," 244.

32. Stokes, "Etnicidad," 184–86, 215–18. For an examination of the deficiencies of census records and "racial redefinition" concerning blacks in Buenos Aires, and the reasons behind those deficiencies, see Andrews, *Afro-Argentines*, chaps. 5 and 6.

33. *El Comercio*, July 22, 1856; Cuche, *Pérou nègre*, 136–39; Cuche, *Poder blanco*, chap. 14; Stokes, "Etnicidad," 220–34, 249.

# Bibliography

## Archives and Special Collections

Archivo Arzobispal de Lima (AAL), Lima
    Especially Causas Civiles (CCiv) and Causas de Negros
Archivo de la Cámara de Diputados (ACD), Lima
    Especially Convención Nacional, 1855, 1856, 1857
Archivo Departamental de Arequipa (AD-A), Arequipa
    Especially Corte Superior de Justicia, Causas Civiles (CCiv)
    and Causas Criminales (CCrim), and Notarial
Archivo Departamental de La Libertad (AD-LL), Trujillo
    Especially División Judicial, Causas Civiles (CCiv) and Causas
    Criminales (CCrim), and División Notarial
Archivo General de la Nación (AGN), Lima
    Especially Temporalidades, Causas Civiles (CCiv), Causas
    Criminales (CCrim), and Notarial
Biblioteca Nacional (BN), Lima, Oficina de Investigaciones
    Bibliográficas and Hermeroteca
Public Record Office, London
    Especially Foreign Office (FO) files 61, 84, 177
Royal Geographical Society (RGS), London
    Clements R. Markham Special Collection (CRM)
Wellcome Institute for the History of Medicine, London
    Clements R. Markham, "Travels in Peru in 1853." 2 vols.

## Primary Sources

Dancuart, P. Emilio. *Anales de la hacienda pública del Perú: leyes, decretos, reglamentos y resoluciones; aranceles, presupuestos, cuentas y contratas que constituyen la legislación y la historia fiscal de la república.* 10 vols. Lima: Imprenta de "La Revista" and Imprenta de Guillermo Stolte, 1902–1908.
————. *Crónica parlamentaria del Perú: historia de los congresos, que han funcionado en la república desde 1822.* 4 vols. Lima:

Imprenta de "La Revista" and Imprenta del Panóptico, 1906–1910.

"Defensa de esclavo." *Revista del Archivo Histórico del Cuzco* 3 (1952): 356–58.

Echenique, José Rufino. *Memorias para la historia del Perú (1808–1878).* Prologue by Jorge Basadre, notes by Félix Denegri Luna. 2 vols. Lima: Editorial Huascarán, 1952.

Fuentes, Manuel A. *Estadística general de Lima.* Lima: Tipográfia Nacional de M. N. Corpancho, 1858.

Great Britain. "No. 656. Account of the Value of Imports and Exports between the United Kingdom and Cuba, Chili, Peru and Columbia Respectively, in Each Year, from 1824 to 1845." *Parliamentary Papers* 60 (1847).

Humphreys, R. A., ed. *British Consular Reports on the Trade and Politics of Latin America, 1824–1826.* London: Offices of the Royal Historical Society, 1940.

Lama, Miguel Antonio de la. *Código civil del Perú con citas, notas, concordancias y un apendice.* Lima: Editado por la Imprenta Gil, 1893.

Markham, Clements R. *Cuzco: A Journey to the Ancient Capital of Peru; with an Account of the History, Language, Literature, and Antiquities of the Incas. And Lima: A Visit to the Capital and Provinces of Modern Peru; with a Sketch of the Viceregal Government, History of the Republic, and a Review of the Literature and Society of Peru.* London: Chapman and Hall, 1856.

———. *Markham in Peru: The Travels of Clements R. Markham, 1852–1853.* Edited by Peter Blanchard. Austin: University of Texas Press, 1991.

*Memorias de los virreyes que han gobernado el Perú, durante el tiempo del coloniaje español.* 6 vols. Lima: Librería Central de Felipe Bailly, 1859.

Montejo, Esteban. *The Autobiography of a Runaway Slave.* Edited by Miguel Barnet, translated by Jocasta Innes. New York: Vintage Books, 1973.

Pando, José María de. *Reclamación de los vulnerados derechos de los hacendados de las provincias litorales del departamento de Lima.* Lima: Imp. Rep. de J. M. Concha, 1833.

Perú. *Código de enjuiciamientos en materia civil del Perú.* Lima: Imprenta del Gobierno, 1852.

———. *Colección de leyes, decretos y ordenes publicadas en el Perú desde su independencia en el año de 1821.* 13 vols. Lima: Imprenta de José Masias, 1831–1842; Huaraz: Imprenta de la Colección por José Manuel Ortiz, 1853.

———. *Colección ó catálogo de leyes, decretos, ordenes, reglamentos e instrucciones, dictadas desde el año de 1820 hasta el de 1831.* [Lima]: Imp. en la Casa de Ejercicios de Santa Rosa, n.d.

———. *Diario de los debates de la cámara de diputados: congreso de 1851.* Lima: n.p., n.d.

Proctor, Robert. *Narrative of a Journey across the Cordillera of the Andes, and of a Residence in Lima, and Other Parts of Peru, in the Years 1823 and 1824.* London: Archibald Constable and Company Edinburgh, 1825.

Rico y Angulo, Gaspar. *Proyecto relativo al comercio, suerte y servidumbre de los esclavos, inclinado a su transición oportuna a libres, durante el tiempo que debe continuar la introducción en territorios españoles.* Cádiz: Imprenta Tormentaria, 1813.

Scarlett, P. Campbell. *South America and the Pacific: Comprising a Journey across the Pampas and the Andes, from Buenos Ayres to Valparaiso, Lima, and Panama; with Remarks upon the Isthmus.* 2 vols. London: Henry Colburn, 1838.

Smith, Archibald. *Peru As It Is: A Residence in Lima, and Other Parts of the Peruvian Republic, Comprising an Account of the Social and Physical Features of that Country.* 2 vols. London: Richard Bentley, 1839.

Tavara, Santiago. *Misión a Bogotá en 1852, a consecuencia de la expedición de Flores al Ecuador, &c.* Lima: Imprenta del Comercio, 1853.

Thomas, John. *Diario de viaje del General O'Higgins en la campaña de Ayacucho.* Translated by Carlos Vicuña Mackenna. Santiago de Chile: Imprenta Universitaria, 1917.

Tristán, Flora. *Peregrinaciones de una paria.* Translated and with notes by Emilia Romero. Lima: Editorial Cultura Antártica, 1946.

Ugarteche, Pedro; and San Cristoval, Evaristo, eds. *Mensajes de los presidentes del Perú*, Vol. 1, *1821–1867*. Lima: Librería e Imprenta Gil, 1943.

Vicuña, Pedro Félix. *Ocho meses de destierro o cartas sobre el Perú.* Valparaíso: Librería del Mercurio, 1847.

Von Tschudi, J. J. *Travels in Peru, during the Years 1838–1842, on the Coast, in the Sierra, across the Cordilleras and the Andes, into the Primeval Forests.* Translated by Thomasina Ross. London: David Bogue, 1847.

## Newspapers

*El Comercio* (Lima), 1839–1849, 1851–1857
*El Conciliador* (Lima), 1830–31, 1833
*Correo de Lima* or *El Correo de Lima* (Lima), 1851–52, 1854
*Correo Mercantil* (Lima), 1822
*El Estandarte* (Lima), 1837
*Gaceta del Gobierno* (Lima and Trujillo) or *Gaceta del Gobierno de Lima* or *Gaceta del Gobierno de Lima Independiente* or *Gaceta del Gobierno del Perú* (Lima), 1821–1826, 1835

*Gaceta Mercantil* (Lima), 1834–35
*El Genio del Rimac* (Lima), 1833, 1835
*El Heraldo de Lima* (Lima), 1854–55
*El Intérprete del Pueblo* (Lima), 1852
*Mercurio Peruano* (Lima), 1827–1829, 1832, 1839
*El Meridiano* (Lima), 1833
*Miscelánea* or *La Miscelánea* (Lima), 1830–1833
*El Murciélago* (Lima), 1855
*El Peruano* (Lima), 1826, 1838–1850, 1854–1856
*La Prensa Peruana* (Lima), 1828–29
*Redactor Peruano* (Lima), 1836
*Registro Oficial* (Lima), 1851–52
*El Republicano Extraordinario* (Arequipa), 1854
*Telégrafo de Lima* or *El Telégrafo de Lima* (Lima), 1827–28, 1832–
    33, 1835, 1838
*La Verdad* (Lima), 1833
*El Voto Nacional* (Lima), 1834–35

## Secondary Sources

Adas, Michael. "From Footdragging to Flight: The Evasive History
    of Peasant Avoidance Protest in South and South-East Asia."
    *Journal of Peasant Studies* 13 (1986): 64–86.
Aguirre, Carlos. "Agentes de su propia emancipación: manumisión
    de esclavos en Lima, 1821–1854." Unpublished paper, 1991.
————. "Cimarronaje, bandolerismo y desintegración esclavista:
    Lima, 1821–1854." In *Bandoleros, abigeos y montoneros:
    criminalidad y violencia en el Perú, siglos xviii–xx*, edited by
    Carlos Aguirre and Charles Walker. Lima: Instituto de Apoyo
    Agrario, 1990.
Albert, Bill. *An Essay on the Peruvian Sugar Industry, 1880–1920,
    And the Letters of Ronald Gordon, Administrator of the British
    Sugar Company in Cañete, 1914–1920.* Norwich: School of So-
    cial Studies, University of East Anglia, 1976.
Andrews, George Reid. *The Afro-Argentines of Buenos Aires, 1800–
    1900.* Madison: University of Wisconsin Press, 1980.
Angrand, Léonce. *Imagen del Perú en el siglo XIX.* Lima: Editor
    Carlos Milla Batres, 1972.
Anna, Timothy E. "Economic Causes of San Martín's Failure in
    Lima." *Hispanic American Historical Review* 54 (1974): 657–81.
————. *The Fall of the Royal Government in Peru.* Lincoln: Univer-
    sity of Nebraska Press, 1979.
Arona, Juan de [Pedro Paz Soldán y Unanue]. *La inmigración en el
    Perú.* Lima: Imprenta del Universo, 1891.
Basadre, Jorge. *Historia de la república del Perú, 1822–1933.* 6th
    ed. 16 vols. Lima: Editorial Universitaria, 1969–70.

————. *Introducción a las bases documentales para la historia de la república del Perú con algunas reflexiones.* 2 vols. Lima: Ediciones P.L.V., 1971.

Bell, W. S. *An Essay on the Peruvian Cotton Industry, 1825–1920.* Centre for Latin American Studies Working Paper 6. Liverpool: University of Liverpool, 1985.

Bergad, Laird W. *Cuban Rural Society in the Nineteenth Century: The Social and Economic History of Monoculture in Matanzas.* Princeton: Princeton University Press, 1990.

Bethell, Leslie. *The Abolition of the Brazilian Slave Trade: Britain, Brazil and the Slave Trade Question, 1807–1869.* Cambridge: Cambridge University Press, 1970.

Bierck, Harold A., Jr. "The Struggle for Abolition in Gran Colombia." *Hispanic American Historical Review* 33 (1953): 365–86.

Bonilla, Heraclio. "Peru and Bolivia." In *Spanish America after Independence, c.1820–c.1870,* edited by Leslie Bethell. Cambridge: Cambridge University Press, 1987.

Bowser, Frederick P. *The African Slave in Colonial Peru, 1524–1650.* Stanford: Stanford University Press, 1974.

Burga, Manuel. "La hacienda en el Perú, 1850–1930: evidencias y método." *Tierra y Sociedad* (Lima) 1 (1978): 9–38.

Burns, E. Bradford. *The Poverty of Progress: Latin America in the Nineteenth Century.* Berkeley: University of California Press, 1983.

Burr, Robert N. *By Reason or Force: Chile and the Balancing of Power in South America, 1830–1905.* Berkeley: University of California Press, 1962.

Campbell, Leon G. "Recent Research on Andean Peasant Revolts, 1750–1820." *Latin American Research Review* 14 (1979): 3–49.

————. "Social Structure of the Túpac Amaru Army in Cuzco, 1780–81." *Hispanic American Historical Review* 61 (1981): 675–93.

Casós, Fernando. *Los amigos de Elena: diez años antes.* Paris: Librería Española de E. Denné Schmitz, 1874.

Castañeda, Jorge Eugenio. "El negro en el Perú." *Mercurio Peruano* 490 (1972): 92–95.

Centurión Vallejo, Héctor. *Esclavitud y manumisión de negros en Trujillo.* Trujillo: n.p., 1954.

————. "Esclavitud y manumisión de negros en Trujillo." *Revista el Instituto Libertador Ramón Castilla* (Lima) 5 (1959): 53–81.

Chavarría, Jesús. "The Colonial Heritage of National Peru: An Overview." *Boletín de Estudios Latinoamericanos y del Caribe* 25 (1978): 37–49.

Conrad, Robert Edgar. *Children of God's Fire: A Documentary History of Black Slavery in Brazil.* Princeton: Princeton University Press, 1983.

————. *The Destruction of Brazilian Slavery, 1850–1888.* Berkeley: University of California Press, 1972.

Cotler, Julio. *Clases, estado y nación en el Perú.* Lima: Instituto de Estudios Peruanos, 1978.

Cuche, Denys. *Pérou nègre: les descendants d'esclaves africains du Pérou des grands domaines esclavagistes aux plantations modernes.* Paris: Editions L'Harmattan, 1981.

——. *Poder blanco y resistencia negra en el Perú: un estudio de la condición social del negro en el Perú después de la abolición de la esclavitud.* Lima: Instituto Nacional de Cultura, 1975.

Curtin, Philip D. *The Rise and Fall of the Plantation Complex: Essays in Atlantic History.* Cambridge: Cambridge University Press, 1990.

Cushner, Nicholas P. *Lords of the Land: Sugar, Wine, and Jesuit Estates of Coastal Peru, 1600–1767.* Albany: State University of New York Press, 1980.

Dávalos y Lissón, Pedro. *La primera centuria: causas geográficas, políticas y económicas que han detenido el progreso moral y material del Perú en el primer siglo de su vida independiente.* 4 vols. Lima: Librería e Imprenta Gil, 1926.

Davis, David Brion. *The Problem of Slavery in the Age of Revolution, 1770–1823.* Ithaca: Cornell University Press, 1975.

——. *Slavery and Human Progress.* New York: Oxford University Press, 1984.

Dean, Warren. *Rio Claro: A Brazilian Plantation System, 1820–1920.* Stanford: Stanford University Press, 1976.

*Diccionario enciclopédico del Peru.* Prepared under the direction of Alberto Tauro. 4 vols. Lima: Editorial Mejía Baca, 1966.

Dobyns, Henry E.; and Doughty, Paul L. *Peru: A Cultural History.* New York: Oxford University Press, 1976.

Eisenberg, Peter L. *The Sugar Industry in Pernambuco: Modernization without Change, 1840–1910.* Berkeley: University of California Press, 1974.

Engelsen, Juan Rolf. "Social Aspects of Agricultural Expansion in Coastal Peru, 1825–1878." Ph.D. diss., University of California, Los Angeles, 1977.

Faron, Louis C. "A History of Agricultural Production and Local Organization in the Chancay Valley, Peru." In *Contemporary Change in Traditional Societies*, vol. 3, edited by Julian H. Steward. Urbana: University of Illinois Press, 1970.

Fisher, J. R. *Government and Society in Colonial Peru: The Intendant System, 1784–1814.* London: Athlone Press, 1970.

Fisher, Lillian Estelle. *The Last Inca Revolt, 1780–1783.* Norman: University of Oklahoma Press, 1966.

Flores Galindo S., Alberto. *Aristocracia y plebe: Lima, 1760–1830 (estructura de clases y sociedad colonial).* Lima: Mosca Azul Editores, 1984.

——. "El militarismo y la dominación británica (1825–1845)." In *Nueva historia general del Perú: un compendio*, by Carlos Araníbar, L. G. Lambreras, Manuel Burga, J. I. López Soria,

Alberto Flores Galindo S., Heraclio Bonilla, E. Yepes del Castillo, Julio Cotler, W. Espinoza Soriano, and S. López. Lima: Mosca Azul Editores, 1979.

Flory, Thomas. "Fugitive Slaves and Free Society: The Case of Brazil." *Journal of Negro History* 64 (1979): 116–30.

Foner, Eric. *Nothing but Freedom: Emancipation and Its Legacy.* Baton Rouge: Louisiana State University Press, 1983.

Freyre, Gilberto. *The Masters and the Slaves: A Study in the Development of Brazilian Civilization.* Translated by Samuel Putnam. New York: Alfred A. Knopf, 1946.

Fuentes, Manuel Atanasio. *Biografía del exmo. e ilustrísimo señor Don Ramón Castilla, Libertador del Perú, escrita por el más fiel de sus adoradores.* Valparaíso: Imprenta y Librería del Mercurio, 1856.

Galloway, J. H. "The Last Years of Slavery on the Sugar Plantations of Northeast Brazil." *Hispanic American Historical Review* 51 (1971): 586–605.

García, Enrique León. *Las razas en Lima: estudio demográfico.* Lima: Universidad Mayor de S. Marcos, Facultad de Medicina, 1909.

Genovese, Eugene D. *From Rebellion to Revolution: Afro-American Slave Revolts in the Making of the Modern World.* Baton Rouge: Louisiana State University Press, 1979.

———. *Roll, Jordan, Roll: The World the Slaves Made.* New York: Vintage Books, 1976.

Gleason, Daniel. "Anti-Democratic Thought in Early Republican Peru: Bartolomé Herrera and the Liberal-Conservative Ideological Struggle." *The Americas* 38 (1981): 205–17.

Gonzales, Michael J. *Plantation Agriculture and Social Control in Northern Peru, 1875–1933.* Austin: University of Texas Press, 1985.

Gootenberg, Paul. *Between Silver and Guano: Commercial Policy and the State in Postindependence Peru.* Princeton: Princeton University Press, 1989.

———. "North-South: Trade Policy, Regionalism, and *Caudillismo* in Post-Independence Peru." *Journal of Latin American Studies* 23 (1991): 273–308.

———. "Population and Ethnicity in Early Republican Peru: Some Revisions." *Latin American Research Review* 26 (1991): 109–57.

———. "The Social Origins of Protectionism and Free Trade in Nineteenth-Century Lima." *Journal of Latin American Studies* 14 (1982): 329–58.

Graham, Richard. "Causes for the Abolition of Negro Slavery in Brazil: An Interpretive Essay." *Hispanic American Historical Review* 46 (1966): 123–37.

Gutiérrez Muñoz, César. "El reglamento de 1825 y la situación del esclavo en el Perú republicano." *Enseñanza de la Historia* (Lima) 3 (1972): 10–19.

Hammel, E. A. *Power in Ica: The Structural History of a Peruvian Community*. Boston: Little, Brown and Company, 1969.

Hobsbawm, E. J. *Primitive Rebels: Studies in Archaic Forms of Social Movement in the 19th and 20th Centuries*. New York: W. W. Norton and Company, 1959.

Hünefeldt, Christine. "Los negros de Lima: 1800–1830." *Histórica* (Lima) 3 (1979): 17–51.

Jacobsen, Nils. "Taxation in Early Republican Peru, 1821–1851: Policy Making between Reform and Tradition." In *América Latina en la época de Simón Bolívar: la formación de las economías nacionales y los intereses económicos europeos, 1800–1850*, edited by Reinhard Liehr. Berlin: Colloquium Verlag, 1989.

James, C. L. R. *The Black Jacobins: Toussaint L'Ouverture and the San Domingo Revolution*. 2d ed. rev. New York: Vintage Books, 1963.

Joseph, Gilbert M. "On the Trail of Latin American Bandits: A Reexamination of Peasant Resistance." *Latin American Research Review* 25 (1990): 7–53.

Kapsoli E., Wilfredo. *Sublevaciones de esclavos en el Perú, s. XVIII*. Lima: Universidad Ricardo Palma, 1975.

Karasch, Mary C. *Slave Life in Rio de Janeiro, 1808–1850*. Princeton: Princeton University Press, 1987.

King, James Ferguson. "The Latin-American Republics and the Suppression of the Slave Trade." *Hispanic American Historical Review* 24 (1944): 378–411.

Klaiber, Jeffrey L. *Religion and Revolution in Peru, 1824–1976*. Notre Dame: University of Notre Dame Press, 1977.

Klein, Herbert S. *African Slavery in Latin America and the Caribbean*. New York: Oxford University Press, 1986.

―――. *Slavery in the Americas: A Comparative Study of Virginia and Cuba*. Chicago: University of Chicago Press, 1967.

Knight, Franklin W. *Slave Society in Cuba during the Nineteenth Century*. Madison: University of Wisconsin Press, 1970.

Labarthe, Manuel. "Castilla y la abolición de la esclavitud." *Publicaciones del Instituto "Libertador Ramón Castilla"* (Lima) (1955): 1–23.

Larrabure y Unánue, E. *Cañete: apuntes geográficos, históricos, estadísticos y arqueológicos*. Lima: Imprenta del Estado, 1874.

Lazo García, Carlos; and Tord Nicolini, Javier. *Del negro señorial al negro bandolero: cimarronaje y palenques en Lima, siglo XVIII*. Lima: Biblioteca Peruana de Historia Economía y Sociedad, 1977.

Levin, Jonathan V. *The Export Economies: Their Pattern of Development in Historical Perspective*. Cambridge: Harvard University Press, 1960.

Lockhart, James. *Spanish Peru, 1532–1560: A Colonial Society*. Madison: University of Wisconsin Press, 1968.

Lombardi, John V. "The Abolition of Slavery in Venezuela: A Nonevent." In *Slavery and Race Relations in Latin America*, edited by Robert Brent Toplin. Westport: Greenwood Press, 1974.

———. *The Decline and Abolition of Negro Slavery in Venezuela, 1820–1854.* Westport: Greenwood Publishing Corporation, 1971.

Lynch, John. *The Spanish American Revolutions, 1808–1826.* London: Weidenfeld and Nicolson, 1973.

Macera, Pablo. "Las plantaciones azucareras andinas (1821–1875)." In *Trabajos de historia*, by Pablo Macera. 4 vols. Lima: Instituto Nacional de Cultura, 1977.

MacLean y Estenos, Roberto. *Negros en el nuevo mundo.* Lima: Editorial P.T.C.M., 1948.

McQueen, Charles A. *Peruvian Public Finance.* Washington: Government Printing Office, 1926.

Mariátegui, Francisco Javier. "Anotaciones a la historia del Perú independiente de don Mariano Felipe Paz Soldán (1819–1822)." In *Colección documental de la independencia del Perú. Tomo XXVI. Memorias diarias y crónicas*, vol. 2, edited by Félix Denegri Luna. Lima: Comisión Nacional del Sesquicentenario de la Independencia del Perú, 1971.

Markham, Clements R. *A History of Peru.* Chicago: Charles H. Sergel and Company, 1892.

Martín, Luis. *The Kingdom of the Sun: A Short History of Peru.* New York: Charles Scribner's Sons, 1974.

Martínez, Miguel A. *La vida heroica del gran mariscal Don Ramón Castilla.* Lima: N.p., 1952.

Martínez-Alier, Verena. *Marriage, Class and Colour in Nineteenth-Century Cuba: A Study of Racial Attitudes and Sexual Values in a Slave Society.* Ann Arbor: University of Michigan Press, 1989.

Mathew, W. M. "Antony Gibbs and Sons, the Guano Trade and the Peruvian Government, 1842–1861." In *Business Imperialism 1840–1930: An Inquiry Based on British Experience in Latin America*, edited by D. C. M. Platt. Oxford: Clarendon Press, 1977.

———. "The First Anglo-Peruvian Debt and its Settlement, 1822–49." *Journal of Latin American Studies* 2 (1970): 81–98.

———. "Foreign Contractors and the Peruvian Government at the Outset of the Guano Trade." *Hispanic American Historical Review* 52 (1972): 598–620.

———. *The House of Gibbs and the Peruvian Guano Monopoly.* London: Royal Historical Society, 1981.

———. "The Imperialism of Free Trade: Peru, 1820–70." *Economic History Review* 21 (1968): 562–79.

———. "A Primitive Export Sector: Guano Production in Mid-Nineteenth-Century Peru." *Journal of Latin American Studies* 9 (1977): 35–57.

Mattoso, Katia M. de Queirós. *To Be a Slave in Brazil, 1550–1888*. Translated by Arthur Goldhammer. New Brunswick: Rutgers University Press, 1986.

Maude, H. E. *Slavers in Paradise: The Peruvian Labour Trade in Polynesia, 1862–1864*. Canberra: Australian National University Press, 1981.

Mellafe, Rolando. *Negro Slavery in Latin America*. Translated by J. W. S. Judge. Berkeley: University of California Press, 1975.

Moreno Fraginals, Manuel. "El esclavo y la mecanización de los ingenios." *Bohemia* (Cuba) 24 (June 13, 1969): 98–99.

———. *The Sugarmill: The Socioeconomic Complex of Sugar in Cuba, 1760–1860*. Translated by Cedric Belfrage. New York: Monthly Review Press, 1976.

Mörner, Magnus. *Historia social latinoamericana (nuevos enfoques)*. Caracas: Universidad Católica Andrés Bello, 1979.

Murray, David R. *Odious Commerce: Britain, Spain and the Abolition of the Cuban Slave Trade*. Cambridge: Cambridge University Press, 1980.

O'Phelan Godoy, Scarlett. *Rebellions and Revolts in Eighteenth Century Peru and Upper Peru*. Cologne: Böhlau, 1985.

Palma, Ricardo. *Tradiciones peruanas: colección completa*. 20 vols. Lima: Empresa Gráfica Editorial S.A., 1957.

Palmer, Colin A. *Slaves of the White God: Blacks in Mexico*. Cambridge: Cambridge University Press, 1976.

Paquette, Robert L. *Sugar Is Made with Blood: The Conspiracy of La Escalera and the Conflict between Empires over Slavery in Cuba*. Middletown: Wesleyan University Press, 1988.

Paredes, Luis Felipe. "Castilla y la abolición de la esclavitud." *Revista Universitaria* (Cuzco) 109 (1955): 9–14.

Patterson, Orlando. *Slavery and Social Death: A Comparative Study*. Cambridge: Harvard University Press, 1982.

Piel, Jean. "The Place of the Peasantry in the National Life of Peru in the Nineteenth Century." *Past and Present* 46 (1970): 108–33.

Pike, Fredrick B. "Heresy, Real and Alleged, in Peru: An Aspect of the Conservative-Liberal Struggle, 1830–1875." *Hispanic American Historical Review* 47 (1967): 50–74.

———. *The Modern History of Peru*. London: Weidenfeld and Nicolson, 1967.

Platt, D. C. M. *Latin America and British Trade, 1806–1914*. New York: Barnes and Noble, 1972.

Quiroz Norris, Alfonso W. "La consolidación de la deuda interna peruana, 1850–58: los efectos sociales de una medida financiera estatal." Tesis para el Grado de Bachiller en Humanidades, Pontificia Universidad Católica del Perú, 1980.

Rebaza, Nicolás. *Anales del departamento de La Libertad*. Trujillo: Imprenta de "El Obrero del Norte," 1898.

Rippy, J. Fred. "The Dawn of Manufacturing in Peru." *Pacific Historical Review* 15 (1946): 147–57.

Romero, Emilio. *Historia económica del Perú.* 2d ed. 2 vols. Lima: Editorial Universo S.A., 1968.

Romero, Fernando. "El mestizaje negroide en la demografía del Perú." *Revista Histórica* (Lima) 28 (1965): 231–48.

———. "Papel de los descendientes de africanos en el desarrollo económico-social del Perú." *Histórica* (Lima) 4 (1980): 53–93.

Rout, Leslie B., Jr. *The African Experience in Spanish America: 1502 to the Present Day.* Cambridge: Cambridge University Press, 1976.

Safford, Frank. "Politics, Ideology and Society." In *Spanish America after Independence, c.1820–c.1870*, edited by Leslie Bethell. Cambridge: Cambridge University Press, 1987.

Sales de Bohigas, Núria. *Sobre esclavos, reclutas y mercaderes de quintos.* Barcelona: Editorial Ariel, 1974.

Scarano, Francisco A. *Sugar and Slavery in Puerto Rico: The Plantation Economy of Ponce, 1800–1850.* Madison: University of Wisconsin Press, 1984.

Schwartz, Stuart B. *Sugar Plantations in the Formation of Brazilian Society: Bahia, 1550–1835.* Cambridge: Cambridge University Press, 1985.

Scott, James C. *Weapons of the Weak: Everyday Forms of Peasant Resistance.* New Haven: Yale University Press, 1985.

Scott, Rebecca J. "Gradual Abolition and the Dynamics of Slave Emancipation in Cuba, 1868–86." *Hispanic American Historical Review* 63 (1983): 449–77.

———. *Slave Emancipation in Cuba: The Transition to Free Labor, 1860–1899.* Princeton: Princeton University Press, 1985.

Sharp, William Frederick. *Slavery on the Spanish Frontier: The Colombian Chocó, 1680–1810.* Norman: University of Oklahoma Press, 1976.

Socolow, Susan M. "Recent Historiography of the Rio de la Plata: Colonial and Early National Periods." *Hispanic American Historical Review* 64 (1984): 105–20.

Sotomayor Roggero, Carmela; and Aranda de los Rios, Ramón. *Sublevación de campesinos negros en Chincha, 1879.* Lima: Universidad Nacional Mayor de San Marcos, 1979.

Stein, Stanley J. *Vassouras: A Brazilian Coffee County, 1850–1890.* New York: Atheneum, 1970.

Stewart, Watt. *Chinese Bondage in Peru: A History of the Chinese Coolie in Peru, 1849–1874.* Durham: Duke University Press, 1951.

Stokes, Susan C. "Etnicidad y clase social: los afro-peruanos de Lima, 1900–1930." In *Lima obrera, 1900–1930*, vol. 2, by Laura Miller, Katherine Roberts, Susan C. Stokes, José A. Lloréns. Lima: Ediciones El Virrey, 1987.

Tannenbaum, Frank. *Slave and Citizen: The Negro in the Americas.* New York: Vintage Books, 1946.

Taussig, Michael T. *The Devil and Commodity Fetishism in South America.* Chapel Hill: University of North Carolina Press, 1980.

Tavara, Santiago. *Abolición de la esclavitud en el Perú.* Lima: Impreso por José María Monterola, Imprenta del Comercio, 1855.

Toplin, Robert Brent. *The Abolition of Slavery in Brazil.* New York: Atheneum, 1975.

————. "Upheaval, Violence, and the Abolition of Slavery in Brazil: The Case of São Paulo." *Hispanic American Historical Review* 49 (1969): 639–55.

Ugarte Eléspuru, Juan Manuel. *Lima y lo limeño.* 2d ed. Lima: Editorial Universitaria, n.d.

Ulloa y Sotomayor, Alberto. *La organización social y legal del trabajo en el Perú.* Lima: Tipográfia de "La Opinión Nacional," 1916.

Valencia Avara, Luis. *Bernardo O'Higgins: el "buen genio" de América.* Santiago de Chile: Editorial Universitaria, 1980.

Walker, Charles. "Montoneros, bandoleros, malhechores: criminalidad y política en las primeras décadas republicanas." In *Bandoleros, abigeos y montoneros: criminalidad y violencia en el Perú, siglos xviii–xx,* edited by Carlos Aguirre and Charles Walker. Lima: Instituto de Apoyo Agrario, 1990.

————. "The Social Bases of Political Conflict in Peru, 1820–1845." Paper presented at the 46th International Congress of Americanists, Amsterdam, July 1988.

Williams, Eric. *Capitalism and Slavery.* Chapel Hill: University of North Carolina Press, 1944.

Wolf, Eric R.; and Hansen, Edward C. "*Caudillo* Politics: A Structural Analysis." *Comparative Studies in Society and History* 9 (January 1967): 168–79.

Yepes del Castillo, Ernesto. *Perú, 1820–1920: un siglo de desarrollo capitalista.* Lima: Campodonicoediciones S.A., 1972.

# Index

Aberdeen, Lord, 52, 160, 178, 179, 181
Abolition, 113; criticism of, 39, 198–99, 212–14, 216; decree, 195; evaluation of, 196–97, 206–7; impact of, 197–99, 211–20; implementation of, 189–207; support for, 4–5, 114, 116, 138, 151–68
Abortion, 82, 97
Acari estate, 101
Adams, William Pitt, 179, 180–81, 183, 184
Africa, 218; culture of, 2–3, 97, 99, 221–22; slaves from, 2, 3, 51, 52, 103, 119, 158, 176, 178, 182
Agriculture: and abolition, 39, 193, 195, 199, 213–16, 219; colonial, 2; confidence in, 21–22, 159; mechanization of, 22, 114, 127–28, 135, 143, 215; problems of, 12, 19–21, 23–25, 29, 53, 77, 98, 131–32, 139, 174
Aguardiente, 77, 132
Alegría, José Agustín, 56
Alvares, Juan José, 161
Alvarez, Gervasio, 159
Anna, Timothy, 6

Aramburu, Isidro, 38, 201, 202, 204
Arana, Joaquina, 216, 219
Arenaza, Juan, 160
Arequipa, 38, 98, 152, 160, 191, 194, 204
Argentina (Argentine Confederation), 6, 183; abolition in, 2, 186; reestablishment of slave trade in, 37. See also Buenos Aires
Aria de Henríquez, Irene, 76–77
Arica, 179–80
Arosemena, Mariano, 183–84
Ayacucho, 10

Baca, Valentín, 114–18
Bakeries, 26, 27, 29, 101–2, 108, 198; imprisonment in, 84, 85, 185, 198
Barton, John, 181–82
Basallo, Gregorio, 66
Benavides, Francisco, 46
Bocanegra, Pablo, 29
Bocanegra estate, 213
Boletos, 42–43, 80, 106
Bolívar, Simón, 3, 5, 9–11, 13, 196; attempt on his life, 98, 111; legislation of, 10–11, 13–14, 42–44, 65, 70, 158

Bolivia, 49, 133, 178; abolition in, 186; Gamarra's invasion of, 52. *See also* Peru-Bolivia Confederation

Bourgeoisie, 136–37

Bracamonte, Hipólito de, 161

Brazil, 24; abolition in, 2, 136, 218; diplomatic pressure of, 171, 174; slave resistance in, 96; slaves in, 95, 128, 144, 181, 218; slave trade from, 50, 55, 163, 176, 183

Buenos Aires: and slave trade, 4, 177

Bustamente, Agustín, 72

Cáceres, Manuel, 48

Cajanleque estate, 114, 165

Calvo, Francisco Javier, 51, 52, 158, 178

Camaná, 23

Cañete Valley, 21, 22, 110, 135; after abolition, 213–14, 220; slaves in, 14, 20, 21, 25, 64, 77, 119

Canning, Lord, 179

Capitalism, 127–29

Casa Blanca estate, 119

Castilla, Ramón, 52, 113, 117, 133–34, 137, 143, 220; abolishes slavery, 195; assists slaveholders, 200–202; conflict with British, 179–80; implements abolition, 198–207, 211, 212, 213; liberalism of, 179, 195–96; rebellion against Echenique, 191–98, 213; reopens slave trade, 54, 181

Cauca Valley, 56

Caucato estate, 135

Caudillos, 38

Chamber of deputies, 52, 85–86, 157, 160, 163, 203, 204, 205

Chancay Valley, 14, 23, 25, 109, 135, 219

Chavalina estate, 68

Chicama Valley, 165; slave rebellion, 113–19, 165

Chiclayo, 159

Chiclín estate, 29, 161

Chile, 4, 6, 27, 132, 177; invasion by, 50, 175, 220; Peru's debt to, 130, 179

Chincha Islands, 142, 143. *See also* Guano industry

Chincha Valley, 14, 22, 135, 220

Chinese, 104, 139–42, 192, 198, 220. *See also* Coolies

Chiquitoy estate, 114

Chocavento estate, 112

Civil Code: of 1852, 45, 58, 70, 81, 163–64, 167, 191, 196, 197

Clinton, Lord Edward, 110

*Cofradías*, 2–3

Colina, Narciso de la, 22

Colombia: abolition in, 2; Peru's debt to, 130; treaty with Peru, 172, 174, 178. *See also* New Granada

*El Comercio* (Lima), 138, 214; abolitionism of, 153, 155, 159–60, 165, 166; advertisements in, 104, 167, 190, 198; inconsistency of, 167, 204

Congress of Panama (1826), 172

Conservatives, 5–6, 49, 50, 152, 163, 191

Consolidation: laws of, 133–34, 191, 215

Constitution: of 1812, 6; of 1823, 9, 13–14, 172; of 1828, 15, 40; of 1834, 15; of 1839, 50, 176, 179; of 1856, 207; Spanish, 6

*Consulado*, 136
Coolies, 25, 77, 113, 197, 214, 218, 222; conflicts with blacks, 102–3, 220; in guano industry, 27, 136, 141; importation of, 139–42, 212, 218
*El Correo de Lima*, 166
Cotton industry, 22, 25, 131, 135, 143
Council of state, 51–52, 53, 158, 177–78
Courts, 45–47, 65–67, 69, 73–75, 76, 80–82, 86–87, 156; criticize slavery, 156–57; used by slaves, 65–66, 74–75
Creoles, 6, 11, 12, 13, 64
Cuba, 24, 128, 178; abolition in, 2, 167; slave resistance in, 96

Dancuart, Emilio, 214
Dávalos y Lissón, Pedro, 213
Dávila, Ruiz, 157
Davis, David Brion, 189–90
Dean, Warren, 144
*Defensor de menores*, 41–42, 45, 73–74, 81, 83, 86–87, 156
Duanes, Juan de Mata, 86

Echenique, José Rufino, 21, 53, 104, 134, 135, 183, 191, 206; Civil Code, 163–64, 191; economic policy, 133–34, 135; and Elías, 117, 144, 184, 191; frees slaves, 163, 192–94; rebellion against, 134, 191–98; and San Pedro estate, 101, 106, 112–13, 135
Echenique, Ramón, 72
Economy, 38, 128–36, 175–76; effect of abolition on, 206, 213, 215–16; expenditures,

131, 133; debts, 38, 130–31, 132–33, 134, 175–76, 179, 202, 206; independence period, 12–13, 129; inflation, 215–16; revenues, 130–31. *See also* Agriculture; Industrialization
Ecuador, 159, 178; abolition in, 2, 166, 186; exodus of slaves from, 30, 50; Peru's debt to, 130; treaty with Great Britain, 53
Elguera, Ceferino, 46
Elías, Domingo: and Chinese coolies, 139, 141–42, 144; and guano industry, 143, 144; as landholder, 22–23, 38, 143, 192, 215; and New Granada slaves, 57, 144, 184; opposition to Echenique, 117, 144, 184, 191; as politician, 117, 143–44, 202; as slaveholder, 38, 117, 144, 197, 202–3
Elmes, Toribio, 75, 84
Escobar, Juan Bautista, 185
Escobar, León, 110

Ferdinand VII, king of Spain, 4, 6
Fonseca, Lucas, 158
France, 110; liberal ideas from, 151, 153, 190
Frederick VI, king of Denmark, 154
Free blacks, 14, 23, 68, 69, 71, 73–74, 105, 110
Free womb law, 7, 155
Fuentes, Manuel Atanasio, 58, 196, 219

Gálvez Egúsquiza, José, 196
Gálvez Egúsquiza, Pedro, 196
Gamarra, Agustín, 50–52, 74, 156, 160, 161–62, 176–79

Gambling, 68, 71, 80, 97
*El Genio del Rimac* (Lima),
    153
Genovese, Eugene, 65, 116
Germany (German Confedera-
    tion): opposition to slave
    trade, 163, 183. *See also*
    Immigrants
González Pinillos, Alfonso,
    119, 165–66
Gootenberg, Paul, 38
Great Britain, 12, 53, 153,
    212; antislavery crusade,
    3, 4, 51, 55, 151, 158, 163,
    171–83; and guano indus-
    try, 132–33; gunboat
    diplomacy, 179–81; lack of
    influence, 175–76, 179;
    loans to Peru, 130, 132,
    133, 175–76; and New
    Granada, 182, 183; trea-
    ties with Peru, 173–75,
    178, 182–83; treaty with
    Ecuador, 53
Guano industry, 135–36, 137,
    141, 143, 199, 200, 203,
    215, 216; boom in (1840s),
    38, 113, 132–34, 136, 143,
    145, 175, 186; slaves in,
    27, 136, 144
Guerrillas. *See Montoneros*

Haiti, 9; after abolition, 40,
    219; slave rebellion in, 95,
    98, 111, 119, 154
*El Heraldo de Lima*, 166, 190,
    193–94, 196–97
Herrera, Bartolomé, 163, 183,
    184
Herrera-Da Ponte Ribeyro
    Convention (1851), 163
Highwaymen, 12, 105–8, 198,
    217
Hobsbawm, Eric J., 109
Huaito estate, 112
Hualcará estate, 135
Huancayo, 160, 195, 196

Huaral, 11
Huarochirí, 191

Ica, 14, 22, 68, 135, 143, 221
Iguaín, José Félix, 180
Immigrants, 53, 55, 57, 138–
    42, 145, 153, 156, 212,
    218; abuse of, 141, 142;
    Asian, 193, 221; German,
    139, 140, 142, 192; Irish,
    139, 140; numbers of,
    139–40; Polynesian, 212,
    222; Portuguese, 104;
    support for immigration,
    128, 138–39. *See also*
    Chinese
Independence Wars, 5–10, 11–
    14, 26, 29, 38, 52, 72, 104,
    115, 185
Indians, 4, 5, 108, 218; on
    coast, 2, 23, 222; head tax
    imposed on, 64, 130, 191,
    195, 206; as highwaymen,
    105, 108. *See also*
    *Serranos*
Industrialization, 134–35, 215
Infantas estate, 102
Infanticide, 82, 97
*Ingenuos*, 74, 163–64, 198
*El Intérprete del Pueblo*
    (Lima), 164, 165
Islam, 99
Islay, 179

Judges: abolitionism of, 156,
    165
Junín, 10
Junta de Manumisión, 202–5

Labor: free wage, 23–24, 27,
    127, 137–39, 159, 200;
    shortage of, 23–24, 50–51,
    70, 159
La Libertad, 14, 139, 155, 157.
    *See also* Trujillo
Lambayeque, 23, 57, 159, 192
*La Miscelánea* (Lima), 31

La Molina estate, 45, 81–82, 102, 105, 107, 108, 112, 113, 192
Lang, Ursula, 142
La Palma, Battle of, 197–98
La Palma bakery, 101–2
La Quebrada estate, 119, 135
Larán estate, 135, 194
La Serna, José de, 11
Lavalle, José Antonio, 202
Lavalle estate, 25
La Ventilla estate, 20
Legislation: abolishing slavery, 195, 198; antislavery, 4; assisting slaveholders, 3, 13–14, 42–43, 49, 52, 53–54, 57–58, 200, 201–2; to control banditry, 106; freeing slaves, 192–93; independence period, 7–9, 10–11; Lima police regulations, 43, 50; protecting *libertos*, 8; protecting slaves, 44, 65. *See also* Civil Code; Consolidation; Free womb law
León, Pedro, 110
Liberalism, 49, 52, 152–53, 162, 167, 190, 196; in Spain, 6
*Libertos*, 14, 161; abuse of, 79, 86, 119, 154; baptized, 46, 72; changing masters, 45–46, 70, 75; criticism of, 39–41, 73; freed, 151, 195, 200, 202, 205; Gamarra's decree affecting, 50–51, 67, 74, 177; from New Granada, 56–57, 181, 182, 184; price of, 28; protection of, 8, 70, 156, 160, 163–64; purchasing freedom, 69, 76; separated from parents, 80–81, 82
Lima, 26, 28, 64, 71, 99, 103, 134, 219; highwaymen threatening, 106; *montoneros* threatening, 110; political domination of, 38; population, 14, 15, 26, 221; society, 30, 129; support for Elías, 143
Lizarzaburu, José María, 85, 115, 117
Lostaunau, Juan Pedro, 82, 87, 107
Lostaunau, Justo, 198
Lotteries, 8, 162, 163

Macera, Pablo, 25, 77, 135, 215
Magdalena Valley, 105, 108
Mala Valley, 24
*María de los Angeles* (ship), 57, 184
Markham, Clements R., 143, 180; and estates, 23–24, 77; and highwaymen, 108; and slaves, 26, 27, 63, 64, 68, 98, 102
Mataratones estate, 214, 215
Mathew, W. M., 133
Mayorazgo estate, 105
Melgar, José Fabio, 204
Menéndez, Manuel, 51, 178
Merchants, 136, 215
Mexico, 152
Montalván estate, 20, 103, 135
Monte Mar y de Monteblanco, conde de, 44
Monterrico Grande estate, 20, 22, 29, 101
*Montoneros*, 12, 97, 108–11, 192, 199, 217
Moreno Fraginals, Manuel, 128
*Morenos*, 72
*El Murciélago*, 219

Nazca Valley, 22, 112
Nepén estate, 78, 165
New Granada, 166, 171; abolition in, 186; export of

New Granada (*continued*)
　　*libertos* from, 56–57, 144,
　　180, 181, 182, 184–85;
　　Great Britain and, 182,
　　183; slaves in, 50, 52, 55,
　　57, 144, 181, 184–85
Nuestro Señor de los Milagros:
　　cult of, 221–22

O'Higgins, Bernardo, 20, 40,
　　103, 135, 161
Orbegoso, Luis José de, 49,
　　110, 111
Osma, Ignacio, 202
Osma, Mariano, 201
Oyague, Manuel, 48

Pacasmayo Valley, 216
Paita, 56, 180
*Palenques*, 97–98, 103, 105
Palma, Manuel, 83
Palma, Ricardo, 3, 25, 196
Palmerston, Viscount, 172–73,
　　176, 182, 183, 198
Palpa estate, 69, 135
Palpa Valley, 22
Pampas Libres estate, 112
Panama, 56, 57, 172
Pando, José María de, 40, 48,
　　49
Pando, Manuela, 79, 201, 204
*Pardos*, 72
Pastor estate, 112
Paz Soldán, José Gregorio, 21,
　　24, 55–56, 138, 181–82,
　　201
Paz Soldán, Pedro, 201, 202
Pedreros estate, 86, 105
Peña, Manuela, 100
Peru-Bolivia Confederation,
　　49–50, 174–75, 181
*El Peruano*, 118–19, 193, 205
Piérola, Nicolás de, 154
Pino, María, 100
Pisco Valley, 14, 20, 22, 100
Piura, 14, 139
Pizarro, Francisco, 2

Platt, D. C. M., 128
Political unrest, 37–38, 49–
　　50, 52, 104–5, 109–10,
　　174, 178–79, 191–98;
　　impact on economy, 21,
　　135
Population, 14–15, 26, 220–21
Portugal: colonists from, 104;
　　opposition to slave trade,
　　183
Proctor, Robert, 26, 27, 63–64,
　　77, 129
Puertas, Micaela, 161

Quintanilla, Juan J., 157
Quirós, Francisco, 137, 201,
　　202, 203

Racism, 39–40, 72–74, 153,
　　157, 218–19
Rape, 83, 84, 216
Religion, 2–3, 71–72, 99, 116,
　　221–22
Religious orders, 22, 97, 203,
　　205, 206; nuns with slaves
　　as domestics, 27
Retes estate, 113
Revoredo, Felipe, 57, 184
Ricketts, Charles Milner, 20,
　　23, 24, 135
Riva Agüero, José de la, 13,
　　109
Rodríguez, Juan, 139, 141
Rodríguez y Riquelme, Rosa,
　　161
Rodulfo, José Antolín, 56–57
Rojas, Juan, 116, 118
Rueda, Manuel, 42
Runaways, 78, 80, 103–4, 107,
　　108, 112; advertisements
　　seeking, 46–48; in colonial
　　period, 5, 103; fines for
　　hiring, 42, 43, 46; in
　　independence period, 12,
　　103, 111
Russia: opposition to slave
　　trade, 163, 183

Sagastaveytia, Francisco, 57, 202
Salas, José Manuel, 202
Salaverry, Felipe Santiago de, 49, 110, 173, 175, 176
Salinas, Antonio, 202
San Antonio de Zárate estate, 29
Sanchez de la Concha, Francisca, 198
Sancho Dávila, José María, 202, 203
San Jacinto de la Nazca estate, 20
San Jacinto de Napeña estate, 29
San Javier de la Nazca estate, 20–21, 71, 72, 78, 143, 192; slaves on, 25, 30, 65, 68, 69–70, 77, 78–79, 111–12, 130
San José estate, 135
San José de la Nazca estate, 20–21, 30, 71, 78, 143; slaves on, 25, 29, 30, 65, 68, 69–70, 72, 75, 77, 78–79, 98, 103, 192
San Juan estate, 105, 107
San Lorenzo Island, 30
San Martín, José de, 11, 20, 54, 151, 167, 196, 204; antislavery legislation, 6–8, 15, 37, 42, 52, 66, 72, 114, 116, 172; declares independence, 1, 5, 6; hostility toward, 12, 13, 41, 42, 54–55
San Nicolás estate, 86, 104
San Pedro estate, 25, 86, 101, 104, 106, 112–13, 135, 192
San Regis estate, 20
Santa Beatriz estate, 20, 104
Santa Cruz, Andrés de, 30, 49–50, 157, 162, 174–75, 177, 179
Santa Rosa estate, 102, 111
Saravia, Manuel, 30

Sartige, Viscount, 110
Sausal estate, 161
Sayán, 11
Scott, James C., 64, 95, 96
Senate, 52, 53, 157, 158–60
*Serranos*, 23, 53, 55, 193, 212, 218, 222
Slaveholders, 43, 75; commitment to slavery, 28, 30, 31, 57–58; criticism of, 155, 204; defense of slavery, 39, 40; freeing slaves, 161, 165–66; ignore laws, 46, 74–75, 76, 114; indemnification of, 201–6; at independence, 6, 8; influence of, 38, 42–48, 57–58, 160, 176–77; protecting property, 30, 42–48, 76–77; support for Castilla, 194, 197
Slavery: criticism of, 154–55, 156–57; defense of, 39–41; profitability of, 25, 28–30
Slaves: after abolition, 197, 198, 200–201, 214, 216–20; abuse of, 73–87, 102, 114, 154; accumulate funds, 68; bartered, 31; change owners, 66, 70, 76–77, 97, 158; as domestics, 2, 4, 14, 19, 27, 63–64, 68, 214; family life of, 71–72, 80–84; humane treatment of, 40, 63–64, 181; illnesses of, 70, 78; manumission of, 67–68, 161–62, 163–65; as muleteers, 25–26; numbers of, 14–15, 25, 26, 203, 205; price of, 28, 29, 70; punishment of, 10, 30, 43, 85–87 (*see also* Whipping); rations of, 10, 25, 65, 77–78, 113; rebellions of, 111–19; rental of, 29–30, 31; resistance of, 2–3, 5, 12,

Slaves (*continued*)
95–120, 192, 219–20;
response of to 1854 law,
194; as robbers, 66, 86,
100–101, 217; sale of,
80–82, 87; self-purchase
by, 5, 44, 68–70, 97, 190–
91; sexual abuse of, 83–
84, 102, 154; as soldiers,
8, 9, 11–12, 13, 14, 49,
192–94, 197; valuation
of, 44, 45, 69–70, 75, 76;
value of, 29; violence of,
12, 98, 101–3, 104, 111–
19, 154–55, 216; wages
of, 30, 55, 68; as water
carriers, 4, 26, 55, 84,
99, 100, 220; as wet
nurses, 2, 4, 27, 30, 47,
67–68, 218. *See also*
Runaways
Slave trade: British crusade
against, 3, 4, 51, 55, 158,
163, 172–83; end of, 57,
182–83; late colonial, 3–
4; opposition to, 153–54,
158–60, 163, 172, 177;
resumption of, 53–54, 56–
57, 181–82; support for,
40, 49, 50, 51–53, 54–56,
158, 173–77, 181
Smith, Archibald, 30, 63, 64,
85
Sociedad de Agricultura, 138
Solar, Pablo del, 57
Soquete (thief), 108
Sotomayor, José María, 38, 57,
202
Stowe, Harriet Beecher, 166
Suárez Fernández, Manuel,
53
Sucre, Antonio José de, 12
Sugar industry, 2, 21, 23, 25,
26, 114, 159; for export,
131, 132; mechanization
of, 135
Sulivan, J. N., 198

Supe Valley, 104
Surco Valley, 109, 217
Swayne, Henry, 22

Tannenbaum, Frank, 73
Tavara, Santiago, 184–85,
196, 215–16, 217, 218
Tejada y Olaya, Gregorio,
114, 116–18
Toplin, Robert Brent, 95
Torre Tagle, marquis of, 9
Trapiche Viejo estate, 101
*Tres Amigos* (ship), 56, 181–
82
Tribunal de Acordada, 217–
18
Tribunal Mayor de Cuentas,
201–2, 204–5
Tristán, Flora, 25, 82, 98
Trujillo, 58, 100, 114–19, 165
Túpac Amaru rebellion, 4–5

*Uncle Tom's Cabin*, 165, 166,
167
United States: antislavery
sentiments in, 151, 153,
163; Civil War, 189, 214;
Peru's debt to, 130; sla-
very in, 2, 65, 95, 160
Ureta, Manuel Toribio, 196,
206
Uriarte, Julián, 116, 118

Valdivia (deputy), 204
Valle, José María del, 201
Venezuela, 9–10; abolition
in, 2, 186; Peru's debt
to, 130; and slave trade,
160, 177
Vicuña, Pedro Félix, 21, 25
Vidal, Francisco de, 110
Villa estate, 45, 98, 102, 105,
107, 108, 113, 192
Villalva, Tomás, 142
Vineyards, 25, 143, 154;
production of grapes, 2,
22, 216

Vivanco, Manuel Ignacio, 52, 56, 104–5, 179, 206
Von Tschudi, J. J., 64, 85

War of the Pacific, 220
Whipping, 43, 44, 85–87; criticism of, 154; legislation concerning, 4, 8, 10, 43, 58, 65, 85

Wilberforce, William, 154
Wilson, Belford Hinton, 110, 173–78

Xenophobia, 41, 171, 180

Yauyos, 191
Yungay, Battle of, 50, 175

Zerpa, Carmen, 45

# Latin American Silhouettes
## Studies in History and Culture

*William H. Beezley and*
*Judith Ewell*
Editors

**Volumes Published**

William H. Beezley and Judith Ewell, eds., *The Human Tradition in Latin America: The Twentieth Century* (1987). Cloth ISBN 0-8420-2283-X Paper ISBN 0-8420-2284-8

Judith Ewell and William H. Beezley, eds., *The Human Tradition in Latin America: The Nineteenth Century* (1989). Cloth ISBN 0-8420-2331-3 Paper ISBN 0-8420-2332-1

David G. LaFrance, *The Mexican Revolution in Puebla, 1908–1913: The Maderista Movement and the Failure of Liberal Reform* (1989). ISBN 0-8420-2293-7

Mark A. Burkholder, *Politics of a Colonial Career: José Baquíjano and the Audiencia of Lima* (1990). Cloth ISBN 0-8420-2353-4 Paper ISBN 0-8420-2352-6

Kenneth M. Coleman and George C. Herring, eds. (with Foreword by Daniel Oduber), *Understanding the Central American Crisis: Sources of Conflict, U.S. Policy, and Options for Peace* (1991). Cloth ISBN 0-8420-2382-8   Paper ISBN 0-8420-2383-6

Carlos B. Gil, ed., *Hope and Frustration: Interviews with Leaders of Mexico's Political Opposition* (1992). Cloth ISBN 0-8420-2395-X Paper ISBN 0-8420-2396-8

Charles Bergquist, Ricardo Peñaranda, and Gonzalo Sánchez, eds., *Violence in Colombia: The Contemporary Crisis in Historical Perspective* (1992). Cloth ISBN 0-8420-2369-0   Paper ISBN 0-8420-2376-3

Heidi Zogbaum, *B. Traven: A Vision of Mexico* (1992).  ISBN 0-8420-2392-5

Jaime E. Rodríguez O., ed., *Patterns of Contention in Mexican History* (1992). ISBN 0-8420-2399-2

Louis A. Pérez, Jr., ed., *Slaves, Sugar, and Colonial Society: Travel Accounts of Cuba, 1801–1899* (1992). Cloth ISBN 0-8420-2354-2 Paper ISBN 0-8420-2415-8

Peter Blanchard, *Slavery and Abolition in Early Republican Peru* (1992). Cloth ISBN 0-8420-2400-X   Paper ISBN 0-8420-2429-8

Sandra McGee Deutsch and Ronald H. Dolkart, eds., *The Argentine Right: History and Intellectual Origins* (1993). Cloth ISBN 0-8420-2418-2 Paper ISBN 0-8420-2419-0

Paul J. Vanderwood, *Disorder and Progress: Bandits, Police, and Mexican Development*. Revised and Enlarged Edition (1993). Cloth ISBN 0-8420-2438-7   Paper ISBN 0-8420-2439-5